Enterprise Level
SECURITY

SECURING INFORMATION SYSTEMS
IN AN UNCERTAIN WORLD

Enterprise Level
SECURITY

SECURING INFORMATION SYSTEMS
IN AN UNCERTAIN WORLD

Dr. William R. Simpson

*Award-winning cybersecurity architect for
high assurance information technology systems*

Institute for Defense Analyses, Alexandria, Virginia, USA

CRC Press
Taylor & Francis Group
Boca Raton London New York

CRC Press is an imprint of the
Taylor & Francis Group, an **informa** business
AN AUERBACH BOOK

Cover design by Rebecca Simpson Steele.

Cover art: Padlock dissolving, copyright John Lund; 6/11/2012 by license.

CRC Press
Taylor & Francis Group
6000 Broken Sound Parkway NW, Suite 300
Boca Raton, FL 33487-2742

© 2016 by Taylor & Francis Group, LLC
CRC Press is an imprint of Taylor & Francis Group, an Informa business

No claim to original U.S. Government works

Printed on acid-free paper
Version Date: 20160217

International Standard Book Number-13: 978-1-4987-6445-2 (Hardback)

Library of Congress Cataloging-in-Publication Data

Names: Simpson, William Randolph, 1946- author.
Title: Enterprise level security : securing information systems in an uncertain world / author, William R. Simpson.
Description: Boca Raton : Taylor & Francis, 2016. | Includes bibliographical references and index.
Identifiers: LCCN 2015041818 | ISBN 9781498764452 (alk. paper)
Subjects: LCSH: Computer networks--Security measures. | Industries--Security measures.
Classification: LCC TK5105.59 .S563 2016 | DDC 005.8--dc23
LC record available at http://lccn.loc.gov/2015041818

Visit the Taylor & Francis Web site at
http://www.taylorandfrancis.com

and the CRC Press Web site at
http://www.crcpress.com

This book is dedicated to my wife who has put up with many missed engagements, and to my partner Coimbatore Chandersekaran who coached and mentored me through many of the processes described herein. His presence is missed, although felt throughout these pages.

Contents

SECTION I BASICS AND PHILOSOPHY

SECTION II TECHNICAL DETAILS

List of Figures

List of Tables

Foreword

Shortly after I joined the Institute for Defense Analyses in February 2008, I sat down with Randy Simpson to learn about his work. Ever the patient teacher, Randy tutored me on the architectural foundation that he and others were designing to define the infrastructure needed to support information assurance (now cybersecurity) in the United States Air Force information enterprise. I didn't understand everything in the 300-page document Randy sent me, but I could easily see the potential value of developing an enterprise-level security model for the Air Force, and eventually for the entire Department of Defense (DoD).

Before I retired from the Office of the Secretary of Defense in 2008, I was responsible for the DoD Data Strategy with a goal of making data visible, accessible, understandable, and trusted across the DoD enterprise. While we had made some progress in implementing this goal, I recognized that it would take years to break down the barriers created by the large number of legacy systems. These systems were never designed to share information, largely because many of them had their roots in the days of mainframe computing and point-to-point data connections; at that time, interfaces between systems were painstakingly negotiated via many bilateral interface agreements. But the world had changed, and Randy was one of the visionaries who recognized that a new security model was desperately needed.

This book condenses more than a decade of research into one document that describes a comprehensive program for enterprise-level security. What makes this book unique is that the research behind it is based on military applications, but the book derives its content from openly published literature sources, which are publically available. The work is now being implemented in the Air Force and is an enterprise security candidate for the DoD Joint Information Environment. By minimizing the military elements as much as possible, the book is equally relevant to businesses and other enterprises looking for a stronger security. This market is select but growing.

This foreword would not be complete without a brief mention of Coimbatore Chandersekaran, Randy's covisionary for the work embodied in this book. Sekar's heart gave out in May 2014, but his spirit lives on.

Margaret Myers
Director, Information Technology and Systems Division
The Institute for Defense Analyses

Preface

This book has been derived from 14 years of research, pilots, and operational trials in putting together an enterprise system. The later chapters (8 through 22) contain information obtained by making painful mistakes and reworking processes until a workable formulation was derived. The early chapters (1 through 7) contain an evolved set of principles and philosophies that were not apparent at the beginning of this project, and I urge the reader not to gloss over these. If you hope to apply any of the material here to a real-world situation, you will need this set to help make decisions that surely are not covered in this book.

From a philosophical standpoint, a number of realizations over the years have shaped the security measures described in the book. They roughly fall into a few basic categories:

1. Complexity—The complexity cannot be reversed and continues to grow. The ship has sailed on simple times and models. The complexity of what we cannot control is immense and there are currently no methods formal or informal that can even verify a majority percentage of the circumstances. The complexity means that we are destined to have flaws and exploits in the future and these are innumerable.

2. Threats—If you are connected, you cannot prevent threats and exploits, you can only mitigate. Strong mitigation becomes very user unfriendly because of the complexity. Mitigate to an extent that users are not overly inconvenienced. Limit damages by distributed approaches and keeping potential values of targets small.

3. Operation—The design must operate in the presence of threats. As described above, the threat is persistent and present. Systems must operate even if threats are present.

4. Sanitization—Regular scans and assessments are a constant part of the process. Keeping clean means regularly sweeping for unknown software and review of logs looking for intrusions and anomalies. It is not enough, but it makes recovery, when needed, easier.

5. Recovery—IT systems must be resilient because they will be the subject of intrusion, abuse, exfiltration, and denial of service. Recovering from this is an important design feature. When exploits are discovered, the damage must be assessed and repaired. The system must be patched, and that exploit must be further mitigated. After that, stand by for the next round.

Acknowledgments

Much of the material in this book has been published in various forms. These include many technical reports and analyses, along with a multitude of coauthors including Coimbatore Chandersekaran (most), Kevin Foltz (many), Andrew Trice, Ceesay Ebrima, Ryan Wagner, and Elizabeth McDaniel. The author thanks them for their insights and acknowledges their contributions to this book. The material herein was derived from the open literature sources that are referenced in each section. The author is especially indebted to Coimbatore Chandersekaran who did not live to see the publication of this book, but contributed to almost every aspect of the work.

The author is deeply indebted to his technical editor, Lynne Russillo. Lynne has turned the technical gobbledygook into real and understandable English and has greatly enhanced its usability and user friendliness.

The author acknowledges the standards producers. These products are valuable and mostly not appreciated, but provide the glue that holds everything together. Standards body standards for OASIS [1], NIST [2], ISO Common Criteria [3], IETF [4], W3C [5], and ISO/IEC [6] are referenced in the standard nomenclature for this book and details can be found in the reference section.

Author

Dr. William R. Simpson earned a BS in aerospace engineering from Virginia Polytechnic Institute and State University, an MS and a PhD in aeronautical and astronautical engineering from The Ohio State University, and an MS in administration from George Washington University. He has held academic positions at George Mason University, Old Dominion University, University of Maryland, and The Ohio State University. He has held industry positions at the US Naval Air Test Center, the Center for Naval Analyses, the ARINC Research Corporation, and the Institute for Defense Analyses. He has held elected or appointed offices at Institute of Electrical and Electronics Engineers (IEEE), American National Standards Institute (ANSI), International Electrotechnical Commission (IEC), and Office of the Secretary of Defense (OSD).

Dr. Simpson has published extensively including several books, and numerous journal papers, conference papers, technical reports, and magazine articles. He has contributed to a number of technical standards.

Through the years he has been a teacher at the graduate and undergraduate levels, program manager, private pilot, public and invited speaker, workshop organizer, session chair, committee chair, standards writer, software capabilities evaluator, and information assurance evaluation validator.

Chapter 1

Introduction

1.1 Problem Description

The World Wide Web (WWW) has been tagged as a miracle of modern technology. Its success can be measured by the pace of its adoption and the pervasiveness of its use in modern society.

1.1.1 Success beyond Anticipation

The Internet's pace of adoption eclipses all other technologies that preceded it. Radio was in existence 38 years before 50 million people tuned in; TV took 13 years to reach that benchmark. Sixteen years after the first PC kit came out; 50 million people were using one. Once it was opened to the general public, the Internet crossed that line in four years. (*The Emerging Digital Economy [7]*)

1.1.2 But, It Started Long before That ...

1.1.2.1 A Brief History of the Development of the WWW

The Advanced Research Projects Agency Network (ARPAnet) was one of the world's first operational packet switching networks, the first network to implement transmission control protocol/Internet protocol (TCP/IP), and the progenitor of what was to become the global Internet. The network was initially funded by the Advanced Research Projects Agency (ARPA, later the Defense Advanced Research Projects Agency [DARPA]) within the U.S. Department of Defense for use by its projects at universities and research laboratories in the United States. The packet switching of the ARPAnet, together with TCP/IP, formed the backbone of how the Internet works. The packet switching was based on the concepts and designs of engineer Paul Baran, British scientist Donald Davies [8,9], and Lawrence Roberts of Massachusetts Institute of Technology Lincoln Laboratory [10]. The TCP/IP set of communication protocols was developed for ARPAnet by computer scientists Robert Kahn and Vinton Cerf [11].

The original ARPAnet connected four computers (1971). They were located in the respective computer research labs of the University of California, Los Angeles (UCLA) (Honeywell DDP 516 computer), Stanford Research Institute (SDS-940 computer), the University of California, Santa Barbara (IBM 360/75), and the University of Utah (DEC PDP-10). As the network expanded, different models of computers were connected, which created compatibility problems. The solution rested in a better set of protocols, TCP/IP, designed in 1982.

Under ARPAnet, several major innovations occurred: email (or electronic mail)—the ability to send simple messages to another person across the network (1971); telnet—a remote connection service for controlling a computer (1972); and file transfer protocol (FTP)—allows information to be sent from one computer to another in bulk (1973).

As nonmilitary uses for the network increased, more and more people had access, and it became no longer safe for military purposes. As a result, MILnet, a military-only network, was started in 1983. Internet protocol software was soon being placed on every type of computer, and universities and research groups also began using in-house networks known as local area networks or LANs. These in-house networks then started using Internet protocol software so that one LAN could connect to another (Figure 1.1).

> In 1986, one LAN branched out to form a new competing network, the National Science Foundation Network (NSFnet). NSFnet first linked together the five national supercomputer centers and then every major university, replacing the slower ARPAnet, which was finally shut down in 1990. NSFnet formed the backbone of what we now call the Internet. (*A Brief History of Network Computing [12]*)

1.1.3 Fast-Forward to Today

Today we have a network and a collection of software products (the system).

- ◼ This system is a robust communication provider.
- ◼ This system is a collection of capabilities whose use has become pervasive, and its capabilities continue to grow.
- ◼ The usefulness of this system is so high that discarding it is inconceivable.
- ◼ System updates and revisions are hindered by the need for backward compatibility, so old vulnerabilities and methods are still embedded while new capabilities are introduced.

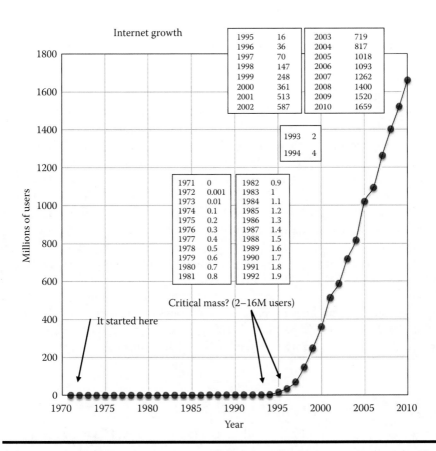

1995	16	2003	719
1996	36	2004	817
1997	70	2005	1018
1998	147	2006	1093
1999	248	2007	1262
2000	361	2008	1400
2001	513	2009	1520
2002	587	2010	1659

| 1993 | 2 |
| 1994 | 4 |

1971	0	1982	0.9
1972	0.001	1983	1
1973	0.01	1984	1.1
1974	0.1	1985	1.2
1975	0.2	1986	1.3
1976	0.3	1987	1.4
1977	0.4	1988	1.5
1978	0.5	1989	1.6
1979	0.6	1990	1.7
1980	0.7	1991	1.8
1981	0.8	1992	1.9

Figure 1.1 Internet growth. *(Internet Growth Data 1995–2010,* **www. internetworldstats.com.** *MIT Internet Growth 1993–1994,* **http://www.mit. edu/~mkgray/net/internetgrowth-raw-data.html.** *Internet Growth Data 1971– 1992,* **extrapolated by author.)**

■ The system supports anonymity. This leads to nefarious behavior and a high potential for misuse with a low potential for getting caught.
■ System complexity and number of underlying protocols and software that ride on top of the network make a rework of the basic approaches and reduced vulnerabilities almost impossible.

In certain enterprises, the network is continually under attack. Examples include

■ The banking industry enterprise
■ Defense industry applications
■ Credit card consolidation processes
■ Commercial point-of-sale processes

- The health industry (privacy and statutory compliance requirements)
- Content distributors (data rights, content theft)

The attacks have been pervasive and often include previously unseen attack vectors. In some cases, nefarious code may be present that is undetected by regular monitoring and system sweeps that clean up readily apparent malware. This omnipresent threat leads to a healthy paranoia of many threats, and these threats may be resistant to observation, work in conjunction with normal software, and masquerade as known entities in the system. The web interface is still the best way to provide access to many of its users despite this highly active threat environment. One way to maintain secure capability in this type of environment is to know and vet not only the users but also the software and devices. Even that has limitations when dealing with the voluminous threat environment. Today, we regularly construct seamless encrypted communications between machines through secure socket layer (SSL) or other transport layer security (TLS). These do not cover the "last mile" between the machine and the user (or service) on one end, and the machine and the service on the other end. This last mile is particularly important when we assume that malware may exist on either machine, opening the transactions to exploits for eavesdropping, exfiltration, session hijacking, data corruption, man-in-the-middle, repeat replay, masquerading, blocking or termination of service, and other nefarious behavior.

1.2 What Is Enterprise Level Security?

Enterprise level security (ELS) is both an architecture and a philosophy that allows the intelligent sharing of information among the entities in an enterprise and among coalition and other partners while maintaining a strong security posture that is both uniformly applied and standards-driven throughout the enterprise. ELS is also the singular approach to security that involves end-to-end public key infrastructure (PKI)-based bilateral authentication, with Security Assertion Markup Language (SAML)-based authorization credentials for access and privilege. This requires standard naming and PKI credentials for all active entities and a presence in the enterprise attribute store for all active entities.

1.3 Distributed versus Centralized Security

1.3.1 Case Study: Boat Design

The original builders of boats had a simple design philosophy. Separate the water from the interior of the boat. In the beginning, boats were watertight by virtue of their being hewn from a single tree trunk, or when constructed from more than one piece of wood, joints were sealed with pitch or other sealants. But boats still leaked—just enough that it continually had to be dealt with. Sealants got better, but boats got more complex as hatches for cargo, weapons, and steerable rudders mounted through the hull were added. Boats still leaked, not much, but just enough that it limited the range or speed, or time in the water without maintenance. Then an epiphany occurred—boats leak so why not design the inside of boats to accommodate leakage. Drains and channels were added to funnel water to an area, the bilge, where the water could be dealt with, manually at first, and then with automated pumps. A well-sealed boat was still required because a high-leakage rate could overwhelm bilge capacity.

1.3.2 Case Study Enterprise Information Technology Environment

The original builders of information technology (IT) systems had no penetrations because the era of the hacker had not yet arrived. This changed quickly. Intruders penetrated unprotected systems. IT system designers tightened the boundaries, monitored the ports, and inspected all transmissions, and developed counter-measures and mitigations. Intruders found ways around these mitigations, often through unexpected means. Boundary protection, boundary monitors, and boundary countermeasures improved. However, as systems became more complex with additional functionality and communication requirements, intruders penetrated systems via unexpected holes left in the systems due to the complexity. The increased capability created a noisy environment and many threats went undetected by hiding in the noise of real traffic and valid messages. Now is the time for an epiphany. Penetrations happen, and intruders will get into IT systems. Systems need to be designed to accommodate this fact. We need to design internal traps and funnels and move intruders toward discovery so they can be eliminated, and the doors and windows revealed by penetration can be closed. However, the system will be penetrated again through another unclosed door. We need a strong perimeter, because without this, our internal measures will be overwhelmed. But with a strong external perimeter, and appropriate internal measures (such as tagging and identifying enterprise traffic), the noise of real traffic will be low enough that intruders can be heard and seen and eliminated before they strengthen and take control.

1.3.3 Security Aspects

Information protection is divided into five primary security categories: confidentiality, integrity, availability, authenticity, and nonrepudiation. To this we add mechanisms (or products) to provide detection and response to violations of the security services. Dividing system security services into standard categories is convenient for this description. A secure cyber system will include products in these categories at a level of strength commensurate with the information resources being protected. They may be provided by a combination of products and environmental considerations, such as placing computer resources in a guarded area.

1.3.3.1 Confidentiality

The confidentiality security service is defined as preventing unauthorized disclosure of data (both stored and communicated). Confidentiality services will prevent disclosure of data in storage, or transiting. One of the most common confidentiality mechanisms is cryptography.

1.3.3.2 Integrity

The integrity security service includes prevention, detection, and notification of unauthorized modification of data (both stored and communicated). One of the most common mechanisms for integrity is check sums, or hash algorithms, together with authoritative data source signature binding.

1.3.3.3 Availability

Availability is timely, reliable access to data and information services for authorized users. A popular attack is called denial of service (DOS), which attempts to make access unavailable.

1.3.3.4 Authenticity

Authenticity is the property that ensures that the identity of a subject or resource is the one claimed. Authenticity applies to entities such as users, processes, systems, and information.

1.3.3.5 Nonrepudiation

Nonrepudiation is the property that ensures actions are attributable to the entity that invokes them.

1.4 Crafting a Security Model

Adversaries to the enterprise already exist "within the wire"; that is, they have infiltrated the online environment, jeopardizing the integrity and availability of enterprise information and systems. Network attacks have been pervasive, and nefarious code may be present even in the face of system sweeps to discover and clean readily apparent malware. Interruption of service has been a particularly successful form of network attacks. The focus of this book is on the security aspects of countering existing as well as known and unknown threats.

1.4.1 The Assumptions

A large part of the problem stems from unknown perpetrators. The current web-based approaches to security are remarkably tolerant of unknown entities. These unknown entities present in the system, can see and report, so surveillance is a give-away. These entities, after gathering their intelligence may insert themselves into the flow of information. Some basic assumptions have been made at the outset for the security model. These are

- Only interactions based on authorization credentials and two way, end-to-end authentication are permitted (this leads to strong requirements for enterprise naming and credentials)
- Impersonation prevents originator attribution and is not allowed
- Least privilege is used to avoid privilege amplification attacks
- Confidentiality of all data/content exchanged is enforced because of the possibility of threats being present
- Eliminate man-in-the-middle attacks and tampering wherever possible
- Guarantee integrity, authenticity, timeliness, and pedigree by process
- Monitoring is a precursor for cyber security
- Eliminate or mitigate Malware by periodic scans and active measures

1.4.2 Tenets: Digging beneath the Security Aspects

Each component of every enterprise solution should be tested against a set of fundamental design criteria or tenets. These tenets are separate from the functional requirements of a specific component; rather, they relate to the attributes of the solution that make it implementable, affordable, and supportive of the fundamental objectives of the architecture.

- The zeroth tenet is that *malicious entities* can look at all network traffic, send virus software to network assets, and perform other nefarious actions. Current threat evaluation indicates that attacks are often successful at all levels; discovering these attacks and their consequences is problematic. In many cases attackers may infiltrate the exploit discovery and patch loop. In other cases, successful phishing and spear phishing attacks have been launched. When the symptoms of these infiltrations are discovered, a thorough cleansing is undertaken (often revealing that the threat has been present for an extended period of time). Even when a system is purged, it is only a matter of time before another malicious entity invades. Rogue agents may be present, but to the extent possible, the enterprise should be able to operate in their presence and maintain confidentiality without precluding their ability to view some activity. This tenet causes us to insist upon strong identity, confidentiality (use of encryption in this case), and integrity. A provider should be able to verify with whom he is talking and what claims to service that identity can support. A provider should be able to verify that what was received was actually what the requester sent.

■ The first tenet is *simplicity*. Added features come at the cost of greater complexity, less understandability, greater difficulty in administration, higher cost, and/or lower adoption rates that may be unacceptable to an organization. Supporting cross-domain and enterprise scenarios will automatically add a certain degree of complexity. On the other hand, a level of complexity is required for security purposes; implementations should not be overly simplified for convenience.

■ The second tenet, and closely related to the first, is *extensibility*. Any construct put in place for an environment should be extensible to the multiple instances and applications, to the enterprise as a whole, and ultimately to the cross-enterprise and partners. It is undesirable to work a point solution or custom approach for each of these constructs.

■ The third tenet is *information hiding*. Information hiding involves revealing to the outside world the minimum set of information needed for making effective, authorized use of a capability. Insider threat aside, since the enemy is always present, revealing information to our own entities may lead to leakage to the outside world. It also involves implementation and process hiding so that this information cannot be farmed or analyzed for secondary information and inference or used for mischief. The user does not need to know the algorithms or internal variables the service uses to implement the capability. Hiding this information keeps these details secret from the user of the capability, makes it harder to exploit, and increases implementation flexibility. Any information that is not shielded from inadvertent discovery may be used in later attacks.

■ The fourth tenet is *accountability*. In this context, accountability refers to the ability to identify and track any entity in the enterprise that has performed a specified operation (e.g., accessed a file or IP address, invoked a service). To enable accountability, it is necessary to prohibit online "impersonation," in which principals share their credentials with another actor rather than delegating their authority. Without a delegation model, it is impossible to establish a chain of custody or conduct effective forensic analysis to investigate security incidents. Proxies and portals cause ambiguity in identity and violate the accountability tenet. This leads us to require active entities to act on their own behalf and not to act on behalf of others. Nor do active entities allow others to act on their behalf, because they will be held accountable. This leads to avoidance of intermediaries and restricting the way we do load balancing and mediation, both of which fulfill the intermediary position in our network.

- The fifth tenet is *minimal detail* (add detail to the solution only to the required level). Minimal detail combines the principles of simplicity and information hiding and preserves flexibility of implementation at lower levels. For example, adding too much detail to the access solution while all of the other information assurance components are still being elaborated may result in vendor lock-in, inability to take advantage of newer processes, or at the least, wasted work when the solution has to be adapted or retrofitted later.

- The sixth tenet is to use a *service-driven* rather than a product-driven solution whenever possible. Using services makes possible the flexibility, modularity, and composition of more powerful capabilities. Product-driven solutions tend to be more closely tied to specific vendors and proprietary technology. However, certain commercial solutions that produce cost efficiencies should be emphasized.

- The seventh tenet is that *lines of authority* should be preserved and information assurance (IA) decisions should be made by policy and/or agreement at the appropriate level. This tenet works with accountability in that decisions made are recorded and accountable. The decision to share information or allow resources to be exploited should be made at the point in the organization where accountability is acceptable.

- The eighth tenet is *need-to-share* overrides need-to-know. Often, effective health, defense, and finance rely upon, and are ineffective without, shared information. Within the enterprise, information is the currency of decision. Shared does not mean released, and the differences must be clear. However, judicious use of release authority and delegated access lead to a broader distribution of information. This leads to a more formalized delegation policy, both within and outside of the enterprise. The development of this delegation policy also allows correction of governance shortcomings without taking the expedient way out on completing sharing requirements. When in doubt, share information, because lack of it leads to bad decisions.

- The ninth tenet is *separation of function*—sometimes referred to as atomicity—this makes for fewer interfaces, easier updates, maintenance of least privilege, and reduced and more easily identified vulnerabilities, and it aids in forensics. Separated functions are easier to share and maintain, and the smaller the scope of the function, the easier to verify and sanitize. It also makes it easier to satisfy the twelfth tenet.

- The tenth tenet is *reliability*—security needs to work even if you and everyone else know how it works. In a large-scale enterprise, information on how a system works needs to be freely shared. Lack of information leads to bad decisions, but obscurity is not a security aspect. The processes should be robust enough to work, even in the face of those who would exploit that knowledge. This is not in conflict with information hiding, which has to do with information elements—not processes. An example of open methods and hidden information would be to publish the use of TLS 1.2 encryption but hide the session keys.

- The eleventh tenet is *trust but verify* (and validate). Trust should be given out sparingly and even then trusted outputs need checking. Verification includes checking: signature blocks, time stamps, to whom information is sent, that the credential identities match (binding), that information received is identical to information sent, etc. Validation includes checking the issuing authority, certificate validity, and identity white and black lists. This tenet essentially precludes the use of identity by self-attestation, which is unverified. This tenet also requires a careful selection of what is trusted, along with a requirement to be able to check these factors.

- The twelfth tenet is *minimizing attack surfaces*. The fewer the interfaces and the less the functionality in the interfaces, the lesser the exposure to threats. This is related to the simplicity tenet, but it is directly applicable to the threat model. Bringing in commercial products with a wide range of capability requires locking down all unneeded interfaces and creates a larger vulnerability space due to configuration errors. Removing code may interrupt the remediation and patching process and invalidate warranties. Better to go with less complicated products. The fewer the interfaces, and the less capability in each interface, the fewer avenues through which an adversary can apply his craft.

- The thirteenth tenet is *handle exceptions and errors*. Handling exceptions and errors involves three basic aspects. The first is logging. The second is alerting, and all security related events should be alerted to the Enterprise Support Desk (ESD). The third is notification to the user. Because malicious entities are present, any exception subject to alert should provide minimal information to the user (information hiding). More exacting information may be used by a penetrator to improve its access. This leads to typical responses to the exceptions such as: *"Unable to complete your request at this time, if this persists, please contact ESD and provide the code 345xyz."* The user (if authorized) can get further information after he is authenticated to the ESD.

- The fourteenth tenet is *use proven solutions*. A carefully developed program of pilots and proofs of concepts was pursued before the elements described in this book were integrated into the enterprise. This process should be followed for new implementations even when expediency dictates a quicker solution. Immediate implementation should always be accompanied by a roadmap for integration that includes this tenet.

- The fifteenth tenet is *do not repeat old mistakes*. From a software point of view, this has many implications. First, never field a software solution with known vulnerabilities and exploits. There are several organizations that track known vulnerabilities and exploits, and an analysis against those indexes should be required for all software. Second, a flaw remediation system is required. After a vulnerability analysis, fixes may be required, and after fielding, fixes will be required as new vulnerabilities and exploits are discovered. These first two are covered in detail in Chapter 18. Third, from an operations standpoint take time to patch and repair, including outputs from the flaw remediation and improvements described in the Security Technical Implementation Guidelines.

1.5 Entities and Claims

Entities in the enterprise environment may be active or passive. Passive entities include information packages, static files, and/or reference data structures. Passive entities are the target of activities; they do not initiate activities and cannot assume the role of requestor or provider. Active entities are those entities that change or modify passive entities, request or provide services, or participate in communication flows. Active entities are users, hardware, and services. All active entities in the enterprise have certificates, and their private keys are stored in tamperproof, threat-mitigating storage. Communication between active entities in the enterprise requires full bilateral, PKI, end-to-end authentication. Active entities must be uniquely named in accordance with enterprise instruction (Figures 1.2 and 1.3).

1.5.1 Credentialing

A credential is a claim (for authentication, the claim is identity) that can be verified as accurate and current. Identity credentials must be provided for all active entities that are established in the enterprise in order to perform authentication. Prior registration as an active entity with a confirmable entity name is required.

Credentials are also needed for claims about authorization (both access and privilege). The form of the credentials will be discussed in the individual chapters for these two subjects (authentication and authorization).

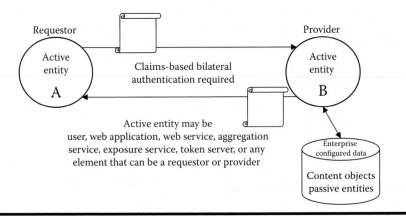

Figure 1.2   Claims for authentication between active entities.

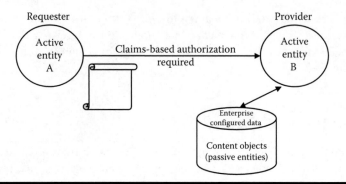

Figure 1.3   Authorization claims active entity A.

1.6 Robust Assured Information Sharing

Transforming enterprise architecture to take advantage of the web services concept while maintaining security requires some rethinking of the problem. Creating a secure and robust infrastructure for information sharing is a daunting goal.

1.6.1 Security Requirements

Security is, in general, a risk management process, which involves the following minimal requirements:

- Two-person verification is preferred for all information assurance (IA) tasks, with one of the persons being in a position equivalent to that of an information assurance manager (IAM).
- No accounts will use username/passwords. All accounts will use strong credentials for authentication. Username/passwords have proven to be insecure.
- There will be no storage of software certificates. Like passwords, these are a primary threat vector, and securing software certificates is improbable.
- Approved methods of authentication include:
  - PKI-based authentication: the use of PKI certificates on an approved hardware token
  - One-time password tokens
  - Biometrics with personal identification number (PIN) or password
- All enclaves will incorporate usage of PKI, digital signature policy, encryption policy, and content management into annual security awareness training.

1.6.2 Security Mechanisms

Mechanisms such as *access control* are implemented to provide the security aspects identified in later chapters. In the context of security, access control means limiting access to resources (hardware and software) and information. In order to provide these basic services, products may provide logs for auditing and tracing events, or even exclusion from access by using accountability. Modern information assurance and computer network defense systems use proactive and predictive capabilities to prevent unauthorized access before it can occur. In many cases, forensic analysis on logs will be used to detect unauthorized access and changes to information, provide estimates of losses, and restore the information to its original integrity.

1.6.3 Goals and Assumptions of IA Architecture

The overarching goal of an *IA strategy* is to evolve the enterprise to a set of smoothly interoperating enclaves. An enclave can be thought of as a set of encapsulated capabilities with (at least) common naming, authentication, authorization, and audit requirements and standards.

- It is assumed that as the enclaves are evolved, they will also employ federation to enable interaction and sharing between enclaves to take place transparently, with appropriate IA mechanisms in place, across all layers of the architecture.
- It is assumed that a service-oriented architecture (SOA) approach will pervade the solutions that will evolve, and this affects IA as well. SOA approaches rely heavily on machine-to-machine communication to realize complex capabilities, while preserving modularity and enabling reuse of functionality. This has two implications for IA efforts. The first is that services will provide the implementation mechanism at many layers in the architecture, each of which will require specific IA capabilities. The second is that while the architecture will make every effort to reuse existing IA mechanisms that have proved successful for human users in the past, some new approaches and standards may be necessary in certain cases.
- It is assumed that no support for anonymous users is required—at least during the first implementation spiral. This will require open interchanges of data between enclaves as part of their trust agreements. Although there may well be applications in which anonymity may be desirable, anonymity is generally at odds with key IA needs such as attribution and auditing.

The desired end state for the enterprise in terms of IA is to build a single, consistent, net-centric IA architecture that supports the key related elements of the enterprise, including integration of the network and command and control capabilities; improving situational awareness; and optimizing transport of authoritative, secure information.

To help realize this vision (which clearly requires many elements of net-centricity), many organizations are moving to an SOA approach. To implement an SOA successfully and coherently, it is necessary to implement a layered architecture, and

OSI model of protocol stack

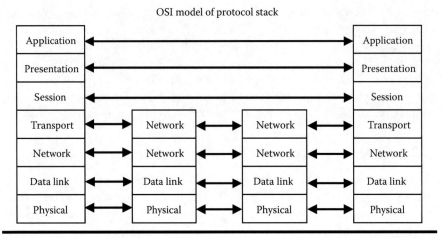

Figure 1.4 Layered system example.

that is the key aspect of the IA strategic plan. Once the roles of (and the ground rules for the usage of) the layers are understood, we can show how each of the other architectural building blocks (e.g., naming, credentialing, and authentication) will make use of them.

Figure 1.4 depicts a standard view of a layered system, the open systems interconnection (OSI) model of a protocol stack. Although this layered architecture primarily contains layers that are not visible to the typical end user, it still is useful for illustrating some of the key benefits of a layered approach. In a layered architecture, each layer (e.g., transport) knows about and relies on only the layer immediately below it (e.g., network); likewise, it knows nothing about any of the layers above it (e.g., session).

Layers communicate by means of well-defined interfaces that specify the functions or services they provide to requestors. Since only its interface is exposed to the requestors, each layer can hide its implementation and technology details from other layers. For example, more efficient internal algorithms can replace the old ones, or a new vendor's technology can be swapped in, as long as the underlying interface of the layer remains the same. In addition, since each layer has a well-defined and limited purpose, layers tend to be more lightweight and reusable than "large-grained" architectural components.

The benefits of a well-designed layered architecture include greater reusability, more vendor flexibility (particularly if the layer interfaces reflect industry standards), greater opportunity to improve or modify the overall implementation without breaking the entire system, greater understandability and modularity, and all of the cost-saving and effectiveness that can accrue from the above.

It is clear that shortcomings at lower levels can be mitigated at the upper levels with confidentiality and integrity in a distributed end-to-end approach. Now that we have introduced the layering concept, we can begin to build up the architectural components of the evolving enterprise and describe how they will communicate and interoperate using the architectural layers to realize IA capabilities.

The lower layers of this model have been worked extensively, standardized, and embodied in commercial products, and they are mostly subject to choice, not customization. For the most part, they will be taken as given, and the upper layers, where we have some latitude, will be the point of discussion. The exception will be when the processes going on at the lower layers in some way interfere with the end-to-end approach or allow vulnerabilities that we want to mitigate.

1.6.4 Assumptions

The enterprise approach is designed under the following assumptions:

- *Complexity continues to escalate, and vulnerabilities and exploits are growing*: The counter to complexity is partitioning and radical simplicity, at least in the areas of concern. This means eliminating complexity and chaos wherever possible. Convenience features add complexity and unintended consequences. Brutally simple rules for complexity reduction are
  - Keep communication to a two-party event. Do not allow intermediaries such as portals, proxies, and others.
  - Establish the identities of both parties as acceptable to each other.
  - Provide confidentiality for this conversation.
  - Establish access and privilege separately from identity.
  While these rules are simple, implementing and maintaining them can get complex.
- *The current approach has failed to keep threats at bay*: The current approach is typified by layered defenses where multiple checks are made at the external boundaries of a computing environment, with little or no defensive measures inside the environment. This is sometimes called a fortress approach, with double firewalls and other gauntlets surrounding the computing assets. The fortress approaches have been strengthened and restrengthened, but the threat has been able to find ways to breach those defenses. Often, unintended consequences in the defenses add vulnerabilities. Concentrating assets has made the concentration a high-value target. Figure 1.5 shows the defensive setup that has been employed in the past. A major concentration of assets has been protected by a demilitarized zone (DMZ), where communications are extensively examined before they are permitted. The intruder has managed to learn these approaches and circumvent their intent. In many cases, intruders learn the rules we employ and know them better than we do.
- *A more distributed defensive posture is needed*: The goal is to distribute the computing requirements, reduce the concentration of assets, reduce the

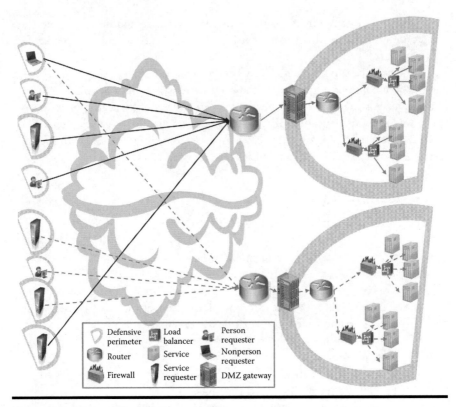

Figure 1.5 Computing centers as a fortress.

attack space, tailor defenses to the specific applications, and minimize losses when they occur. This is generally accomplished by distributing the defenses as shown in Figure 1.6. A quick glance at Figure 1.6 shows that the DMZ fronting the computing center has been removed; however, the functionality has been included in the application defenses, as discussed in 21. This distributed approach levies separate requirements on other network entities, as we shall see. Physical protection of the computing center is still required.

■ *The enterprise controls its user community*: The users and their activities are known; the information that needs to be shared is known; and the enterprise controls the physical environment, including the edge environment. The control of the user communities and physical edge environment allows the enterprise to implement more stringent security while making information and services more accessible to authorized users.

■ *The use of commercial, open standards is preferred*: Proprietary standards and protocols will be excluded where possible from the implementation of the baseline.

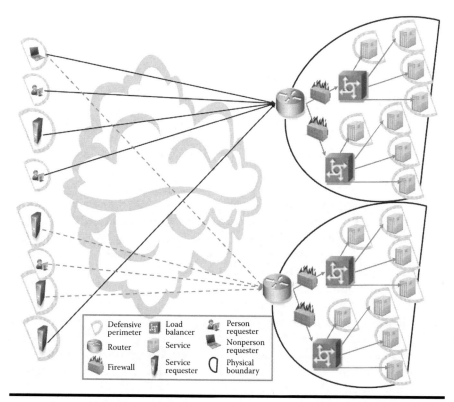

Figure 1.6   Distributed defenses.

■ *The use of commercial-off-the-shelf products is preferred*: Specialized development or customization of commercial products is not recommended. Open
source implementation methods are pursued where feasible.
■ *External users will adhere to enterprise standards for authorization and authentication*: Exposing information and services to users external to the enterprise will be accommodated as long as the requesting community can meet
the information assurance standards and requirements established by this
approach.

1.6.5 A Framework for Entities in Distributed Systems

The framework is related to entity behavior and comes from the basic security
model and is a combination of security definitions, aspects, and the design tenets
as applied to all active entities.

■ All active entities are named in accordance with an enterprise naming
standard.

- All active entities have a presence in the enterprise attribute store.
- All enterprise passive entities are registered for asset management.
- All active entities within the enterprise have unique identities. All active entities have only one identity and access to only one private key.*
- All active entities private keys are stored in tamperproof, threat-mitigating storage to which only the associated entity has access.
- Anonymous is not an identity (there are no active entities without names).
- Identity is verified by challenging the holder to prove he holds the private key.† Authentication tokens are not allowed. Traditional single sign-on is not allowed.
- Authorization in the operational environment is implemented by a verifiable access and privilege claims-based process. All active entities that act as requesters of any other active entity that requires claims have attributes that support the computation of claims in the enterprise attribute store. The claims objective requirements are provided by the data owner. All active entities that act as providers of any other active entity that requires claims have objective requirements in the enterprise registry.
- A trusted third party examines the attributes of an entity and determines whether the requirement is satisfied. All active entities that have objective requirements in the enterprise registry support claims rendering via an enterprise claims engine. A trusted third party provides a claim in a SAML.
- All active entities that act as a provider of any other active entity that requires claims have a SAML handler installed.
- All active entities that act as a provider of services to any other active entity require a definition of claims and privileges.
- Accountability is needed to unambiguously identify and track which active entity in the enterprise performed any particular operation.
- All active entities have provisions for logging security relevant events.
- No active entity acts on behalf of any other active entity. Proxies and portals cause ambiguity in identity and violate the accountability tenet. All active entities act on their own behalf.
- Verify and validate all inputs. All active entities evaluate all inputs for consistency with intended function before acting on any input. All active entities evaluate all outputs for consistency with intended function before transmitting any output.
- Identity by self-attestation is precluded. All active entities have credentials from approved certificate-issuing authorities. The challenge for holder-of-key is the basis of positive identity. This latter point precludes single-sign-on operations.

---

* Multiple personas such as an individual who is both a contractor and retiree may be handled by either persona representation or separate identities (and separate certificates).
† This requirement eliminates the ability to use single-sign-on paradigms.

■ Being able to be verified and validated is a requirement for trusted entities. All active entities that are designated trusted must have verifiable credentials.

1.7 Key Concepts

The key concepts for ELS are based on the tenets listed in Section 1.4.2. Tenets that are related to the key concepts are shown in brackets. These key concepts (and thus tenets) relate directly to requirements as well, forming a bridge between the high-level tenets and the technical requirements. The key concepts are as follows: *Label, description (tenet cross-reference).*

0. *ELS-specific concepts* (see next section) (2, 6, 14).
1. *Naming*: A standard naming process is applied to active entities (2, 4, 11).
2. *AuthN1—AuthN Claims*: Authentication is implemented by a verifiable identity claims-based process (0, 2, 4, 11).
3. *AuthN2—AuthN Vetting*: Identity claims are tied to a strong vetting process to establish identity (0, 4, 11).
4. *AuthN3—AuthN Verify IDs*: Active entities verify each other's identity (0, 4, 11).
5. *AuthN4—AuthN Private Key*: The verification of identity is by proof of ownership of the private key associated with an identity claim (4).
6. *AuthN5—AuthN Own Behalf*: Active entities act on their own behalf (0, 1, 12).
7. *AuthZ1—AuthZ Data Owner Rqt*: The claims objective requirement is provided by the data owner (7, 8).
8. *AuthZ2—Access and Privilege*: Service providers use identity and authorization credential claims to determine access and privilege (0, 1, 2, 3, 8, 11, 13).
9. *AuthZ3—AuthZ Claims Service*: A trusted entity examines the attributes of an entity and determines if the claims objective requirement is satisfied (2, 3, 5, 6, 9).
10. *AuthZ4—Claims Imply Access*: A claim in an authorization credential is a statement that an access requirement has been satisfied (1, 3, 5, 8, 11).
11. *AuthZ5—AuthZ Claims*: Authorization is implemented by a verifiable identity, access, and privilege claims-based process (0, 2, 3, 4, 8, 11).
12. *AuthZ6—AuthZ Additional Info*: The data owner may request as part of his requirement definition, additional information about the requesting entity (1, 2, 11, 12).
13. *AuthZ7—AuthZ Credential Creation*: Authorization credentials are created by a trusted entity for a specific requester, a specific target resource, and a specific level of access (0, 6, 9, 10).
14. *Web Functionally*: Functionality is provided through web services (6).
15. *Noncustom*: It is undesirable to work a point solution or custom approach (1, 2, 5, 14).

16. *Delegation*: A formalized delegation policy both within and outside of the enterprise is a requirement (0, 2, 4, 7, 11).
17. *Trust*: The ability to be verified and validated is a requirement for trusted entities (0, 4, 11).
18. *Confidentiality*: Active entity interactions require confidentiality of data/content exchanged (0, 3, 10).
19. *Guarantees*: Integrity, authenticity, timeliness, and pedigree are to be guaranteed (0, 2, 4, 10, 11).
20. *Monitoring*: Monitoring is a required element of cyber security (0, 4, 10, 11, 13).
21. *Sanitize*: Eliminate or mitigate malware (0, 15).

1.7.1 ELS-Specific Concepts

Of particular interest is the set of ELS-specific concepts. They relate directly to tenets 2, 6, and 14 as defined in Section 1.4.2. These ELS-specific concepts are choices based on current technology, and they are subject to change (however, they do drive requirements and architecture) and expansion as technology changes and the ELS model is developed further. They are considered as a single concept in the previous section, and are expanded here for additional clarity. The ELS-specific concepts are

a. Use PKI credentials as the primary identity credential for active entities
b. Use SAML credential for claims and privileges
c. Use TLS v1.2 for end-to-end confidentiality and integrity
d. Use a trusted entity (security token service [STS]) for generating authorization credentials
e. Exceptions to ELS requirements must be documented with a plan and schedule to become compliant

1.7.2 Mapping between Tenets and Key Concepts

The concepts derive directly from the tenets as shown in Figure 1.7.

1.7.3 Enterprise-Level Derived Requirements

As in the previous discussion, these key concepts may be used to derive enterprise-level requirements. Many are directly or indirectly related to the framework for entities in distributed systems (Section 1.6.5). References to associated key concepts are indicated by numbers within parentheses ().

1. Active entities shall be named in accordance with a naming standard (1).
2. All active entities within the enterprise shall have unique identities (1).

Tenets

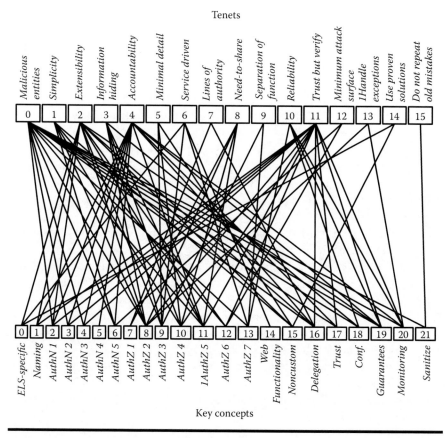

Figure 1.7 Key concepts as derived from security tenets.

3. Active entities shall use credentials from approved certificate-issuing authorities (1, 2).
4. Active entity communication shall use two-way end-to-end PKI authentication (0, 2, 4, 5, 15).
5. No active entity shall be anonymous (3, 4, 6, 20).
6. Authentication tokens shall not be allowed (4, 5).
7. Traditional single sign-on shall not be allowed (4, 5).
8. Private keys shall be stored in tamperproof, threat-mitigating storage to which only the associated entity has access (5, 6).
9. No impersonation of active entities through sharing of private keys or issuing of duplicate credentials shall be allowed (3, 6).
10. No proxies or portals shall be allowed; they cause ambiguity in identity (6).
11. Active entity authentication shall use only primary or derived credentials (2, 3).

12. Any active entity without authorization credential claims shall access only identity-based services (8).
13. Active entities that act as a provider of any other active entity that requires claims shall have objective requirements in the enterprise registry (7, 8, 9, 15).
14. Active entities that act as a requester of any other active entity that requires claims shall have attributes that support the computation of claims (8, 9, 10).
15. Each active entity that acts as a provider for any other active entity and requires claims shall have a SAML handler installed (8, 11, 14, 15).
16. Access and privilege to applications and services shall be provided by SAML-based verifiable claims from a trusted STS (0, 8, 9, 10, 11, 12, 15).
17. Authorization credentials shall conform to least privilege so that only the relevant claims for the target are included (13).
18. Each active entity that acts as a provider for any other active entity and requires claims shall have a list of trusted STSs (0, 11).
19. Each expedient solution shall have an accountable decision authority and a roadmap for bringing the solution into the basic approach for security (0, 15).
20. Delegation services shall be used for (and only for) assignment of duties not based on existing attributes and for temporary assignments not met by existing claims and attributes (14, 15, 16).
21. Active entities that are designated trusted shall have credentials that are verifiable (17).
22. All active entity interactions shall occur over end-to-end TLS v1.2 connections (0, 18, 19).
23. Active entities shall have provisions for logging security relevant events (20).
24. Monitoring of all active entities shall be performed (20).
25. A carefully developed and executed program of pilots and proofs of concepts shall precede integration into ELS (15, 21).
26. Active entities shall evaluate inputs for consistency with intended function before acting on any input (21).
27. Active entities shall evaluate outputs for consistency with intended function before transmitting any output (21).

1.7.4 Mapping between Key Concepts and Derived Requirements

Although many of the key concepts are directly or indirectly related to the framework for entities in distributed systems, for security modeling purpose, those elements are not used in the traceability of derived requirements. The derived requirements follow directly from the key concepts as shown in Figure 1.8.

Key concepts

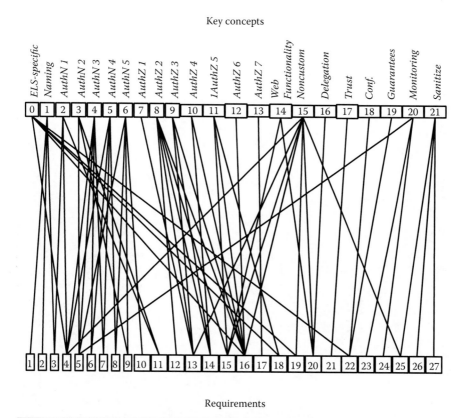

Figure 1.8   **Enterprise-derived requirements mapped from key concepts.**

1.8 Two Steps Forward and One Step Back

The material in this book has evolved over the last 14 years. Many experiments have led to a few successes. They roughly followed the path shown below (but not without backtracking and reconfiguring). The material below is for context and is covered in detail in later chapters (Figure 1.9).

1.9 The Approximate Time-Based Crafting

Figure 1.10 provides a time-based roll-out of elements that are discussed in the various chapters of this book. The times, of course, do not include the iterations for refinement.

(b)

Field	Required content	Notes
SAML: Assertion		
subject	(content)	Identity
SAML: Attribute statement		
subject	Common name	For identification in log files
Attributes: DAC and MAC	(content)	
End SAML: Attribute statement		
End SAML: Assertion		

Security Assertion Markup before vulnerability studies (not in the text)

(a)

Certificate authority PKI

Unambiguous identity (Chapters 2 and 8)

(c)

Field	Required content	Notes
SAML: Assertion		
Version ID	Version 2.0	Required
ID	(unique value)	Required
Issue instant	Timestamp	Required
Issuer	(content)	Required
Signature	(content)	Required
Subject	(content)	Required—must contain the X.509 distinguished name
SAML: Attribute statement		
Subject	Common name	For identification in log files
Attributes: DAC and MAC	(content)	
End SAML: Attribute statement		
SAML: Conditions		
Notbefore	(content)	Timestamp – minutes
Notafter	(content)	Timestamp + minutes
Audience	(content)	Target service
End SAML: Conditions		
End SAML: Assertion		

Security Assertion Markup after vulnerability studies (Chapter 9)

(d)

Web service context

HTTPS Protocol

Logging server handler

SAML validation handler

Signature validation handler

Web service

Web service and handler configuration files

Log records and alerts

Common framework—server side

Security Assertion Markup handlers (Chapters 9 and 18)

Figure 1.9   (a–d) Key processes coaxed from experimentation. *(Continued)*

(f)

Requester — Provider

Active entity A — Active entity B

PKI — PKI

Claims-based bilateral authentication required

Active entity may be: user, web application, web service, aggregation service, exposure service, token server, or any element that can be a requester or provider

Requester — Provider

Active entity A — Active entity B

Claims-based authorization required

SAML

Enterprise configured data

Content objects (passive entities)

(h)

Web application or aggregation service

Service to service / Service logic

Exposure service — Service logic

Exposure service — Service logic

User device — Browser

STS

Claims-based security for high assurance (Chapters 9 and 10)

Nonperson entities—web services paradigm (Chapter 11)

(e)

SS/TLS pipe (RED) with secure message flow inside

Bilateral authentication

Web application or aggregation service

Service to service / Service logic

Exposure service — Service logic

Exposure service — Service logic

SAML creation and movement

User device

STS

Bilateral authentication

User at a browser or presentation system

Embedded Security Assertion Markup handlers (Chapter 18)

(g)

Alerts

Web service and handler configuration files

Web service context

Web service

Log records and alerts

Service ACLs

Other handler(s) — Logging server handler — SAML validation handler — Claims validation — Signature validation handler — XML validation handler

Common framework—server side

H T T P S P r o t o c o l

Claims-based assets ELS handlers (Chapter 18)

Figure 1.9 **(e–h) Key processes coaxed from experimentation.**

(Continued)

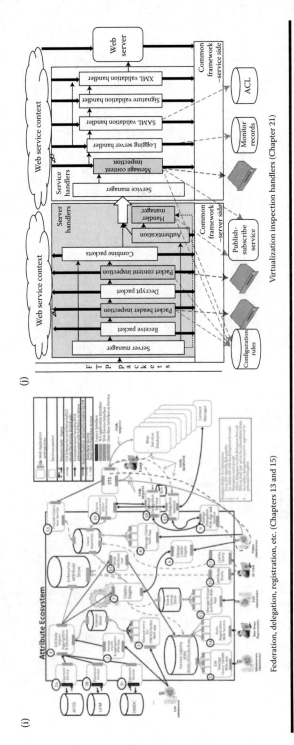

Federation, delegation, registration, etc. (Chapters 13 and 15)

Figure 1.9 (i–j) Key processes coaxed from experimentation.

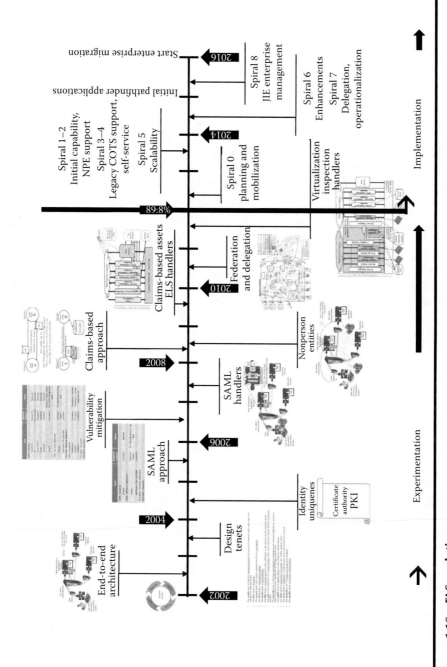

Figure 1.10 ELS evolution.

1.10 Summary

The fortress approach has worked well for a period of time. Increasing complexity and new computing hardware and techniques have made an impenetrable barrier impossible. The new approach to security is more distributed and has no need for passwords or accounts. Losses, when they occur are localized, and global attacks are much more difficult. The security approach is derived from a set of tenets that form the basic security model requirements. Many of the changes in authorization within the enterprise happen automatically as identities move within the enterprise structure. At each step in the computing process, we determine identities and claims for access and privileges. Many, but not all, of the techniques in this book have been piloted. These techniques have been proven to be resilient, secure, extensible, and scalable. The operational model of a distributed computer environment defense is currently being implemented on a broad scale for a particular enterprise.

BASICS AND PHILOSOPHY

Chapter 2

Identity

The material in this chapter is new and has not been previously published in association with these security approaches. However, the literature is absolutely bursting with identity documents and processes—to the point of overwhelming confusion. This chapter sets the context for identity as used in this security model. It may very well be applicable in other contexts too.

2.1 Who Are You?

Identity is complex. If you Google *identity* you can well come away more confused than when you first started. Identity commonly includes a number of attributes that may change over time, like job description, feelings, marital status, etc. In IT, we need to separate things that are static from things that are temporal in nature. The simplest definition presented by Merriam-Webster [15] is probably the best place to start: "Identity is who someone is: the name of a person." For IT purposes, the identity is a label that is unique and attached to only one entity or object. This is the static part of identity, and it can be tied to something you know, something you have, or something you are. Each of these proper-ties is an attempt to bind the name (and associated data and credentials) to the entity. For purposes of computation, this is the element we rely upon. There are familiar identities (recognized in my domain) and unfamiliar or less familiar identities (not recognized in my domain or not recognized at all). Establishing identity is a necessary first step in IT security activities. The basic security measures relate directly:

■ *Confidentiality*: The confidentiality security service is defined as preventing unauthorized disclosure of data (both stored and communicated). Confidentiality services will prevent disclosure of data that is in storage or is transiting. One of the most common confidentiality mechanisms is cryptography. Familiar identities have the privilege of accessing data both stored and communicated.

■ *Integrity*: The integrity security service includes prevention of unauthorized modification of data (both stored and communicated), and detection and notification of unauthorized modification of data. One of the most common mechanisms for integrity is check sums, or hash algorithms, together with authoritative data source signature binding. Familiar identities have created or transmitted the data. Familiar identities need to know that unfamiliar identities have not modified the data.

■ *Availability*: Availability is timely, reliable access to data and information services for authorized users. A popular attack is called *denial of service* (DOS), which attempts to make access unavailable. Of course, authorized users are familiar identities and unauthorized users are unfamiliar identities.

■ *Authenticity*: Authenticity is the property that ensures that the identity of a subject or resource is the one claimed. Authenticity applies to entities such as users, processes, systems, and information.

■ *Nonrepudiation*: Nonrepudiation is the property that ensures actions are attributable to the identity of the entity that invokes them.

Identity also applies to many of the system tenets:

■ Malicious entities—unfamiliar identities.
■ Accountability—attributing actions to familiar entities.
■ Lines-of-authority—an accountability chain.

Many exploits take advantage of confusing identities through *masquerade, man-in-the-middle* (MITM), and other approaches. In a secure environment, actions that provide access and privilege should always be preceded by a strong identity check. Since we know the enemy is present (see Chapter 1, Section 1.4.2), we must avoid any mechanisms that get in between known, vetted identities, like proxies and portals. These often confuse the identity issue and lead to vulnerabilities and exploits.

2.2 Naming

Naming provides the initial address for most entities and is one of the fundamental abstractions for dealing with complexity. The name for an entity (an individual, organization, or facility) provides a pointer into a set of labeled properties, managed by a registration service. Names provide the handle by which further certificates and other data concerning the entity can be accessed. *Integrity, quality, performance,* and *scalability* all hinge on a solid design for directory namespace and schema.

Architecturally, software components such as the directory service agent (DSA) depend on the schema to provide access controls and security to directory data. A namespace design determines the structure of the directory information tree (DIT) and how an organization can partition the directory for replication.

We often take for granted the name associated with a uniform resource locator—an identity. The power of the web was fully realized when the web developers defined the uniform resource locator (URL). This is a registry that assigns names to a resource and enforces the uniqueness of that name [4j]. This provides a way to specify where you wish to go without ambiguity and "...the relationship between uniform resource identifiers (URI)s, URLs, and uniform resource name (URN)s, describes how URI schemes and URN namespaces identities are registered...." The lack of ambiguity is the principle thing. Computers and their associated software get unpredictable when a label can mean more than one thing.

2.3 Identity and Naming: Case Study

When Sam Cinco first came to XYZ Corporation, he was provided an identity in accordance with the company policy. His Name was Sam.Cinco3579. The resources people were careful about uniqueness in this case because there may well be another Sam Cinco. The extra digits ensured that his identity would always be unique. He first worked in corporate services, where he did a stellar job of providing payroll data and other financial services. After 4 years, his job was taken by a newer hire and he moved to the executive suite, where he provided services connected with dashboards for executive desktops. When he moved, the resources department recorded his new functional location, his new network affiliations, his equipment upgrades, and his new responsibilities. Sam is a server automated machine made by Cinco, and there are 20 or so at XYZ Corporation. Although they are 20, each is unique and accountable for its own actions. The resources department here was the IT resources department, and it had parallel function to the human resources department. Sam was more than an identity—he had a collection of attributes that provided his location, functionality, responsibilities, and privileges within the XYZ Corporation.

There are two points from this example

■ The first is that all entities, human or machine, need unique identities. Uniqueness cut across space and time, in that we do not wish old identities to be reused even when the old identity is thought to no longer be part of the

system. At best, reusing an identity can create an identification ambiguity and at worst it can open the system to masquerade attacks.
■ The second is that identity is not enough. Attributes that may change over time must be available to each entity regarding its place, function, capabilities, and privilege.

2.4 Implications for Information Security

A number of implications can be derived from the case study.

1. We need some way to recognize an identity as being part of our ecosystem. When John.Smith1234 wishes to interact with Sam.Cinco3579, each has to have a concrete way of identifying who the other is.
2. This is critical to the XYZ Corporation (the enterprise); it is up to the enterprise to provide credentials that can be used in securing this identity. A secret handshake may be possible, a Kerberos ticket may suffice, but the identity must be recognizable, and according to our tenets, it must be able to be verified and validated. Passwords and secret handshakes do not pass muster. Credentials that can be verified and validated must be provided by an enterprise authority or an enterprise trusted authority.
3. Point 2 requires a credential of some form for each and every entity that might take part in a transaction. This credential can have a relatively long life in that identity is unique and does not change over time.
4. Identity credentials require a trusted identity credentialing agent, a registry, and software services associated with verification. They also require a way to challenge the presenter of a credential to prove that he is the owner of that credential.
5. Identity is only part of the issue. Knowing the identity of an entity is not the same as knowing the attributes of that entity. This implies that a provider of services in a transaction must have some measure of what the entity's attributes are, either the data itself or some claim.
6. Data or claims must be presented in a manner that can be verified and validated.
7. Point 6 requires an attribute or claims credential. This credential must have a relatively short life because entities move around and change their locations, functionalities, responsibilities, and privileges. Claims and attributes are not unique and change over time.
8. Care must be taken that attribute or claims credentials are not reused with the same or other identities.
9. Point 8 requires a trusted attribute or claims credentialing agent that can generate a credential at the time a request is made.

10. Point 9 requires a registry and software services associated with creation of the credential.
11. Point 9 also requires a way to bind the presenter of an attribute or claims credential to the same identity that presented and verified the identity credential.

2.5 Personas

Some attributes are so important that they may alter the expected behavior of an identity. This can be typified by an individual with multiple roles. The example given often is a former active duty military person, who is an active National Guard member and a defense contractor. But the two aspects of the described person could be expressed as attributes related to multiple assignments in the enterprise. John. Jones123 may be an administrator for the payroll system, and a user of that system for his own data. Everybody is a user in that they fill in time sheets and check their leave, etc. These may not overlap (John.Jones123 may be administrator for the executive department and reside in the IT department). This may be by design, with enterprise policy preventing John.Jones123 from administering his own accounts. The software may give him all the privileges of both personas (this is difficult for the software to do and prone to error). In the event that the software is not that clever, the software will need to know which persona it is dealing with. At one level, a persona could be considered another identity (say John.Jones123a). The enterprise could issue credentials for each persona and provide them to John.Jones123 to use as needed. However, this has a number of implications, not the least of which is maintaining duplicate attribute files, and tracking multiple credentials. The easiest way to handle these things is to ask John.Jones123 which persona he wants to be. Since John.Jones123 has both personas and the privileges that accrue to each, John should be asked to mitigate the ambiguity that the persona issue creates. If he were issued multiple credentials, he would decide which one to use.

2.6 Identity Summary

This all sounds very complicated and confusing, but in reality we are seeking to know with whom we are dealing. As in most human transactions, not knowing this can lead to problems, and it is easier to confuse and masquerade in the IT world than in person. As each of the security issues is reviewed, the implications of Section 2.4 should be considered.

Chapter 3

Attributes

The development of attributes that can be associated with the identity of active entities in the enterprise is a governance problem. Some attribute definitions and their implications are generally specific to an enterprise, such as office, pay grade, and corporate function. Other attributes are common across many enterprises, such as assignment and date of birth.

3.1 Facts and Descriptors

"An attribute is a quality or characteristic given to a person, group, or some other thing" [146]. Entity attributes in an enterprise system may include many things. Certainly, position within the organization, function, phone numbers, and maybe even the reporting chain both above and below are primary considerations. The one thing they have in common is that they are needed for access control. In order to be useful, they must come from an authoritative source. Sources include HRs, IT resources, and others. The key is that they are maintained by an individual or group to the level of detail consistent with their use in enterprise operations. To the extent that these data sources do not meet the requirements for a robust authoritative content source, they may have to be mediated and sanitized. The sudden promotion of a person from the mailroom to the board of directors has to be verified. If the HR system is not well protected, the changes to the HR information might happen (just as grades have been changed in educational environments with lax security). Attributes generally change infrequently (although several attributes may change at once for an individual, and reorganizations cause many individuals' data to change at once) and are relatively static. The exception is discussed in Section 3.3.4.

3.2 An Attribute Ecosystem

Figure 3.1 identifies the following elements of a fully developed attribute ecosystem (AE):

- Service Number 1 is an exposure service that draws attributes from the authoritative content store (ACS). Each exposure service is triggered by a call from the AE Data Import Aggregation and Mediation (Service Number 4). The call may be scheduled or it may be triggered by a system administrator who requests the schedule or demand through the Manage Import and Aggregation Web Application (Service Number 2). The purpose is to bring information into the AE, mediate and sanitize as appropriate, and place it into the interim store for later upload to the EAS. These will be referred to as import agents and are assigned the symbol to the right. There are similar agents (1b, 1c, …) for other ACSs. Currently, all ACSs are assumed to be legacy, and the import agents must conform to the legacy process. In the future, they may become web service (WS) and ELS enabled. Import agents may be used elsewhere in the enterprise environment.
- Service Number 2 is an AE service for managing import of data from the ACS for later dissemination to the EAS. The call for attribute updates may be scheduled or triggered by a system administrator. The purpose is to bring information into the AE, mediate and sanitize as appropriate, and place it into the interim store for later upload to the EAS. A second purpose is to schedule or demand an upload of sanitized and mediated information to the EAS and to trigger the claims engine for recomputing the claims.
- Service Number 3 is a web application that allows manual entry of attributes and entities by the EAS administrator. This is not the preferred method, which is the import of identity and attributes. Note that at times, import from authoritative content sources may be inadequate or inaccurate. Because these are not automatically checked, they should be logged and reviewed from time to time for currency. The changes are placed in the interim store for later upload, as described in service 2.
- Service Number 4 is an EAS service for requesting ACS that updates, sanitizes, and holds attributes from the ACS for later dissemination to the EAS. The call for attribute updates may be scheduled or triggered by a system administrator who requests the schedule or demand through the Manage Import and Aggregation Web Application (Service Number 2). The purpose is to bring information into the AE, mediate and sanitize as appropriate, and place it into the interim store for later upload to the EAS. A second purpose is to upload sanitized mediated information to the EAS. The call for AE updates may be scheduled or triggered by a system administrator who requests the schedule or demand through the Manage Import and Aggregation Web

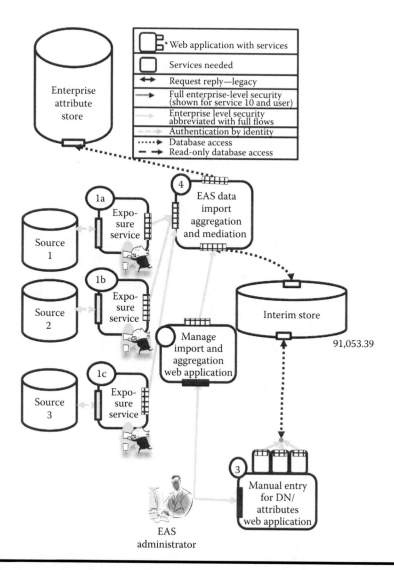

Figure 3.1   Attribute ecosystem.

Application (Service Number 2). A third purpose is to trigger the claims engine for recomputing the claims. The call for AE update may be scheduled or triggered by a system administrator who requests the schedule or demand through the Manage Import and Aggregation Web Application (Service Number 2). This service creates a tagged list of identities where one or more attributes have changed (for a new identity all attributes are new), and sends it to the claims engine (discussed in Chapter 9) where information for an identity has changed.

3.3 Data Sanitization

The EAS consists of multiple sets of information. It contains user attributes imported through customizable guards from authoritative sources to the EAS. The guards may include cross-domain and other logic checks as appropriate. These guards and the integrity of the EAS data are the subject of this section. User information such as employment level, assignment, training, assigned roles, and other information, are often contained in more than one ACS and are updated on different schedules. An agent triggers the import on demand, periodically, or when updates are made to the ACS. Temporal-based information such as temporary duty assignments, locations, time of access, and assigned devices are included. These data are used when the policy requires them to be considered in access control decisions.

Because most ACSs are legacy, attributes included in the import process are used in computations based on rules and filters previously established by administrators of the Authoritative Content Systems. These rules and filters may differ from the rules and filters applied to stores within the EAS. Legacy wrapper services act as both mediation and remediation of the legacy data and the security process and are termed exposure services. These wrappers meet ELS on the enterprise side and legacy security on the ACS side. These wrappers are not required when ACSs are developed as web services that meet enterprise security requirements.

3.3.1 Guarded and Filtered Inputs

Because numerous errors and inconsistencies may exist, a software guard is placed on the import process. A knowledgeable person with an authority to remedy discrepancies may be required in some instances. Handling of these discrepancies depends on the nature of the discrepancy, and corrections may be required before the data can be imported. The EAS administrator can override any of these checks when justified. The override is logged, and the logs are reviewed. Guard functionality is discussed below.

The EAS has access to the enterprise service registry (ESR) (stored elsewhere and may be centralized or distributed), containing distinguished names, X.509 certificates, WSDLs,* XSDs,† access control lists (ACLs), access control requirements (ACRs), and other WS-based information. These are imported from physical storage media provided by the WS administrator. The EAS administrator

---

* Web Service Description Language (WSDL) is an Extensible Markup Language (XML) format for describing network services as a set of endpoints operating on messages containing either document-oriented or procedure-oriented information. The operations and messages are described abstractly, and then bound to a concrete network protocol and message format to define an endpoint—World Wide Web Consortium (W3C) [5].

† XML Schema Definition (XSD), a recommendation of the W3C [5], specifies how to formally describe the elements in an XML document. It can be used by programmers to verify each piece of item content in a document.

develops the rules for claim mappings and places them in the ESR through a secure interface.

3.3.2 Guard Administrator Web Interface

The EAS administrator (or a separately credentialed role with administrator privileges) adjudicates anomalies detected by the guard function.

3.3.3 Integrity in Attribute Stores

For an access control system to operate properly, the information used must be reliably available, accurate, and unambiguous. Integrity is achieved when all information sources are trusted and accurate, secure methods are used in the data acquisition, and content from the many sources agrees. However, this is not the case with authoritative content today and steps must be taken to assure integrity that may have discrepancies inserted by an adversary (through poor security) or by input entry errors (without adequate checking). The first step is secure data acquisition. The initial standup of the EAS may not have such integrity. By integrity, we mean that the authoritative content has been checked for discrepancies and repairs have been made where discrepancies exit. However, recursive use of the techniques below, instantiation of learning algorithms, and a push to clean up the ACSs all evolve the EAS to a higher level of integrity.

3.3.4 Secure Data Acquisition

All communication within the enterprise conforms to ELS requirements.

Figure 3.2 shows how this is achieved with legacy systems that do not conform to ELS requirements. A wrapper system is front ended to ensure proper authentication (bilateral) and access control through claims-based approaches. If the ACS is ELS compliant, then a direct import may be possible. These latter steps only ensure secure data gathering—not integrity, which can be achieved in several ways.

3.3.5 Integrity at the Source

An authoritative source may be secured, protected against tampering, and has adequate sanitization, anomaly detection, and corrective processes to be trusted. In this case, the principal concern is to ensure that the data received by the EAS are the data that are acquired from the ACS. To do this, data must be signed by the trusted ACS, and the signature must be verified by the guard on the EAS side. The guard may wish to check for consistency across all the ACSs it uses. While trusted ACSs are desirable, they are not a reality. However, each ACS should be worked to improve its level of trust, including its own secure implementation, sanitization of data, anomaly detection, secure protection

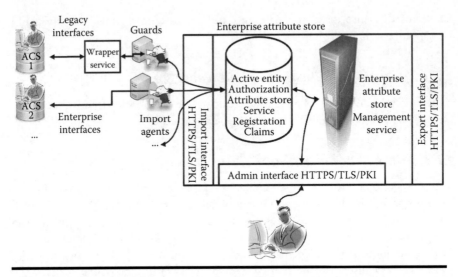

Figure 3.2   Data acquisition process for the EAS.

against tampering, and data accuracy, as well as signature processes for assured transmission.

3.4 Temporal Data

Most data about an entity are quoted as of its last update, which may have been hours, days, or even weeks earlier. Some data about an entity can be quoted only as of the moment, such as the current location. If such data are needed, the process described for the EAS for acquiring and distributing the data is inadequate and the time needed for current information is considerably shortened. When these data are needed, the AE must rely on services that will be run at the time the data are needed. When data that change more rapidly than or outside of updates to ACS are needed, these must be checked when the service is invoked. Such data include location of the requester, device, and software being used. The provision for temporal data in the access rules is discussed in Chapter 4.

3.5 Credential Data

Credential data are generally stored separately and associated with the developer of the credential. This may include certificate stores (for reference by services) and/or trust chains for verification and validation.

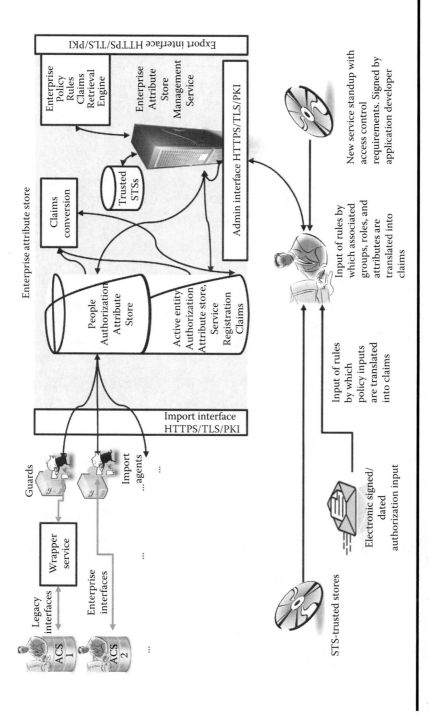

Figure 3.3 Enterprise attribute store.

3.6 Distributed Stores

Figure 3.3 illustrates a centralized store of attributes. If security is well handled, or not an issue, the data may be retrieved as needed from the ACSs, which are often called distributed stores. In our experience, the security and performance of the ACSs is an issue. The centralized store for both security and the precomputing of access claims is discussed in detail in Chapters 8 and 9.

Chapter 4

Access and Privilege

A large number of access and privilege processes have been documented. Many of these are complex and bewildering. The initial desire to make access and privilege responsive to changes in the enterprise in an automated manner drove our choices [17,18].

4.1 Access Control

Access control commonly involves two areas: the physical and the logical. When dealing with physical access control, an individual presents himself/herself and his/her mission (reason for being there) at a facility and to a guard or clearance individual, along with his/her credentials. These may be supplemented by attributes in a database that support his/her identity and his/her mission. Identity-based access control (IBAC) in these cases is perfectly reasonable. A human interpretation based on experience, the individual facility, and its missions provide a clear basis for decision making. Restricted information policies can be overridden or enforced, depending on the nature of the individual, the mission, or the reason for the requested entry (e.g., too close an inspection of covert operatives is not desirable—supporting the tenet of information hiding). In this case, time is a commodity that can be used to consider what decisions are to be made, and suspect cases can be examined in greater detail.

In IT systems, we deal with logical (as opposed to physical) access. Logical access control occurs when a documented (certificated) entity (human or nonhuman, e.g., a software program) presents itself to a software service and the software service needs information upon which to base a decision on whether to provide a service or not (and if so, which kind of service). This decision often involves transfer of information, and that transfer may be in quantity. If the service examines only a particular set of attributes, it may not be sufficient to support a decision. The decision may be made using a complex Boolean algebra* that is subject to complexity and error and based on custom-developed processes rather than commercial processes (this does not support the tenet of simplicity). The process we just described invites wholesale transmission of attributes (such as birth date or social security number), which does not support the tenet of information hiding.

4.2 Authorization and Access in General

Access is granted through an authorization process that is generally reviewed through the appropriate level of authority. Thus, local access to local databases may be resolved at the local level. Enterprise-wide access to enterprise data will be resolved at a much higher level. The authorization model in general requires the user, either directly or through an authenticated source, to supply credentials and authorization information sufficient for the service to make an access decision. Many models exist, including the following:

- *Default access control (anyone preregistered can have access)*: This lacks the discrimination and flexibility necessary for an effective IA policy. Revocation is done by removing preregistration. Delegation is difficult in this model (basic tenet of accountability).
- *IBAC*: Access is based solely on identity, and it may be accompanied by a weak authentication such as password only. Others may use a strong authentication, including PKI smart cards, biomeasures, or combinations in a multilevel authentication scheme. Passwords that use additional questions for the requester are still weak in general. One-time passwords are a bit stronger. Identity has some valuable properties and should be included in many of the other access control methods. However, multiple tasking can lead to multiple personas. See the concept of least privilege in Section 4.6 and personas in Section 2.5.
- *Group-based access control (GBAC)*: All members for a specific access privilege (under a registered group) are enumerated. Individual revocation is done by removing group link to identity. Group revocation is done by removing the group from the registration authority. All privileges for an individual must be accomplished by an enumeration service, and they are given by the enumeration of the privilege groups held by an individual. Both delegation and/or inheritance are possible. Groups are dynamic and expected to change over time. Groups are formed by use cases, which are dynamic. Coalition and

---

* Is the entity over 25 OR emancipated, OR has his boss provided a waiver AND does he work in the Human Resources Dept.? ... [(AGE ≥ 25).OR. (Eman = 'YES') .OR. (APPR = 'YES')] .AND. (Job = 'HR') ...

cross-enterprise trust relationships are specific use cases that can be designated as group access privileges. Identity may be considered as one of the properties under groups and roles.

■ *Role-based access control (RBAC)*: This is a special form of the group, where privileges are accrued by virtue of job requirements. Revocation is done by removing the role from the individual entity (in reality removing attributes that make up the role). Difficulties come when individuals assume multiple roles (often solved by assigning separate identities—see persona discussion in Chapter 2, Section 2.5). When treated as group access, membership in multiple groups is not a problem. Both delegation and/or inheritance are possible. Roles may be credentialed, and role credentials may be used in place of individual credentials. Roles are less dynamic than groups in general, but they do change over time. Roles may exist independent of membership, but in any instance of time, the collection of members serving a role may be treated as a group.

■ *Attribute-based access control (ABAC)*: This is a form of access control that is based on enumerated attributes rather than identity. Revocation is done by modifying a particular attribute or creating an exception list. All members who have a particular access privilege must be enumerated through a separate service. A separate use case for each type of access must be developed. Enumeration of all privileges for an individual is very problematic. Both delegation and/or inheritance are difficult and problematic.

■ *Policy-based access control (PBAC)*: Privilege is based on policy and is described by the context, currency, and priorities of the command structure together with the other attributes that the entity may have. One group of policies may be deemed attribute control, and others may be context driven. The policy-based privilege is the most difficult to automate because the semantics and grammar of an arbitrary policy-based authorization have not been defined.

■ *Claims-based access control (CBAC)*: Privilege is based on a predefined access control rule set and may include membership in roles and groups, as well as policy constraints and other factors such as training or exceptions. Basically, the owner defines the access control requirement. An example would be VOYEUR II = company employee for 3 years AND (executive pay scale OR waiver by CEO) AND (training in finance OR waiver by finance and accounting) but NOT (sales or marketing). The requester would present a trusted claim of VOYEUR II to gain access.

■ *Others*: These are basically combinations of the above.

Commercial software in general is proficient at handling group-based (GBAC) and role-based access (RBAC) along with identity; so, products exist that can use these features in a general access approach. This is not true for attribute-based, policy-based, or CBAC, all of which require specialized rule sets.

4.3 Access Control List

The service has either within or externally an ACL that consists of conditions that must be met for access. This may include conditions that deny access (such as not USCITIZEN). External positioning of this ACL is easier to maintain and update. Access control may include both mandatory and discretionary access. *Mandatory* takes precedence and *deny* in both takes precedence as discussed below. Presented credentials may use groups and/or roles for access decisions.

4.3.1 Group Requirements

A group is a shorthand label that represents a collection of individual entities. Examples are all individuals assigned to the New York Offices of Merrill Lynch (NYML) or all printers at Deloitte Lisbon (DelLis). An enterprise registry or service is needed to avoid ambiguities and to provide services to delegation, claims, and other enterprise utilities. Services include *memberof* (identity), which returns all groups the identity is listed in, and *memberof* (GroupName), which returns all members of a group, among others. The uniqueness of group names must be maintained over all enterprise computing and time, with no circularity in their definitions; this allows the retrieval services mentioned previously to bring unambiguous information for evaluation. Ambiguity is often a vulnerability that can be exploited. Groups may contain other groups in their lists, but they cannot be circular or self-referential. Changes to group membership must be flagged for claims computation.

4.3.2 Role Requirements

A role is an assignment to an entity. The role represents the position filled by an individual in the enterprise management system or an assignment provided by a higher authority. Examples are *Purchasing Office Head* or *Building Maintenance Officer NY Bldg 3*. An enterprise registry or service is needed to avoid ambiguities and to provide services to delegation, claims, and other enterprise utilities. Services include *rolesfor* (identity), which returns all roles in which the identity is listed, and *rolesin* (RoleName), which returns all members of a role, among others. The uniqueness of role names must be maintained over all enterprise computing and time, with no circularity, and provide the retrieval services mentioned previously. Roles may contain other roles in their lists, and may contain the context of a group (Executives NY Branch, Board of Directors in NY, etc.). Changes to role membership must be flagged for claims computation.

4.3.3 ACRs and ACLs

The data owner is responsible for stating the ACRs for access to and privileges allowed to each requester for service. The requirements must be unambiguous and clear and will result in the computation of a claim (the simplest claim is that an individual meets the set of requirements). It gets a little more complex than that, and claims are discussed in detail in Chapters 8 through 11. Each WS is provisioned with an ACL for discretionary access control (DAC) and mandatory access control (MAC). The ACLs contain the names of the claims for which access is either granted or denied. ACLs are developed to permit claim holders access and privilege with a specific web service. The initial ACLs are specified by the organization that is the owner of the information. In order to make a comprehensive process for access claims, the conditions and rationale are stored in an ACR at the enterprise level. This ACR is used to compute the claims for entities that may wish to make a request for service. ACRs are the collection of attributes, roles, and policies that provide a basis for service use and include access, authorities such as read/modify/write/delete, sharing restrictions, and other permissions. Each set of factors represents a set of capabilities to be applied to a class of users. The name of the claim in the ACR corresponds to one element of the ACL. The designation of an assignment to a billet with certain roles is sufficient in many cases. ACLs are stored at the software service and are intended for comparing presented claims (computed from the ACR) to acceptable claims (stored in the ACL). The WS contains an administrative interface to the service for maintenance of these data. These data are stored with the service in an appropriate place.

4.3.4 Discretionary Access Control and Mandatory Access Control

In order to allow for full flexibility, access controls are divided into two categories: discretionary and mandatory. Either can allow or deny access, but each has its own unique properties. Denies are always treated first and cannot be overridden by any allow. Most DAC is allowed, but occasionally a DAC may be specified that denies access. For example, DAC may deny access to anyone without proper training, regardless of where they work or who their boss is. If untrained is in the discretionary list, then no further evaluation is made. The computer will treat these two categories differently. DAC is treated as a mathematical OR. After evaluating the denials (any one of which can terminate access), the allows are evaluated. Any allow will permit access (although privilege may be different). For example, a claim of user or administrator or auditor will allow access. Table 4.1 provides the data elements for this area.

Table 4.1 Discretionary Access Control Store

DAC	Description	DAC	Description
DAC 1	Allows access	DAC a	Denies access
Claim 2	Allows access	DAC b	Denies access
…	Up to 512 attributes	…	Up to 512 attributes

Some web services are provisioned with an MAC store. MACs are requirements that must be met, in aggregate—all MAC claims must be met— before other considerations can be evaluated. MACs are treated as a mathematical AND. MACs include, but are not limited to, citizenship, age, and clearance. MACs are developed to allow claim holders with appropriate MAC access and to deny access to a specific WS for those that do not meet the MAC criteria (even if other claims can be made). The initial MACs are specified by the organization that owns the information. In order to make a comprehensive process for access claims, the conditions and rationale are stored in ACRs. Each set of factors represents a set of capabilities to be applied to a class of users. The label applied to the MAC requirements corresponds to one element of the MAC. MACs are in addition to the DACs when they exist; if they do not exist, the MAC requirement is assumed to be "none." Access is granted only when there is a match between the requester MAC and the provider MAC store or the content MAC requirement. When MACs exist, they are evaluated first since they normally deny access. This is a computational efficiency since access is only allowed when all MACs are satisfied and at least one DAC is satisfied. Any expression of deny takes precedence. An example of a deny MAC might be dual citizenship. Table 4.2 provides the data elements for this area.

Access control proceeds first with mandatory and then with discretionary access. Mandatory access has both *allow* and *deny*. Deny takes precedence. For example, Non-USCITIZEN may deny access—the access control decision is over and access is denied. It does not matter what is in the rest of the mandatory and discretionary data stores. Any denial terminates the decision. Next, the allow values are evaluated. For MAC, all are needed (they act like a mathematical AND or EACH). For example, if claims on the allow side of the MAC contain trade secret and executive only, then the claims in the SAML must have both. If both are absent, the access is denied with no need to check discretionary access. Assuming there is no denial of access at this point, the discretionary access is evaluated. Deny takes precedence. For example, if Non-Flag denies access, the access control decision is over and access is denied. It does not matter what is in the rest of the discretionary data stores. Any denial terminates the decision. Assuming that there is no denial of access at this point, the claims on the allow side of discretionary access are evaluated. Any match between the presented claim and the ACL allows access (a match acts like a mathematical OR or ONEOF). One match is all that is required.

Table 4.2 Mandatory Access Control Store

MAC	Description	MAC	Description
MAC1	Allows access	MAC a	Denies access
MAC2	Allows access	MAC b	Denies access
...	Up to 512 attributes	...	Up to 512 attributes

4.4 Complex Access Control Schemas

More complicated expressions may require a Boolean engine to accomplish the concept of (Role a AND Role b) but not (Group i OR Group j). An open-ended computation may take the following form:

Format for ACL at the Services
Nomenclature:*

```
expression ::= and_expression (('or' | '||') and_expression) *
and_expression ::= comparison ( ('and' | '&&') comparison)*
comparison ::= sum ('=' | '!=' | '<>' | '>' | '<' |
                    '>=' | '<=' | 'match' | 'like' ) sum
        | sum 'between' sum 'and' sum
sum ::= product ( ('+' | '-') product)*
product ::= atom ( ('*' | '/') atom)*
atom ::= '(' expression ')'
        | string
        | '-'? number
        | number
        | attribute_name
        | ('!' | 'not') atom
        | 'in' group_name
        | 'defined' attribute_name
        | 'now'
```

Attribute and group names are case insensitive.

```
! is equivalent to not,
|| is equivalent to or,
&& is equivalent to and,
<> is equivalent to !=.
```

If an attribute is not defined in the context, the evaluation of the expression raises an exception.

The && operator evaluates until the first false argument, while || operator—until the first true, for example, not-defined location and location != "Thailand" evaluates to true even when the location is undefined.

String literals may be enclosed either in quotes or apostrophes, for example,

```
'Hello,' + "Dolly!"
```

Date literals are represented by strings, for example,

```
"June 15, 2012", '5:30 pm', "12/21/2012",
now between "9am" and "17pm"
        now <= "25 Dec, 2012, 23:59:59"
```

---

* Based on http://msdn.microsoft.com/en-us/library/windows/desktop/dd981030(v = vs.85).aspx.

"Match" comparison exploits regular expressions, "like" comparison exploits wildcards, for example,

```
greeting match '^(Hi|Hello)\b.*!$'
product like 'soft*'
```

Such a complex representation can be reduced to a claim by placing a label on the rule. This concept will be exploited later for CBAC.

4.5 Privilege

Once access is accomplished, privilege can be computed in a number of ways. Privilege allows the requester to read, write, update, or create entries in one or more databases or flat files or to request complex analytics or presentations. The approaches are listed below:

1. Account based—The service maintains an account for each individual that contains the privileges in as much detail as needed.
2. Role- or group based—Privilege is based on the same elements that are used for granting access.
3. Gathering of additional data—Once access is allowed, further data may be sought from the attribute stores to define privilege. This is often combined with IBAC, where identity is the basis for access.
4. Credential presentation that contains additional data for privilege—This may be combined with the credential for CBAC.

4.6 Concept of Least Privilege

In computer science and other fields, the principle of minimal privilege, also known as the *principle of least privilege* or just *least privilege,* requires that in a particular abstraction layer of a computing environment, every module (such as a process, user, or program on the basis of the software layer being executed) must be able to access only such information and resources as are necessary to its legitimate purpose. The principle of least privilege is widely recognized as an important design consideration in enhancing the protection of data and functionality from faults and malicious behavior.

In operating systems such as Windows, there is no security enforcement for a code running in kernel mode, and therefore, such a code always runs with maximum privileges. The principle of least privilege therefore demands the use of user-mode solutions when given the choice between a kernel-mode and user-mode solution if the two solutions provide the same results.

Least-privilege issues occur when an individual is assigned two or more roles with differing privilege sets within the organization. Under ideal conditions, the role being executed should determine privilege. For example, a user (defined role) may modify his own information, and an administrator (defined role) may modify the information of any entity.

4.6.1 Least Privilege Case Study

Major Clint Jones has several assignments within the unit, including enclave administrator and database administrator, and he is also just a user. He, and the unit, would like to limit his authority so that while checking his e-mail, he does not accidently format a hard drive (which an enclave administrator is allowed to do). The solution may well be to give Major Jones two identities or personas, but as shown in Section 2.5, this can lead to extra complications and duplicate stores. The computer or software application could just ask Major Jones when he requests services which role he is making requests for, or the computer or software service could try to figure the context and limit his authority when he appears to be working in his own accounts. There are no simple answers. All require code, governance, policy, and accountability for actions.

Chapter 5

Cryptography

Cryptographic services have been around for some time, but they have not been used to the extent recommended in this book. Cryptography alone will not solve security problems, but cryptography can provide methods for ensuring confidentiality and integrity in communication. Cryptography is well documented in the literature. It is seldom used to the extent advocated in this book. It became apparent that an openly published version was necessary for distribution to vendors and application owners. Some of the material in this chapter was originally published in 2013 [19].

5.1 Introduction

Cryptographic services are pervasive in a high-assurance enterprise. Standard terms used in the chapter include the following:

- Plaintext—The material that is to undergo cryptographic operations
- Key—The unique mathematical parameter used in the cryptographic operations to generate a ciphertext
- Cipher—The algorithm that is used to apply a key and a cryptographic operation
- Encryption—The act of applying the cipher to the key and plaintext, resulting in ciphertext
- Ciphertext—The results of encryption of a plaintext
- Decryption—The act of applying the cipher to the key and the ciphertext, resulting in plaintext

Cryptographic services and functions need to be standardized to ensure interoperability. These services provide security protection for data and messages and support security properties such as confidentiality, integrity, nonrepudiation, authentication, and authorization. Functions to sign, validate, and timestamp messages are provided via mechanisms approved for enterprise usage. Authentication and signature cryptographic functions employed in the enterprise are based on the use of the PKI public/private key pairs. The strength of the protection mechanisms for these functions relies on the private key portion remaining secret. For services and devices, private keys are kept in a secure store. Cryptographic functions in WS security—protection for service calls follows the WS security standards [1] for protecting messages. Several supporting services are required, including XML Canonicalization [5c], Hashing function, Secure Hash Algorithm (SHA)-512 [4e], and strong random number (RN) generation (strong implies uniform distribution of values over the appropriate range). Java™ provides many cryptographic services through the Java Cryptography Architecture (JCA) framework. The libraries used to do cryptographic operation must be certified [2h]. Data at rest may be encrypted to protect the confidentiality and integrity of the data. If encrypted, the keys are derived from the primary credentials of the owner of the data. All data in motion are encrypted and transported using TLS with mutual authentication [4m]. End-to-end encryption is used for all active entity communications. This chapter is divided into the following sections, which describe handling of dependent functions: cryptographic keys, encryption, decryption, hash function, signatures, and key lengths.

5.2 Cryptographic Keys and Key Management

Each active entity has an asymmetric key pair issued as part of their Enterprise X.509 [4g] PKI certificate. These keys are RSA 2048-bit asymmetric keys. Symmetric keys are generated for TLS and other forms of communication because their computation is more efficient.

5.2.1 Asymmetric Key Pairs

Asymmetric key pairs are generated in a secure process, and PKI certificates are issued for all active entities. All current-enterprise PKI certificates use RSA 2048-bit asymmetric key generation. Users are issued smart cards through the normal identification issuance process. All other active entities (machines, devices, servers, web services, and other OSI level-5+ software) are issued Enterprise X.509 PKI certificates.

5.2.1.1 RSA Key Generation

RSA involves a public key and a private key. The public key can be known to everyone and is used for encrypting messages. Messages encrypted with the public key can be decrypted only by using the private key. The keys for the RSA algorithm are generated in the following way:

Choose two distinct prime numbers p and q. For security purposes, the integers p and q should be chosen at random, and should be of similar bit length. Prime integers can be efficiently found using a primality test.[*]

$$\text{Compute } n = pq, \qquad (5.1)$$

n is used as the modulus for both the public and private keys.

$$\text{Compute } \varphi(n) = (p-1)(q-1), \qquad (5.2)$$

where φ is Euler's totient or phi function. Choose an integer e such that $1 < e < \varphi(n)$ and gcd $(e, \varphi(n)) = 1$, that is, e and $\varphi(n)$ are coprime.

e is released as the public key exponent. The bit length for the enterprise cryptographic operation is 2048.

$$\text{Determine } d = e - 1 \bmod \varphi(n), \qquad (5.3)$$

that is, d is the multiplicative inverse of $e \bmod \varphi(n)$. This is more clearly stated as solved for d given $(d{*}e) \bmod \varphi(n) = 1$.

d is kept as the private key exponent. The public key consists of the modulus n and the public (or encryption) exponent e. The private key consists of the private (or decryption) exponent d, which must be kept secret.

5.3 Symmetric Keys

Symmetric keys are developed for a number of uses. One of the main reasons to do so is the algorithms for encrypt and decrypt are faster using symmetric keys than similar algorithms for asymmetric keys for the same effective key lengths.

5.3.1 TLS Mutual Authentication Key Production

TLS mutual authentication requires that the TLS client side holds a certificate (all active entities are required to hold Enterprise X.509 certificates).

---

[*] The key pairs may also be weak due to weaknesses in the random number or because the pair is weak, and these should be checked for weakness and regenerated as necessary. Many checklist and other algorithms for weak key pairs exist such as Debian-weak-key check or checking-generated keys against a list of known weak keys. Most primality tests are probabilistic; so, another potential weakness is choosing a composite number that tests prime. This would cut the effective bit length to less than half.

TLS involves three basic phases:

- Peer negotiation for algorithm support
- Key exchange and authentication
- Symmetric cipher encryption and message authentication

During the first phase, the client and server negotiate *cipher suites*, which determine the ciphers to be used, the key exchange and authentication algorithms, and the message authentication codes (MACs). The key exchange and authentication algorithms are typically public key algorithms. The MACs are made up of cryptographic hash functions using the HashMAC (HMAC) construction for TLS and a nonstandard pseudorandom function for SSL.

Typical algorithms are given below:

- For key exchange: RSA, Diffie–Hellman, ECDH, SRP, and PSK (e.g., RSA [20])
- For authentication: RSA, DSA, and ECDSA (e.g., RSA)
- Symmetric ciphers: RC4, Triple Data Encryption Standard (DES), Advanced Encryption Standard (AES), IDEA, DES, or Camellia (e.g., AES)
- For cryptographic hash function: HMAC– Message Digest 5 (MD-5) and/or HMAC–SHA are used for TLS (e.g., MD-5 and SHA 256/512 [4e]). MD-5 is not to be used except in combination with SHA for HMAC*

The key information and certificates necessary for TLS are handled in the form of X.509 certificates, which define required fields and data formats.

TLS has a variety of security measures:

- The client may use the certificate authority's (CA) *public* key to validate the CA's digital signature on the server certificate. If the digital signature can be verified, the client accepts the server certificate as a valid certificate issued by a trusted CA.
- The client verifies that the issuing CA is on its list of trusted CAs.
- The client checks the server's certificate validity period. The authentication process stops if the current date and time fall outside the validity period.
- The client protects against a downgrade of the protocol to a previous (less secure) version or a weaker cipher suite.
- The client numbers all the application records with a sequence number, and uses this sequence number in MACs.
- The client uses a message digest enhanced with a key (so only a key holder can check the MAC). This is specified in RFC† 2104 [4].

---

* For IPSec, HMAC-SHA 256/512 is preferred.
† RFC—request for comment.

■ The message that ends the handshake ("Finished") sends a hash of all the exchanged handshake messages seen by both parties.

In order to generate the session keys used for the secure connection, the client encrypts an RN with the server's public key and sends the result to the server. Only the server can decrypt it (with its private key: this is one fact that makes the keys hidden from third parties, since only the server and the client have access to these data). The client knows the public key and RN, and the server knows the private key and (after decryption of the client's message) RN. A third party may know only the public key, unless the private key has been compromised. From the RN, both parties generate key material for encryption and decryption.

5.3.2 *Other Key Production*

Symmetric keys may be generated for a number of other reasons, including the safe store of data during operations and encryption of memory for protection. Keys must be generated using a strong RN generator and should be at least 256 bits in length. When an RN generator is used in the key generation process, all values are generated randomly or pseudorandomly such that all possible combinations of bits and all possible values are equally likely to be generated. Intermediate key generation states and values are not accessible outside the module in plaintext or an otherwise-unprotected form [4m].

5.4 Store Keys

All asymmetric keys are generated in a security-hardened store* such as a hardware storage module, hardware security module (HSM), or other store that is hardened against theft, tampering, or destruction. Session keys are usually stored in memory by the server and browser, and they should be stored in a memory space that is unavailable to other programs. When contained within a cryptographic module, secret and private keys may be stored in plaintext form. These plaintext keys are not accessible from outside the module. A means is provided to ensure that all keys are associated with the correct entities (i.e., person, group, or process) to which the keys are assigned. Any cryptographic key that is stored in a repository must be protected from disclosure for the life of the key. This includes encryption of the key, restricted access controls, password protection, dispersion, and obfuscation, among other measures, to prevent it from falling into nefarious hands.

---

* Security hardened means that the store is unavailable to unauthorized requestors, and the contents are not retrievable, even with physical access, or modifiable. Preferably, it should not be physically accessible by unauthorized personnel.

5.5 Delete Keys

A cryptographic module of any web service in an enterprise utilizes an internal capability to zeroize all plaintext cryptographic keys and other unprotected critical security parameters within the module when the keys are no longer in use. Zeroization of cryptographic keys and other critical security parameters are not required if the keys and parameters are either encrypted or otherwise physically or logically protected (e.g., contained within an additional embedded Federal Information Processing Standard [FIPS] 140-2 cryptographic module [2h]).

5.6 Encryption

In cryptography, encryption is the process of transforming information (plaintext) using an algorithm (cipher) to make it unreadable to anyone except those possessing special knowledge, usually referred to as a key. The result of the process is ciphertext. Encryption can be used to protect data "at rest," such as files on computers and storage devices, or to protect data in transit, such as data being transferred via networks. There have been numerous reports of data in transit being intercepted in recent years [21]. Encryption can protect the confidentiality of messages, but other techniques are still needed to protect the integrity and authenticity of a message; for example, verification of MAC or a digital signature.

5.7 Symmetric versus Asymmetric Encryption Algorithms

Symmetric encryption algorithms encrypt and decrypt with the same key. The main advantages of symmetric algorithms are security and high speed. Asymmetric encryption algorithms encrypt and decrypt with different keys. Data are encrypted with a public key, and decrypted with a private key (or vice versa). Generally, symmetric encryption algorithms are much faster to execute than asymmetric ones. In practice, they are often used together; so, a public key algorithm is used to encrypt a randomly generated encryption key and the random key is used to encrypt the actual message using a symmetric algorithm.

5.7.1 Asymmetric Encryption

Asymmetric encryption keys come in pairs. What one key encrypts, only the other can decrypt. Frequently the keys are interchangeable, in the sense that if key A encrypts a message, then B can decrypt it, and if key B encrypts a message, then key A can decrypt it. Asymmetric encryption is also known as public key cryptography, since entities typically are assigned a matching key pair and make one public while keeping the other secret. Entities can "sign" messages and send secret messages by encrypting a message with the recipient's public key. The requisite to the successful use of asymmetric encryption is a key management system, which implements a public key infrastructure [4g,4h].

A number of algorithms are in use.* Keys that are RSA compatible [20] are generated for Enterprise X.509 certificates. Additional material may be found in Reference 22.

5.7.2 RSA Asymmetric Encryption

RSA uses public and private keys that are functions of a pair of large prime numbers based on the difficulty of factoring large integers. The keys used for encryption and decryption in RSA algorithm are generated using random data. The key used for encryption is a public key. Public keys are stored anywhere publicly accessible. The sender of a message encrypts the data using a public key, and the receiver decrypts it using his/her own private key.

5.7.3 Combination of Symmetric and Asymmetric Encryption

If we want the benefits of both types of encryption algorithms, the general idea is to create a random symmetric key to encrypt the data, and then encrypt that key asymmetrically. Once the key is asymmetrically encrypted, we add it to the encrypted message between a sender and a receiver. The receiver gets the message and the encrypted key, decrypts it with his private key, and uses it to decrypt the message.

5.7.4 Symmetric Encryption

Symmetric encryption uses the same secret key to encrypt and decrypt information, or there is a simple transform between the two keys. A secret key can be a number, a word, or just a string of random letters. Symmetric algorithms require both the sender and the receiver to know the secret key.

Symmetric key algorithms [22] can be divided into stream algorithms (stream ciphers) and block algorithms (block ciphers).

5.7.4.1 Stream Ciphers

Stream ciphers encrypt the bits of information one at a time, operating on 1 bit (or sometimes 1 byte) of data at a time (encrypt data bit by bit). Stream ciphers are faster and smaller to implement than block ciphers; however, they have an important security gap. If the same key stream is used, certain types of attacks may cause the information to be revealed. This document does not specify stream ciphers.

---

* Rivest, Shamir, and Adleman—(RSA), digital signature algorithm—(DSA), and pretty good privacy—(PGP).

5.7.4.2 Block Ciphers

Block cipher (method for encrypting data in blocks) is a symmetric cipher that encrypts information by breaking it down into blocks and encrypting data in each block. A block cipher encrypts data in fixed-sized blocks (commonly of 64 bits). The most-used block ciphers are Triple DES and AES. The enterprise uses AES for block ciphers.

5.7.5 AES/Rijndael Encryption

AES stands for Advanced Encryption Standard. AES is a symmetric key encryption technique that replaces the commonly used DES. It was the result of a worldwide call for submissions of encryption algorithms issued by the U.S. Government's National Institute of Standards and Technology (NIST) in 1997 and was completed in 2000. The winning algorithm, Rijndael, was developed by two Belgian cryptologists, Vincent Rijmen and Joan Daemen [24]. The AES algorithm uses three key sizes: 128-, 192-, and 256-bit encryption key. Each encryption key size causes the algorithm to behave slightly differently; so, the increasing key sizes not only offer a larger number of bits with which to scramble the data, but they also increase the complexity of the cipher algorithm.

5.7.5.1 Description of the AES Cipher

AES is based on a design principle known as a substitution permutation network. It is fast in both software and hardware. Unlike its predecessor, DES, AES does not use a Feistel network. AES has a fixed block size of 128 bits and a key size of 128, 192, or 256 bits, whereas Rijndael can be specified with block and key sizes in any multiple of 32 bits, with a minimum of 128 bits. The blocksize has a maximum of 256 bits, but the keysize has no theoretical maximum. AES operates on a 4×4 matrix of bytes, termed the state (versions of Rijndael with a larger block size have additional columns in the state). The AES cipher is specified as a number of repetitions of transformation rounds that convert the input plaintext into the final output of ciphertext. Each round consists of several processing steps, including one that depends on the encryption key. The key cipher algorithm process involves matrix transformations [24]. Hardware for performing these functions exists, and may be used. Intel cores have added instruction sets to speed the algorithms.

5.7.6 Data Encryption Standard

Derived in part from Reference 23, additional material may be found there. DES is a symmetric block cipher developed by IBM. The algorithm uses a 56-bit key to encipher/decipher a 64-bit block of data. The key is always presented as a 64-bit block, every eighth bit of which is ignored. The algorithm is best suited to implementation in hardware. DES is the most widely used symmetric algorithm in the world, despite claims that the key length is too short. Ever since DES was first announced, controversy has raged about whether 56 bits is long enough to guarantee security. NIST[*] recommended that DES be replaced by Triple DES, a modified version employing 112- or 168-bit keys. DES's versatility was also limited because it worked only in hardware, and the explosion of the Internet and e-commerce led to a much greater use and versatility of software than could have been anticipated by DES's designers. As DES's vulnerabilities became apparent, NIST opened an international competition in 1997 to find a permanent replacement for DES (see AES cipher above).

5.7.6.1 Triple DES

Triple DES [2d] is a variation of DES. It uses a 64-bit key consisting of 56 effective key bits and eight parity bits. The size of the block for Triple DES is 8 bytes. Triple DES encrypts the data in 8-byte chunks. The idea behind Triple DES is to improve the security of DES by applying DES encryption 3 times using three different keys.

5.7.6.2 Description of the Triple DES Cipher

Those who consider the exhaustive key-search attack to be a real possibility can make the problem more difficult for an adversary by using double- or triple-length keys [23]. The use of multiple-length keys leads us to the Triple DES algorithm, in which DES is applied 3 times. If we consider a triple-length key to consist of three 56-bit keys, K1, K2, and K3, then encryption is as follows:

1. Encrypt plaintext with K1
2. Decrypt the result in 1 with K2
3. Encrypt the result in 2 with K3 to provide ciphertext

Setting K3 equal to K1 in these processes gives us a double-length key K1 and K2. Setting K1, K2, and K3 all equal to K has the same effect as using a single-length (56-bit) key. Thus, it is possible for a system using Triple DES to be compatible with a system using single DES. The key cipher algorithm process involves matrix transformations [2d].

5.8 Decryption

Decryption is the complement of encryption. In cryptography, decryption is the process of transforming encrypted information. (*Ciphertext*) uses an algorithm (*cipher*) to make it readable to an entity that possesses special knowledge (*key*). The result of the process is decrypted information (in cryptography, referred to as *plaintext*).

---

[*] National Institute of Standards and Technology.

5.8.1 Asymmetric Decryption

Since we have specified that asymmetric encryption and decryption is performed using the PKI properties of the enterprise certificate, for active entities, we use the RSA algorithm by inverting the encryption process and using the complementary key. That is, if the material was encrypted using the *private* key, then it is decrypted using the *public* key. The properties of the PKI will also allow the material that was encrypted using the *public* key to be decrypted using the *private* key.

5.8.2 Symmetric Decryption

For symmetric encryption, we have limited the possible algorithms to AES and Triple DES.

The AES decryption algorithm is applied as follows:

> Recall: The AES cipher is specified as a number of repetitions of transformation rounds that convert the input plaintext into the final output of ciphertext. Each round consists of several processing steps, including one that depends on the encryption key. A set of reverse rounds is applied to transform ciphertext back into the original plaintext using the same encryption key.

The Triple DES decryption algorithm is applied as follows:
Decryption is the reverse of the encryption process (see Section 5.7.6.2):

1. Decrypt ciphertext with K3
2. Encrypt the result of 1 with K2
3. Decrypt the result of 2 with K1 to provide plaintext

Setting K3 equal to K1 in these processes gives us a double-length key K1 and K2. Setting K1, K2, and K3 all equal to K has the same effect as using a single-length (56-bit) key. Thus, it is possible for a system using Triple DES to be compatible with a system using single DES. The key cipher algorithm process involves matrix transformations [2d].

5.9 Hash Function

A hash function is any algorithm or subroutine that maps plaintext to a value, called the hash, hash value, or hash code. For example, a value can serve as an index to a list of plaintext items. Hash functions are mostly used to accelerate table lookup or data comparison tasks such as finding items in a database, detecting duplicated or similar records in a large file, finding similar stretches in deoxyribonucleic acid (DNA) sequences, and so on. In cryptographic services, a hash is used to nearly uniquely identify the content of a plaintext. Some hash functions may map two or more plaintexts to the same hash value, causing a collision. Cracking a hash code would be devising a set of rules by which one change can be compensated with other changes to make the hash the same. Such hash functions try to map the plaintext to the hash values as evenly as possible because, as hash tables fill up, collisions become more frequent.

5.9.1 Hash Function Algorithms

For most types of hashing functions, the choice of the function strongly depends on the nature of the input data, and their probability distribution in the intended application. In this case, we use *plaintext*, which might be SAML tokens, messages in Simple Object Access Protocol (SOAP) envelopes, log records, etc. The hash is part of the almost-unique identifier bound to a signature.

5.9.2 Hashing with Cryptographic Hash Function

Some cryptographic hash functions, such as SHA-3/SHA-512, have stronger uniformity guarantees than checksums or fingerprints, and thus can provide very good general-purpose hashing functions. A cryptographic hash function is a deterministic procedure that takes an arbitrary block of data (plaintext) and returns a fixed-size bit string—the (cryptographic) hash value—such that an accidental or intentional change to the data changes the hash value. The data to be encoded (plaintext) are often called the "message," and the hash value is sometimes called the message digest, digest, or hash. The ideal cryptographic hash function has four main significant properties; it is deterministic, easy to compute, strong uniformity, and will provide an unambiguous answer. The algorithm is unlikely to generate a message that has a given hash, change a message and not change the hash, or find different messages with the same hash. There are a large number of cryptographic hash algorithms; but for the enterprise, we restrict the usage to two such constructs:

- MD-5
- SHA-512 bits

5.9.2.1 MD-5

The MD-5 message-digest algorithm is a widely used cryptographic hash function that produces a 128-bit (16-byte) hash value. MD-5 is commonly used to check data integrity. In an attack on MD-5 published in December 2008, a group of researchers used this technique to fake SSL certificate validity. US-CERT[*] has

---

[*] Carnegie Mellon's United States Computer Emergency Readiness Team.

advised that MD-5 "should be considered cryptographically broken and unsuitable for further use," and most U.S. enterprise applications now require the SHA-2 family of hash functions. For this reason, MD-5 is not to be used in stand-alone operations but may be used in HMAC construction for TLS.

5.9.2.2 SHA-3-Defined SHA-512

In cryptography, the Secure Hash Algorithm (SHA)-2 is a standard that defines a set of cryptographic hash functions by bit strength (SHA-224, SHA-256, SHA-384, and SHA-512), which was designed by the National Security Agency (NSA) and published in 2001 by NIST as a U.S. FIPS. SHA-2 includes a significant number of changes from its predecessor, SHA-1. In October 2012, NIST chose a new algorithm (Keccak) as the algorithm to be used in the SHA-3 standard [24]. A notable problem in moving from SHA-1 to SHA-2 is that both of them used the same algorithmic approach (Merkle–Damgard) to process message text. This means that a full attack on SHA-1 becomes a potential threat for SHA-2. While no successful attacks against a full-round SHA-2 have been announced, there is no doubt that attack mechanisms are being developed in private. For the enterprise, the goal is that SHA-3/SHA-512 be used for all signature data. The SHA-3 standard has yet to be published, even though the algorithm has been chosen. However, because of the compromises of other hash algorithms, and the time required to implement new models, a transition to SHA-3-defined SHA-512 should be undertaken. It may be combined with MD-5 for HMAC applications in TLS.

5.10 Signatures

A digital signature is an information element that can be added to a document that can be used to authenticate the identity of the generator or the signer of a document and to ensure that the original content of the document that has been sent is unchanged. Digital signatures are easily transportable and cannot be imitated by someone else. The digital signature has specific content elements that include an encrypted hash of the document, hash details, a time stamp, and the X.509 certificate of the signer. An important feature of each signature is the ability to validate the signature. The attachment of the X.509 of the signer must be verified and validated through a number of steps:

- The certificate is issued by a trusted CA.
- The certificate date is valid, and the distinguished name of the signer matches the certificate.
- The certificate is not revoked.

■ The hash must be validated by decrypting with the public key of the signer and comparing it to an independently computed hash. For the enterprise, we consider three basic signatures:
  - XML signatures
  - Secure/multipurpose Internet mail extension (S/MIME) signatures
  - E-content signatures

5.10.1 XML Signature

XML signatures are digital signatures designed for use in XML transactions. They are defined by a standard schema for capturing the result of a digital signature operation applied to arbitrary (but often XML) data. Like non-XML-aware digital signatures (e.g., PKCS), XML signatures add authentication, data integrity, and support for nonrepudiation to the data that they sign. However, unlike non-XML digital signature standards (DSSs), those for the XML signature have been designed to both account for and take advantage of the Internet and XML. A fundamental feature of XML signature is the ability to sign only specific portions of the XML tree rather than the complete document. The entire return may be encrypted for security [5b].

5.10.2 S/MIME Signature

S/MIMEs provide a consistent way to send and receive secure MIME data. On the basis of a popular Internet MIME standard, S/MIME provides the following cryptographic security services for electronic-messaging applications: authentication, message integrity and nonrepudiation of origin (using digital signatures), and data confidentiality (using encryption). S/MIME can be used by traditional mail user agents (MUAs) to add cryptographic security services to mail that is sent and to interpret cryptographic security services in mail that is received. However, S/MIME is not restricted to mail—it can be used with any transport mechanism that transports MIME data, such as Hypertext Transfer Protocol (HTTP). S/MIME [4n] provides one format for enveloped-only data, several formats for signed-only data, and several formats for signed and enveloped data.

5.10.3 E-Content Signature

The DSS [2j], developed by NIST, is used for general E-content signing. This standard specifies algorithms for applications requiring a digital signature rather than a written signature. A digital signature is represented in a computer as a string of bits. A digital signature is computed using a set of rules and a set of parameters that allow the identity of the signatory and the integrity of the data to be verified. Digital signatures may be generated on both stored and transmitted data. Signature generation uses a private key to generate a digital signature; signature verification uses a public key that corresponds to, but is not the same as, the private key. Each signatory possesses a private and public key pair. Public keys may be known by the public; private keys are kept secret. Anyone can verify the signature by employing the signatory's public key. Only the user who possesses the private key can perform signature generation. A hash function is used in the signature generation process to obtain a condensed version of the data to be signed; the condensed version of the data is often called a message digest. The message digest is input to the digital signature algorithm to generate the digital signature. The hash functions to be used are specified in the Secure Hash Standard (SHS) [2i]. FIPS-approved digital signature algorithms are used with SHA-512. The digital signature is provided to the intended verifier along with the signed data. The verifying entity verifies the signature by using the claimed signatory's public key and the same hash function that was used to generate the signature. Similar procedures may be used to generate and verify signatures for both stored and transmitted data [2i].

5.11 A Note on Cryptographic Key Lengths

For the high-assurance process, all communications are encrypted using TLS 1.2 for confidentiality. Private keys are stored in HSMs. All cryptography is done locally (no enterprise cryptographic services). Software cryptographic suites used are FIPS-140 approved. In order to develop an enterprise solution, all processes, including the cryptographic procedures, must be published and openly available. As a result, adversaries know the processes and algorithms used.

5.11.1 Encryption Key Discovery

In a large-scale enterprise, all crypto methods (algorithms—e.g., AES 256) and all message types must be published. This is needed to get all administrators, software developers, and providers on the same path. Two approaches or lines of attack are possible. The first is to find a flaw in the algorithm or computer code. The second is to try all possible combinations of key values (brute force attack). The algorithmic or code flaw approach requires very few computations to discovery. Assuming the code is clean and the algorithm is tight, we can try guessing the key.

The second approach or brute force decryption requires a known number of compute cycles.

1. Pick a feasible key (not all keys may be feasible). Example—asymmetric keys must be prime
2. Apply the decryption algorithm

Table 5.1　Encryption Key Discovery by Brute Force

Key = xxxxxxxxxxxx (n bits)
A compute cycle 1 Key = 0000000000000 (n bits)
A compute cycle 1 Key = 0000000000001 (n bits)
A compute cycle 1 Key = 0000000000011 (n bits)
A compute cycle 1 Key = 0000000000010 (n bits) ...
Total guesses = 2^n compute cycles expect to do 50% of guesses
For 20 bits expect 2^{19} compute cycles

Normal Computing	Fast Computing	High Performance Computing
Assume 1 ms/compute cycle	Assume 1 μs/compute cycle	Assume 1 ps/compute cycle
20 bits = 8.73 mins	20 bits = 0.5 s	20 bits = 0.0005 s
30 bits = 6.2 days	30 bits = 8.9 mins	30 bits = 0.5 s
32 bits = 24.9 days	32 bits = 3.5 h	32 bits = 12.6 s
256 bits = 1.8358715e + 66 years	256 bits = 0.8358715e + 63 years	256 bits = 1.8358715e + 60 years
Etc.	Etc.	Etc.

Time can be reduced by choosing only feasible keys. Finding a flaw in the computer algorithm can be very quick.

3. Examine the output and look for a recognizable material
   a. If the output is recognized (maybe the header on a JPEG or other file)—Key has been identified—apply key to all session packets
   b. If not recognizable—go to 1

Continue until all feasible keys are tried or discovery occurs. Table 5.1 provides a summary.

5.11.2 The High-Performance Dilemma

The locality of cryptographic services makes scaling through high-performance multicore thread management easier and eliminates the need for front-end load balancing. However, maintaining confidentiality with such computing capability available to an adversary is problematic. The encryption methodology must be standard and published so that all elements of the enterprise can obtain the proper software and hardware to perform the needed operations. Rogue agents (including insider threats) may be present, and to the extent possible, we should be able to operate in their presence, although this does not exclude their ability to view and export some activity. Key extraction from encrypted data is inherently a parallel function. For example, all the possible keys can be distributed to many cores and each of them can spend a few cycles attempting to decrypt encrypted packets. When one recognizes the decrypted content, then the key is presumed discovered (this assumes that recognizable is the correct translation, which is almost always true). This parallel decomposition may be across cores in a parallel array.

5.11.3 Parallel Decomposition of Key Discovery

For a given key length, m, the number of possible keys is given by $2m$, which represents the sequential computational burden for trying each possible key. Further, the first n bits may be distributed among cores (c) for processing at the scale of $c = 2n$. The remaining bits ($m - n$) may be sequentially processed with a total processing burden on each processor equal to $2m - n$. This results in a confidentiality effectiveness loss of n bits. Note that this loss is independent of the original key length, m.

If the key length is only 10 bits, then the number of possible keys is 1024. If this is spread over 1024 cores, then a single decrypt cycle (a decrypt cycle includes applying the decryption process and applying a recognition algorithm to the answer; this could be 10 machine cycles or less) reveals the key and provides an adversary a way to overcome confidentiality. If the key length is only 12 bits, then the possible keys that encrypted the packet is 4096. If this is spread over 1024 cores, then four decrypt cycles reveal the key and provide an adversary a way to overcome confidentiality. This latter is equivalent to weakening the cryptographic key by 10 bits. Table 5.2 provides a summary of the discovery process.

From Table 5.2, it can be seen that high-performance computing over $500k$ cores is equivalent to a loss of 19 bits in the strength of encryption, and a million cores essentially reduce bit effectiveness by 20 bits. The response is to increase the bits in the encryption process. The number of bits needed is related to the time it takes for brute force key discovery, which should be supplemented by 20 bits. The increased bit length adds computational burden to the normal computational process, increasing the need for high-performance computing. This could be mitigated by developing a nonparallel decomposable decryption process, which is not currently available. The cryptographic key lengths noted in this document have been increased by 20 bits and rounded to the next power of 2. Reports of compromise of crypto methods happen with increasing frequency, and these reports may result in a recommendation for a different algorithm or increased bit lengths.

5.12 Internet Protocol Security

Internet Protocol Security (IPsec) is a protocol suite for securing IP communications by authenticating and encrypting each IP packet of a communication session. IPsec also includes protocols for establishing mutual authentication between

Table 5.2 Loss of Bit Effectiveness

Distributed Key Bits (n)	Values Spread over Cores (c)	Confidentiality Effectiveness Loss (bits)	Distributed Key Bits (n)	Values Spread over Cores (c)	Confidentiality Effectiveness Loss (bits)
1	2	1	16	65,536	16
2	4	2	17	131,072	17
3	8	3	18	262,144	18
4	16	4	19	524,288	19
5	32	5	20	1,048,576	20
6	64	6	21	2,097,152	21
7	128	7	22	4,194,304	22
8	256	8	23	8,388,608	23
9	512	9	24	16,777,216	24
10	1,024	10	25	33,554,432	25
11	2,048	11	26	67,108,864	26
12	4,096	12	27	134,217,728	27
13	8,192	13	28	268,435,456	28
14	16,384	14	29	536,870,912	29
15	32,768	15	30	1,073,741,824	30

agents at the beginning of the session and negotiation of cryptographic keys to be used during the session. IPsec is an end-to-end security scheme operating in the Internet layer of the IP suite. It can be used in protecting data flows between a pair of hosts (host to host), between a pair of security gateways (network to network), or between a security gateway and a host (network to host). Although the methods of encryption described in this document may be used, there are mandatory requirements for standards compliance (DES in CBC mode, HMAC with MD-5, HMAC with SHA-1, NULL authentication algorithm, and NULL encryption algorithm). Additionally, there are specific headings and synchronization requirements, and the reader is referred to IETF RFC 2406 [4f] for details. The preferred operational implementation is AES256 and HMAC with SHA-256/512.

5.13 Other Cryptographic Services

Java is heavily used in the operational software. Java provides many cryptographic services through the JCA framework (JCA Reference Guide for Java Platform 6, Sun Microsystems). This version includes the Java Cryptography Extensions (JCEs) library. The libraries used by web services to do cryptographic operations are not required to be JCE- or JCA compatible, but they must be standards certified [2h].

5.14 The Java Cryptography Extension

JCE provides a framework and implementations for encryption, key generation and key agreement, and MAC algorithms, as well as hashing and RN generation. Support for encryption includes symmetric, asymmetric, block, and stream ciphers. The software also supports secure streams and sealed objects. Most of the requirements for cryptographic services can be met by the JCE. The use of commercial packages that meet the software vulnerability detection and remediation in Chapter 18 are sufficient with the proviso that the key store be securely protected and robust. JCE is based on the same design principles found elsewhere in the JCA: implementation independence and, whenever possible, algorithm independence. It uses the same "provider" architecture. Providers signed by a trusted entity can be plugged into the JCE framework, and new algorithms can be added.

5.15 Data at Rest

Data at rest may be encrypted to protect the confidentiality and integrity of the data. If encrypted, the keys are derived from the primary credentials of the owner of the data (e.g., an exposure service for an authoritative database). All files containing configuration data for web applications and/or services that are stored local to the service (on the server) are encrypted in storage with AES-256 protected with the public key of the service.

5.16 Data in Motion

All data in motion are encrypted and transported using TLS with mutual authentication [4m]. End-to-end encryption is used for all active entity communications.

The form of communication to and from a user host device is TLS based on PKI using the common access card (CAC) with a user-supplied PIN. The form of communication between active entities is TLS based on PKI using the enterprise certificates for the entities. In some legacy cases, the SSL may use passwords.

The operational systems use the SSL/TLS bilateral encrypted dialog, where the enterprise (forest or enclave) knows the public key because the entity has prior registration with the enterprise. Certificates and keys for these exchanges are RSA 2048-bit credentials. For users, the private keys are stored and cryptographic operations take place within validated crypto modules [2h] when possible. Private keys never exist in an unencrypted form outside the crypto module.

Chapter 6

The Cloud

Cloud computing is becoming a multipurpose buzzword, but almost all forms of cloud computing involve someone else handling and protecting your data. The recent rush to place everything in somebody else's hands is a bit mystifying in view of the serious breaches that have been reported. These cloud offerings by multiple different vendors, have been made appealing by promises of reduced costs and improved efficiencies while distributing the accountability for security factors. These were discussed in three papers [25–27].

6.1 The Promise of Cloud Computing

Cloud computing has come to mean many different things. To some, it is simply putting one's data on a remote server. However, in this chapter, we use the definition provided by NIST [2g]. They define five essential characteristics of a cloud-computing environment:

- On demand self-service
- Broad network access
- Resource pooling
- Rapid elasticity
- Measured service

It is important to note that multitenancy and virtualization are not essential characteristics for cloud computing. For our discussion, we will assume no multitenancy and no virtualization, since the latter adds the most complexity.

The discussions below do not require either. Cloud computing is, at its core, a service. There are three primary models of this service. At the lowest level of infrastructure as a service (IaaS), storage, computation, and networking are provided by the cloud provider to the cloud consumer. At the next level, platform as a service (PaaS), all the trappings of IaaS plus an operating system, and perhaps some application-programming interfaces (APIs) are provided and managed by the cloud provider. The highest-level service model is software as a service (SaaS), in which the cloud provider also provides an end-user service such as webmail. The higher the service model, the more control the cloud provider has as compared to the cloud consumer. Currently, there are four different models for deploying cloud services (with more variants in development):

- *Public cloud*: In a public cloud, the infrastructure—although generally not the data on it—may be used by anyone willing to agree to its terms of use. Public clouds offer the lowest threat mitigation levels and the weakest security posture.
- *Private cloud*: Private cloud infrastructure is used by only one organization. It may exist either on or off the organization's premises. Private clouds offer the highest threat mitigation levels and the strongest potential security posture.
- *Community cloud*: In a community cloud, a group of organizations with similar interests or needs share a cloud infrastructure, which is not open to the public.
- *Hybrid cloud*: In a hybrid cloud, two or more cloud deployment models are connected in a way that allows data or services to move between them. An example of a hybrid cloud is an organization's private cloud that makes use of a community cloud during high utilization.

6.2 Benefits of the Cloud

Cloud-computing benefits emerge from economies of scale [26]. Large cloud environments with multiple users are better able to balance heavy loads, since it is unlikely that a large proportion of cloud consumers will have simultaneously high utilization needs. The cloud environment can therefore run at a higher overall utilization, resulting in better cost-effectiveness. In many cloud environments, this balancing is done by virtualization and the use of a hypervisor.

In a large cloud-computing environment, staffing allows greater flexibility. Rather than having a number of information technology generalists, the cloud provider has the ability to specialize staff in a number of areas, including security, databases, and others. The staff can become even more specialized and spend more time hardening platforms to secure them from attacks.

Investments in tools for security management and other tasks can be amortized over larger application bases. In the homogeneous cloud environment, patches can be rolled out quickly to the nearly identical hosts.

6.3 Drawbacks of Cloud Usage

Cloud computing is not without its drawbacks. In cases where services are outsourced to a cloud provider, there is a degree of loss of control by the user/consumer. This can affect compliance with laws, regulations, and organizational policies. Cloud systems have additional levels of complexity to handle intra-cloud communications, scalability, data abstraction, and more. To be available to cloud consumers, cloud providers may need to make their services available via the Internet. And critically, many clouds use multitenancy, in which multiple organizations simultaneously utilize a single host and virtualization. If one tenant organization is compromised or malicious, it may be able to compromise the data or applications of the other organizations on the same host. The load balancing may use a single identity for all instances of a service, whether it is virtual or real.

6.3.1 Differences from Traditional Data Centers

Cloud computing relies on much of the same technical infrastructure (e.g., routers, switches, operating systems, databases, and web servers) as traditional data centers, and as a result, many of the security issues are similar in two environments. The notable exception in some cases is the addition of a hypervisor for managing virtual machines. The Cloud Security Alliance's security guidance states Security controls in cloud computing are, for the most part, no different than security controls in any Information Technology (IT) environment. Cloud computing is about gracefully losing control while maintaining accountability even if the operational responsibility falls upon one or more third parties. While many of the controls are similar, two factors are at work that make cloud computing different: perimeter removal and trust. With cloud computing, the concept of a network or information perimeter changes radically. Data and applications flow from cloud to cloud via gateways along the cloud perimeters. However, since the data may be stored in clouds outside the organization's premises or control, perimeter controls become less useful. In exchange for the lack of a single perimeter around one's data and applications, cloud consumers must be able to trust their cloud providers. A lack of trust in a cloud provider does not necessarily imply a lack of security in the provider's service. A cloud provider may be acceptably secure, but the novelty of cloud computing means that many providers have not had the opportunity to satisfactorily demonstrate their security in a way that earns the trust of cloud consumers. Trust must be managed through detailed service-level agreements (SLAs), with clear metrics and monitoring mechanisms, and clear delineation of security mechanisms [25].

6.3.2 Some Changes in the Threat Scenario

There are clear differences between many of the threat scenarios, as detailed below [2f].

1. Loss of governance (or visibility and/or control of the governance process)
2. Lock-in (threats may be present and locked into the cloud environment)
3. Isolation failure (e.g., hypervisor attack, lack of accountability)
4. Compliance risks (if the provider cannot provide compliance evidence or will not permit audit by the customer, lack of accountability)
5. Management interface compromise (and/or inheritance of threats and/or malicious code from other users of the cloud)
6. Data protection (How does the customer verify protection, lack of accountability?)
7. Insecure or incomplete data deletion
8. Malicious insider (often the cloud insider that is part of the cloud provider ecosystem is not vetted as well as the organizational insider, and insiders from other cloud customers that share cloud resources could bring in contagious viruses—see 5 above)

6.4 Challenges for the Cloud and High Assurance

Despite the obvious advantages of cloud computing, the large amount of virtualization and redirection poses a number of problems for high assurance. In order to understand this, let us examine a security flow in a high-assurance system.

The application system consists of a web application (for communication with the user) and one or more aggregation services that invoke one or more exposure services and combine their information for return to the web application and the user. The exposure services retrieve information from one or more ACSs.

Once the authentication is completed, a TLS connection is established between the requestor and the service provider, within which a WS-Security* package will be sent to the service. The WS-Security [26,27] package contains an SAML† token generated by the STS in the requestor domain. The primary method of

---

* Web Services Security (WS Security, WSS) is an extension to SOAP to apply security to web services. SOAP is a protocol specification for exchanging structured information in the implementation of web. Both WSS and SOAP are standards developed by the OASIS foundation [1].
† Security Assertion Markup Language is also part of the OASIS series of standards [1].

authentication will be through the use of public keys in the X.509 certificate, which can then be used to set up encrypted communications (either by X.509 keys or a generated session key). Session keys and certificate keys need to be robust and sufficiently protected to prevent malware exploitation. The preferred method of communication is secure messaging using WS Security, contained in SOAP envelopes. The encryption key used is the public key of the target (or a mutually derived session key), ensuring only the target can interpret the communication.

The problem of scale-up (opening up applications and data access to ever-larger numbers of users) and performance is the issue that makes cloud environments and virtualization so attractive. The cloud will bring on assets as needed and retire them as needed.

Figure 6.1 shows only the web application, although the same rules apply to all the communication links between any active elements. The simplest form of dividing the load is to stand-up multiple independent instances and divide users into groups who will use the various instances. Dependent instances that extend the thread capabilities of the server are considered single independent instances. Remember, all independent instances are uniquely named and credentialed and provisioned in the attribute stores. A representation that is closer to the cloud environment is shown in Figure 6.2.

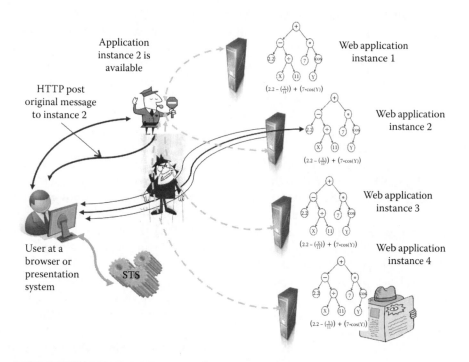

Figure 6.1   High assurance load balancing.

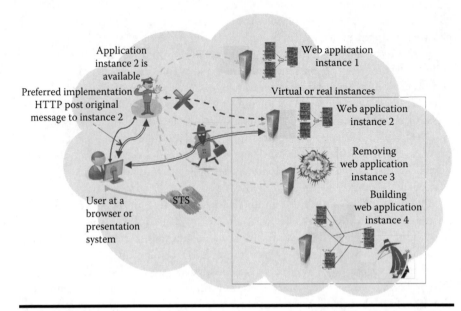

Figure 6.2   High assurance virtualized hypervisor activity.

A traffic cop (load balancer) monitors activity and posts a connection to an available instance. In this case, everything works out since the new instance has a unique name, end point, and credentials with which to proceed. All this, of course, needs to be logged in a standard form and parameters passed to make it easy to reconstruct for forensics. The figure shows a couple of threats that need mitigation, such as one eavesdropping on a communication and trying to insert itself into the conversation (MITM). This highlights the importance of bilateral authentication and encrypted communications. The second is present on instance 4 and highlights the need to protect caches and memory spaces.

When a cloud environment runs out of resources for computing, it builds additional instances, some of these may be thread extension schemas, and some may be independent instances. The traffic cop here is often called a hypervisor, and it keeps track of the instances and connections. Figure 6.2 notionally shows how this operation works. When thread capacity is saturated at the server, the hypervisor would nominally redirect the request to an independent virtual or real instance of the web application. If none exists, it will build one from elements in the resource pool as depicted in instance 4 on the chart. If the last user signs off of an independent virtual or real instance (instance 3 in the figure), the hypervisor tears down the instance and places the resources back into the resource pool. This provides an efficient reallocation of resources.

Several steps must be taken to preserve security, if we are interested in a high-assurance computing environment. The number of independent instances must be anticipated. Names, credentials, and end points must be assigned for their use.

The attribute stores and HSMs* must be provisioned with properties and the key to be used. The simple redirect must be changed to a repost loop as in Figure 6.2. The user will then have a credentialed application to authenticate with bilaterally and an end point for end-to-end message encryption. Key management is complex and essential. When a new independent instance is required, it must be built and activated (credentials and properties in the attribute store, as well as end point assignment). All these activities must be logged in a standard format with reference values that make it easy to reassemble the chain of events for forensics. When a current independent instance is retired, it must be disassembled and deactivated (credentials and properties in the attribute store, as well as end point assignment).

All these activities must be logged in a standard format with reference values that make it easy to reassemble the chain of events for forensics. The same threats exist, and the same safeguards must be taken. In fact, in Figure 6.2, a nefarious code is built right into the virtual or real instance 4, which underscores the need for trusted and verified software to do the virtualization, and protection of the resources while they are in the resource pool.

A recap of these challenges is listed below:

1. Shared identities and credentials break the accountability paradigm.
    a. Each independent instance of a virtual or real machine or virtual or real service must be uniquely named [28,29] and provided a PKI certificate for authentication. The certificate must be activated while the virtual machine is in being and when that machine is deactivated to prevent hijacking of the certificate by nefarious activities. Each instance of an independent virtual or real machine or virtual or real service must have a unique end point. This means that simple redirect will not work. Extensions of the thread mechanism by assigning resources to the operating system may preserve this functionality.
2. Multitenancy (multiple tenants using a single host) must be prohibited.
3. Virtualization across machines is particularly risky, opening up vulnerabilities in the hypervisor and a possible proliferation of vulnerabilities in each of the machines (each virtual machine must reside in a single real machine).
4. Each potential independent instance of a service must have an account provisioned with appropriate elements in an attribute store. This is required for SAML token issuance.
5. A cloud-based STS needs to be installed and implemented, and it must meet all the requirements listed here for uniqueness of names and end points. This is true for each instance of an STS (certificates and cryptographic capability).

---

* A HSM is a physical computing device that safeguards and manages digital keys for strong authentication and provides cryptoprocessing. These modules traditionally come in the form of a plug-in card or an external device that attaches directly to a computer or network server [Wikipedia].

6. The importance of cryptography cannot be overstated, and all internal and external communications should be encrypted to the end point of the communication. Memory and storage should also be encrypted to prevent theft of cached data and security parameters.

7. Private keys must reside in HSM.

   a. Stand-up of an independent virtual or real machine or virtual or real service must link keys in HSM and activate credentials preassigned to the virtual service.

   b. Stand-down of an independent virtual or real machine or virtual or real service must delink keys in HSM and deactivate credentials preassigned to the virtual service.

   c. Key management in the virtual environment is a particular concern, and a complete management schema, including destruction of session keys, must be developed.

8. Proxies and redirects break the end-to-end paradigm. When end points must change, a reposting of communication is the preferred method.

9. Resource pools must be protected from a persistent malicious code.

10. All activities must be logged in a standard format with reference values that make it easy to reassemble the chain of events for forensics.

6.5 Cloud Accountability, Monitoring, and Forensics

The goal of computer forensics is to perform a structured investigation while maintaining a documented chain of evidence to find out exactly what happened on a computing system and who or what was responsible for it [26]. This process is called forensic reconstruction. Several steps must be taken to preserve the state, if we are interested in a forensic reconstruction of the computing events.

6.5.1 Accountability

In order to ensure accountability, the number of independent instances must be anticipated. Names, credentials, and end points must be assigned for their use. The attribute stores and HSMs must be provisioned with properties and the key to be used. The simple redirect must be changed to a repost loop as shown in Figure 6.2. The requester will then have a credentialed application to authenticate with bilaterally and an end point for end-to-end message encryption. Key management is complex and essential. When a new independent instance is required, it must be built and activated (credentials and properties in the attribute store, as well as end point assignment). All these activities must be logged in a standard format with reference values that make it easy to reassemble the chain of events for forensics. When a current independent instance is retired, it must be disassembled and deactivated (credentials and properties in the attribute store, as well as end point assignment).

6.5.2 *Monitoring*

All these activities must be logged in a standard format with reference values that make it easy to reassemble the chain of events for forensics. The same threats exist, and the same safeguards must be taken. Figure 6.2 illustrates that a nefarious code may be built right into the virtual or real instance 4 of Figure 6.2, which underscores the need for trusted and verified software to do the virtualization, and protection of the resources while they are in the resource pool.

6.5.3 *Knowledge Repository*

The knowledge repository (KR) is a single integrated source of all information on the operation of the cloud (Figure 6.3). Instrumented agents feed the database on a schedule or on demand. The knowledge base is where all information related to the enterprise SOA is stored. This includes the following:

■ Hardware/software current status from the cloud or enterprise
■ Current reports on test activities including response times, frequency of the test, etc.
■ Current reports of usage data from service agent monitors and service logs, including the number of users, session times, response times, etc.
■ Hardware/software historical data
■ A list of current alerts for the entire enterprise
■ Historical data on alerts
■ Current monitoring records

Many of these feed-monitoring records are directed to status displays for the network monitoring and the enterprise support desk. They can provide a basis for real-time management and network defenses, as well as forensics.

Figure 6.3   Knowledge repository.

6.5.4 Forensic Tools

Tools are needed for KB query, correlation, and anomaly detection. Each tool should be functionally specified together with outputs and based on the standard defined records described in the next section.

6.6 Standard Requirements for Cloud Forensics

Standards provide a basis for commercial applications, as well as a market for developed tools, and they provide an interoperability process for generated files. Standards need to be developed, and they are required for a number of cloud operations:

1. Standards for identity issuance of virtual objects. The current practice of overloading the identity makes the development of forensic strategies difficult or problematic. The standards should include credentialing and establishment of identity attributes.
2. Standards for a number of details associated with cloud monitoring. These requirements are based on monitoring requirements derived for enterprise application, as shown in Table 6.1. They include the following:
   a. Standard lists of events that must be logged and alerted, including event-specific data (these may be separated into minimal, rich, and robust categories). The events should include all the agility events such as stand-up and teardown of services, as well as credentialing and establishment of identity attributes.
   b. A standard process for automatic escalation of monitoring under predefined circumstances.
   c. Standard-monitoring record content (i.e., separate from event-specific content), including date/time, record number, thread number, sequence number, active entity name, event name, and ID of service requestor.

Table 6.1 Example Audit Records

All Records:
Record number, thread number, sequence number, active entity name, event name, ID of service requestor, date/time, and other pertinent data (OP$_i$)

Event	Content
Start-up of the audit functions within the service	Event Name = "Start Up Audit," OP1 = ID of Service Requestor, OP2 = Level of Audit
Shutdown of the audit functions within the service	Event Name = "Shut Down Audit," OP1 = ID of Service Requestor

    d. Standard identifiers for monitoring content (to assist upload to a centralized KR).

    e. Standard processes for protection, access, and integrity of monitor records.

    f. Standards for continuous operations and recovery of the monitoring system and its records.

3. Standards for KR construction, KR update process, forensics tools, and analysis processes.

4. Standards for protection, access, and integrity of stored resources that will be used in agile virtualization.

A more complete discussion of monitor records and their use is provided in Chapter 19.

Chapter 7

The Network

The original goal of creating a secure web-based computing environment was to develop a secure enterprise based on the application layers and not on the network layers. The network is a requirement, and transport must be provided. The project members believed that most of the software and processes were well developed and standards based. They were embodied in commercial software over which we had little or no control. For the most part, the development team held to that; however, certain things kept coming up that were related to the network and the devices that were the broader part of the Internet communications system. A general discussion is provided below, together with some cautionary substantiation of our original tenet lists. A more detailed discussion of the security impacts is provided in Chapter 21.

7.1 The Network Entities[*]

Network entities that exist beyond the confines of an owned computing center or private cloud are often used in providing a connected network. These entities are mostly out of an enterprise architect's control; however, there are some principles and concerns that should be accommodated for security. The communication path contains an almost incomprehensible array of entities. As networks have grown, so have niche markets for specific functionality. Although not all of these are contained in all networks, many will be in between your users and the applications as part of the connectivity process from outside the network. In most cases, your

---

[*] The term "entity" was defined in Chapter 1. For Chapters 7 and 21, we are discussing nonperson entities that may be hosted on a hardware device designed to accommodate the entity (often termed appliances), or on a general-purpose device.

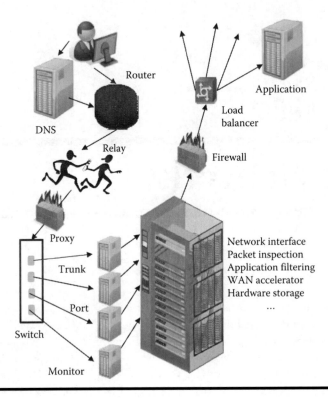

Figure 7.1   Devices along the way.

computing environment has little or no control because the network entities belong to another party, adhere to network or de facto standards, and there are few options for the enterprise to secure these entities. Some steps can be taken to mitigate (not preclude) WHAT? Some are reviewed in this chapter and others are covered in detail in Chapter 20.

Figure 7.1 shows a notional setup with numerous entities coming between a requester for service and his intended service provider. Many more are possible; a few are listed below.

7.1.1 Most Passive Elements

The least intrusive of these entities are the facilitators, path finders, connectors, and switches [30].

Hub: Hubs connect computers together in a particular topology called a network. They provide the plumbing and switching for these connections.

Network interface card: A network interface card (NIC) is a computer hardware communication component that allows computers to communicate over a network.

It allows users to connect to each other and network devices by using either wireless or cable inputs.

Basic switch: Switches redirect, duplicate, and pass communications along to other devices. Similar to a hub, switches provide a central connection between two or more devices on a network.

Bridge: Bridges can "merge" two of their ports together at very high speed.

Multilayer switch: A multilayer switch (MLS) is a computer-networking device that switches and provides extra functions on higher layers.

Basic router: Routers efficiently direct traffic to end points or intermediaries.

Basic dynamic host configuration protocol server: Basic dynamic host configuration protocol (DHCP) is a standardized networking protocol used on IP networks for dynamically distributing network configuration assignments, such as IP addresses for interfaces and services.

Domain name system server: Domain name system (DNS) translates an often humanly meaningful, text-based identifier into a numeric identification or addressing component. This allows many of the traffic and routing components to work more efficiently.

Repeater: A repeater is an electronic device that receives a signal and retransmits it at a higher level and/or higher power or higher fidelity, or onto the other side of an obstruction, so that the signal can cover longer distances.

Power over Ethernet: Power over Ethernet (PoE) is a way to reduce cabling by transmitting power over the data signal. It is useful on IP cameras. Power over Universal Serial Bus (USB) is also a way to reduce cabling.

Spanning tree protocol: The spanning tree protocol (STP) is a network protocol that ensures a loop-free topology for any bridged Ethernet local area network. The basic function of STP is to prevent bridge loops.

Modem: A modulator–demodulator is a device that converts between digital and analog frequencies (normally in the sound range) that can be transmitted over telephone lines and once received on the other side, converts those sounds back into a form used by a USB, Ethernet, serial, or network connection.

Wireless access point: A wireless access point usually connects to a wired network, and it can relay data between the wireless devices (such as computers or printers) and wired devices on the network.

Virtual local area network: In computer networking, a single layer-2 network may be partitioned to create multiple distinct broadcast domains, which are mutually isolated so that packets can pass between them only via one or more routers; such a domain is referred to as a virtual local area network, virtual LAN, or VLAN.

Channel service unit/data service unit: A channel service unit/data service unit (CSU/DSU) is a digital-interface device used to connect a data terminal equipment device (DTE), such as a router, to a digital circuit, such as a T1 or T3 line.

Trunking: Trunking is a method for a system to provide network access to many clients by sharing a set of lines or frequencies in a fiber instead of providing them individually. Examples of this include telephone systems and the very high-frequency (VHF)* radios commonly used by police agencies.

7.1.2 Issues of the Most Passive Devices

Most of these are completely passive. The major concern here is that all of them have administrator and/or other interfaces. Vendors indicate that these interfaces are out of band, but they are almost always accessible to the administrators without their being physically present. Since these switches will direct traffic (some to places where you do not want the traffic to go), authentication, integrity, and confidentiality are of major concern. Even within the data center, the insider threat is an issue for exploiting these administrative interfaces. Mitigations include the following:

- *Limitation of administrator privilege*: Most individuals given administrator jobs are provided superusers privileges, meaning they have access and privileges for everything. Some mitigation is provided by dividing these functions among several administrators.
- *Two-person administration*: This can be used on sensitive or vulnerable devices; all actions must be authorized by more than one person. Mitigation is improved, but collusion can counter this.
- *Detailed monitoring of all administrator actions*: Of course the records need to be periodically reviewed.

7.1.3 The Convenience Functions

Potentially more concerning are the convenience functions [30].

Content switch: Some switches can use up to OSI layer 7 packet information; these may be called layer 4–7 switches, content switches, content services switches, web switches, or application switches. Encrypted traffic makes it difficult to use the content switch unless content tags appear in the headers.

Media converters: Media converters are simple networking devices that make it possible to connect two dissimilar media types such as a twisted pair with fiber-optic cabling. Encrypted traffic makes it difficult to use the media converters based on content. This functionality should be performed before it is sent out on the network.

Bandwidth shaper: Traffic shaping (also known as "packet shaping") is a computer network traffic management technique that delays some or all datagrams to bring them into compliance with a desired traffic profile. Traffic shaping is a form of rate limiting. The process by which shaping is determined is of concern. Encryption of messages and packets make content analysis impractical as a shaping factor.

---

* VHF.

Proxy server: A proxy server is a server that makes Internet connections on behalf of client PCs. All the requests for Internet access that are made by a client on a network are executed by the proxy server. In other words, a proxy server acts as a point of contact between a private and a public network such as the Internet. This proxy arrangement is usually done by allowing the proxy to identify itself as the requester (masquerade). The proxy is bad from a standpoint of accountability and end-to-end integrity. Many network operations stand up a proxy in order to inspect packets in an attempt to monitor employee computer usage. This MITM approach actually uses nefarious behavior in the name of computer security.

Port mirroring: Port mirroring is used on a network switch to send a copy of network packets seen on one switch port (or an entire VLAN) to a network-monitoring connection on another switch port.

Network monitors: Network monitors are generally appliances that duplicate and analyze packets for throughput and other network measurements. Many monitors are expanding to packet and content inspection, which is problematical.

7.1.4 Issues for the Convenience Functions

Care should be taken when allowing convenience functions. Appliances that inspect the content of traffic are often placed at the initial access point of the computing center for the convenience of the network administrators. Traffic inspection should never be done by giving away private keys and allowing end-to-end communication to be interrupted or corrupted or the integrity chain to be broken.

7.1.5 Content Analyzers

The final category is of particular concern. If you were to walk into your data center, you may well see one or more racks of appliances in this category. A wide range of appliances that are claimed to be network defenders are used to provide functionality ranging from quality of service to the user to quality of protection of network resources and servers. These appliances are often placed in-line and some require access to content to provide their service.

The number of appliances can be quite high [31–51]. Below is a partial list of functional types:

- *Header-based scanner/logger*: Header-based scanner/loggers view only the unencrypted portion of traffic. They may be applied in both synchronous and asynchronous operation. They scan for suspicious behavior and log traffic.
- *Content-based scanner/logger*: Content-based scanner/loggers view the decrypted content of traffic. They are applied in synchronous operation. They scan for suspicious behavior and log traffic and/or content.
- *Header-based firewall*: Header-based firewalls view only the unencrypted portion of traffic. They are applied in synchronous operation. They scan for and block suspicious behavior.

- *Content-based firewall—block only*: Content-based firewalls view the decrypted content of traffic. They are applied in synchronous operation. They scan for suspicious behavior and block (terminate) connection.
- *Content-based firewall—modifies malicious content*: These view the decrypted content of traffic. They may be applied in both synchronous and asynchronous operation. They scan for suspicious behavior and block (terminate) connection or remove suspicious content while preserving the connection.
- *Web accelerator*: These view the decrypted content of traffic. They are applied in synchronous operation. They modify content for improved performance.
- *Wide area network (WAN) accelerator*: These view the decrypted content of traffic. They may be applied in synchronous operation. They use a multiparty system. They modify content representation between parties, but do not do end-to-end modification.
- *Load balancers*: These distribute loads among destination end points to improve throughput and reduce latency. Some load balancers may decrypt content and combine encrypted flows through an "encryption accelerator" or distribute content by request to different servers based on load. These load balancers are considered active entities. Some load balancers may avoid decryption of content by using "sticky" or end point balances that route all requests from an entity to the same server.
- *Hardware storage module*: This is the best defense for premature decryption of content. This appliance stores certificates and private keys in a secure tamper-proof module.

7.1.6 Issues for Content Analyzers

Entities that are not active end points and decrypt traffic should be a particular concern. The method by which these entities obtain the capability to decrypt encrypted traffic is an issue. In many cases, the entities are provided access to the private keys of the servers. This is a serious security breach and should be alarming to any security analyst. This will be discussed in the later chapters.

TECHNICAL
DETAILS

Chapter 8

Claims-Based Authentication

Authentication is the process that deals with the establishment of identities. All entities have identities, and when communicating in IT systems, it is important that each part establish the identity of the communicating partner. However, because identities may be misrepresented and spoofed, it is important that these identities be validated and verified. The processes described here have been in use for some time, and PKI is an established part of those processes. The new requirements are the bilateral strong authentication and the requirement for unbroken end-to-end encrypted communication. Because the basic authentication processes have been in use for some time, the publication of the tailoring came later (2013) [52].

8.1 Authentication and Identity

Authentication is responsible for establishing the identity of an entity. Authentication is achieved by receiving, validating, and verifying the identity credentials. Identity credentials are issued for named entities in the enterprise. The name must be unique in space and time. Any ambiguity in identity will lead to a problem in accountability. To ensure this uniqueness, the certificate issuing authority (CA) must check its registry for other instances of the name. Once a certificate is issued, the name is added to that registry so that it is never used again. For certificates, validation is achieved by encrypting a message with the private key of the requester and transmitting it to the provider. The provider can then validate that it was sent by the requester by decrypting it with the requester's public key. This ensures that the requester is the holder of the private key. Verification is achieved by verifying the trusted agent that issued the certificate, this authentication is two-way (the requestor authenticates the provider and the provider authenticates the requestor). In certain cases, additional claims may be examined (multifactor identification), including biometric measures.

8.2 Credentials in the Enterprise

A credential is a claim (in this case of identity) that can be verified as accurate and current. Credentials must be provided for all active entities that are established in the enterprise in order to perform authentication. Prior registration as an active entity with a confirmable entity name is required. The forms of credentials in use include certificates, Kerberos tickets, and hardware tokens. Users are issued hardware tokens (Smart Cards) that have CA-issued certificates stored on them with the private keys stored in hardware on the card. Machines and services are issued software certificates that contain the public key with the private key generated and remaining in hardware storage modules. Figure 8.1 shows the bilateral exchange of PKI certificates. This allows all active entities to identify the partner in communication.

8.3 Authentication in the Enterprise

Authentication is responsible for establishing the identity of an entity. Authentication is achieved by receiving, validating, and verifying the identity credentials. For certificates, validation is achieved by encrypting a message with the private key of the requester and transmitting it to the provider. The provider can then validate that it was sent by the requester by decrypting it with the requester's public key. This ensures that the requester is the holder of the private key. Verification is achieved by verifying the trusted agent that issued the certificate, this authentication is

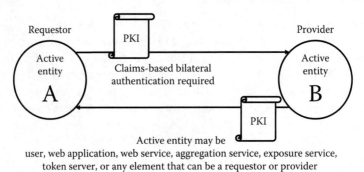

Figure 8.1   Claims for authentication using PKI.

two-way (the requestor authenticates the provider and the provider authenticates the requestor). In certain cases, additional claims may be examined (multifactor identification), including biometric measures.

8.3.1 Certificate Credentials

The required credential for enterprise personnel is an enterprise-issued X.509 (currently version 2.1), RSA-based certificate. X.509 certificates are used to bind an entity name to a public key in the PKI and to hold additional attributes (such as organizational unit data and other data encoded in the identity). The certificates are used by authentication and authorization services, digital signing, and other cryptographic functions. Enterprise certificate credentials for users must be obtained through designated trusted CAs. The CA provides the enterprise PKI credentials for users, devices, and services. Certificate credentials contain nonsecret (publicly available) information. A hardware token that contains the certificate is preferred to software-only certificates. For enterprise users, the method of credential storage is an enterprise-issued card with a highly secure tamper-proof hardware store, which is FIPS 140-2 Level 2 validated for cryptographic tokens [2h].

Software certificates (used in addition to hardware tokens) are in the PKCS#12 [20] formats and must be installed in certificate storage associated with the entity that owns the certificate or its host device (which must also be credentialed). A user may have a software certificate issued by a designated CA that is installed in certificate storage in the user's host device. For devices and services that are established in the enterprise, a software certificate is acquired from a designated CA and is installed in certificate storage on the device itself and on the host device. For hardware elements outside the enterprise, PKCS#12 files may be maintained as backup offline—but, in general, they should not be stored on the hardware device attached to the network. The certificate credential for an entity must contain the enterprise-unique and persistent identifier in the certificate subject identity field (for users, this is the extended common name, and for devices and services, this is the universally unique identifier [UUID]) in accordance with the enterprise naming standard (an example is provided in Reference 53).

8.3.2 Registration

The registration function is a service that creates and maintains the information about the identities of entities in the enterprise. There are three main issues to consider:

- *Kerberos tickets*: Kerberos is a network authentication protocol originally developed by the Massachusetts Institute of Technology, and now documented in several Internet Engineering Task Force (IETF) Internet Drafts and RFCs [4k]. Kerberos tickets are used with enterprise active directory (AD) forests.

■ *Authentication and attribute assertion tokens*: Once authentication is established, the attributes of the identities are used to produce authorization claims. The primary method for expressing authorization claims in the enterprise uses derived credentials based on attribute assertion tokens at the message layer. These tokens contain security assertions and are obtained from an STS. These tokens are based on the SAML (current version) standard [1a–i]. Although the standard allows for authentication elements in the SAML token, they are not used in this formulation. SAML is used only for authorization. A binding to authentication is achieved by performing a match between the distinguished name used in SAML and the authentication commonly called a holder-of-key (HOK) check.

■ *Interoperability of credentials*: Public key cryptography depends on the ability to validate certificates against a trusted source. The use of PKI is discussed in Reference 54. External information sharing includes authentication based upon a federation agreement that specifies approved primary and derived credentials. The credentials will be configured for such federations.

8.3.3 *Authentication*

The enterprise supports two general methods for authentication: Kerberos-based and direct PKI. Authentication relies on certificates.

■ *Devices and services authentication PKI*: Devices and services are configured to authenticate themselves to the identity provider of the enterprise using bilateral TLS [4m]. The authentication relies on enterprise-issued PKI certificates.

■ *User initial authentication to the domain*: The user authenticates using the PKI-enabled logon program, which asks the user for a passcode that is, in turn, used as an index to a Kerberos key. This is a hybrid approach in which the hardware token is read and user ownership is sought by presenting an input screen for the passcode associated with the hardware token. An underlying program is invoked, completing the authentication by PKI (Kerberos supports both password-based user authentication and PKI-based principal authentication with the PKINIT extension) using the certificate stored on the card. The Kerberos-based authentication uses the PKINIT and Kerberos protocols. For enterprise operations, users authenticate to the identity manager with the enterprise hardware token. The hardware token credential is used only by human users, and either soft certificates or certificates stored in hardware storage modules are used for other entities. The user authenticates to the domain controller using a smartcard logon program such as the common access card (CAC) or another approved active card and authenticates using the hardware token and a user-supplied passcode. Multifactor authentication is not currently implemented, but it may be used at this point. Biometric measures will increase the strength of authentication. The PKI initiation program is invoked, completing the authentication by PKI. External users (users communicating from outside the enterprise) are then provided a virtual private network (VPN) tunnel and treated as if they were within the domain. Kerberos supports both password-based user authentication and PKI-based principal authentication (with the PKINIT extension); however, the enterprise uses only PKI-based principal authentication. Successful completion of the logon procedure signifies successful authentication of the user to the domain controller (a timeout will occur at preconfigured period—more details are provided in Reference 55).

■ *User authentication to services using PKI*: It is assumed at this point that the user has successfully authenticated to the identity manager using PKI. If the user wishes to access any other web service through the web browser, he/she does so using hypertext transfer protocol secure (HTTPS). All entity drivers will be configured to use TLS mutual authentication. This additionally provides Transport Layer confidentiality, compression, and integrity (through message authentication) for subsequent message layer traffic over HTTPS. This validates the user's certificate and passes the certificate to the web service being accessed.

■ *Service-to-service authentications*: Requesters make requests for capabilities from web services. In all cases, any capability request is preceded by TLS mutual authentication. Services may request other web services for capabilities (service providers). Services may include web services, utility services, and others.

8.4 Infrastructure Security Component Interactions

Figure 8.2 shows the basic authentication flows required prior to all interactions. This flow is the basic TLS setup.

When a requester wishes to use another service, four active entities come into play. Details are provided in Figure 8.3. The active entities are listed below.

■ For a user:
  - The user (requester) web browser—a standard web browser that can use the hypertext transfer protocol (HTTP) and HTTPS drivers (including the TLS driver) on the platform
■ For a service:
  - The requester host platform
  - The STS in the requester's domain

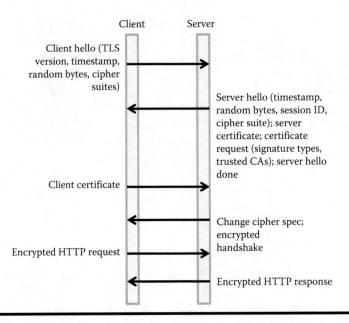

Figure 8.2   Authentication flows.

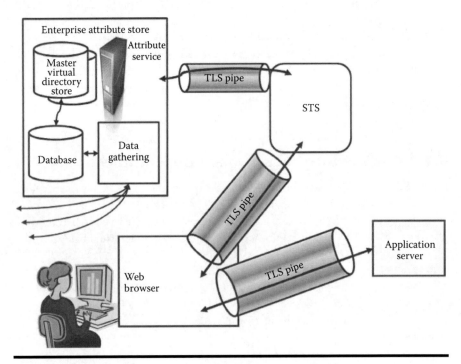

Figure 8.3   Web browser request for service message flows.

- The EAS
- The requested service (application server) in the resource application environment

8.4.1 Interactions Triggered by a User Request for Service

The user first makes a request to STS. Included in that request is an identifier (the URI [4c]) or a token referring to this identifier of the target service. The STS will generate the SAML credentials and return them to the browser with instructions to redirect to the service and post the SAML in this request to the application server (see Figure 8.3). If HTTPS messages are used, then bilateral authentication and establishment of Joan Daemen TLS encryption using AES 256, as discussed in Chapter 5, takes place based on the configuration of the servers and the web browsers.

8.4.2 Interaction Triggered by a Service Request

This is similar to the flow in Figure 8.4, except that instead of a browser requesting a service, another service formulates and makes the request. Note that authentication has nothing to do with authorization, which is performed via a SAML token as discussed in Chapter 9. Authentication tokens are issued to ALL active entities and are called authentication or PKI certificates.

The web application or service (on application server 1) sends a service request to the web service (on application server 2) as shown in Figure 8.4. This request is followed by bilateral authentication and the establishment of a TLS encrypted session. The encryption uses AES 256, as discussed in Chapter 5. This is then followed by an authorization credential, as discussed in Chapter 9.

8.5 Compliance Testing

Authentication testing verifies that the bilateral PKI-based authentication is working properly in the enterprise. This includes testing TLS on every connection in the security flows. Packet captures are done on nodes in the flow, and then TLS traffic is checked for certificate exchanges and encryption. Further checks for currency are made by calling the online certificate status protocol (OCSP) responder, which is an Internet protocol used for obtaining the revocation status of an X.509 digital certificate. Calls and returns verify that certificate status is being checked correctly. The packet captures are executed for a request to the STS. Authentication testing covers revoked and expired certificates as well as certificates that have been modified or tampered. Captures show OCSP traffic for the revoked certificate.

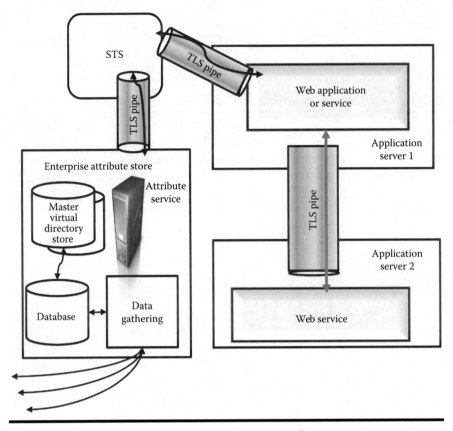

Figure 8.4 Web service request for service message flows.

8.6 Federated Authentication

Federated communications must meet all of the enterprise requirements, including the following:

■ Naming PKI certificates
■ Certificates issued by a recognized certificate issuer
■ Valid, not-revoked, dates
■ TLS mutual authentication
■ Multifactor authentication as required
■ SAML tokens from designated authorized STSs that meet all of the above requirements

The federation partner must present a PKI certificate that meets enterprise requirements as described below and is issued by a trusted certificate authority. Trust is signified by including the certificate authority in the trust list. When required, enforcement of multifactor authentication is undertaken at this point. In cases in which a trusted certificate authority cannot be found, the federation partner must be issued an enterprise PKI certificate and be included in the enterprise attribute stores.

8.6.1 Naming and Identity

Identity is established by the enterprise or the requesting agency as agreed to in the federation agreement. In the enterprise, this is primarily through the enterprise naming contained in the enterprise-issued X.509. These names should be standardized throughout the enterprise and satisfy the property of uniqueness over space and time. For people, this name is the enterprise standardized name, but naming schemes for other certificate authorities are accepted based on federation agreements. The identity used by all federated exchanges is the distinguished name as it appears on the primary credential provided by the certificate authority. If there is a collision, mapping of federation names is required.

Credentials are an integral part of the federation model. Each identity requiring access is credentialed by a trusted credentialing authority. Further, the STS used for generating SAML [1a–i] tokens is also credentialed (as are all active entities in the enterprise). The primary exchange medium for setting up authentication of identities and setting up cryptographic flows is the PKI embodied in an X.509 certificate. The certificate authority must use known and registered (or in specific cases, defined) certificate revocation and currency-checking software.

8.6.2 Translation of Claims or Identities

Identities are translated as indicated in the federation agreement. For simple federation, where requests are across the enterprise domains, there is no mapping, because the identities are already in the appropriate form. In any event, the mappings will be rare if distinguished names are used and will only be needed when anonymity is a requirement or a collision occurs between the names provided by designated certificate authorities.

8.6.3 Data Requirements

Configuration files are developed and maintained as specified in enterprise requirements.

All configuration files and stored data are appropriately protected using cryptographic services. Even though these files are distributed for proximity to the relevant service, they are centrally maintained by an appropriate service agent mechanism.

8.6.4 Other Issues

All code that is generated is subject to code assurance review/tools, with risks identified and resolved.

WS-Reliable Messaging [1k], WS-Secure Conversation [1l] is used for communication between active entities. The selection of either WS-Reliable Messaging or WS-Secure Conversation is based on session efficiency.

Chapter 9

Credentials for Access Claims

There are, of course, many credentials from which to choose. The requirements, however, are rather stringent. The credential must be standards-based and in fairly widespread use. It needs to be able to establish integrity and be verified and validated by the recipient. SAML met these requirements. A concern was that the principal usage had been for authentication using a single sign-on (SSO) approach that had been subject to spoofing and MITM attacks in the past. This formulation went through a number of iterations and was published in 2008 [56], again in 2010 [57], and finally in 2012 [58].

9.1 Security Assertion Markup Language

The primary method for presenting access control claims is the SAML token [1a–i]. The SAML token described herein is not the SSO identity token. SAML* holds the dominant position in terms of industry acceptance for federated identity deployments. SAML is deployed in tens of thousands of SSO connections. Thousands of large enterprises, government agencies, and service providers have selected it as their standard protocol for communicating identities across the Internet. This wide-scale adoption ensures that the standard will be supported and enhanced. SAML is XML-based, which makes it a very flexible standard [1f].† This flexibility led

---

* Derived in part from https://www.pingidentity.com/resource-center/SAML-Tutorials-and-Resources.cfm.
† OASIS is the name adopted by the standards organization, advancing open standards for the information society.

to pieces of the SAML standard, such as the SAML assertion format, being incorporated into other standards such as WS-Federation. SAML tokens are issued by the STS on a per invocation basis and used to establish an authorized session. SAML tokens contain claims asserting attributes, membership in groups, and roles and extended claims that include authorized and trusted claims. The STS is a trusted application whose signature is recognized by all the users of SAML. SAML token format is based on the current SAML standard. The use of SAML tokens follows the WS-Security (WSS) framework[*] for web service access using SOAP envelopes. The enterprise uses the WS-Security SAML Binding package [1d]. The SAML token is included in a SOAP message request. The SAML token is signed using the XML Signature standard,[†] and the contents are protected using the XML Encryption standard.[‡] Table 9.1 describes the contents common to enterprise SAML assertions. While other information is included in the SAML standard (such as authentication data), only the information in the Table 9.1 is used in the enterprise. Many of the elements in the SAML are based upon vulnerability analyses. Handling such a complex set of data is not simple. In the enterprise we developed, the SAML handlers are provided to the web service developers. The use of handles was such a success that it was extended to inspection and several other processes. A discussion of SAML handles is contained in Chapter 17. A discussion of content inspection handlers is covered in Chapter 20.

9.2 Access Control Implemented in the Web Service

Upon receipt of the SAML token, the provided Java or .NET executable process compiled into the service (if the service is non-ELS capable commercial or legacy, it is fronted by a wrapper service that performs these functions) identifies the signer of the token and extracts the signer's public key. If the public key is in the local security store, the signer is recognized.

- If the signer is recognized, the provided software validates the SAML token (signature validity, validity period, and revocation status). If all checks are successful, the validation is successful; otherwise an authorization fail message is sent.
- If the signer is not recognized, the SAML token is sent to the Federation STS for possible federation resolution. The Federation STS returns either a new SAML token that it has signed (start over again) or an authorization failure message.

---

[*] Web Services Security: SOAP Message Security 1.1, OASIS Standard, February 2006.
[†] XML Signature Syntax and Processing (Second Edition) W3C Recommendation, June 2008.
[‡] XML Encryption Recommendation 1, W3C, December 2002.

Table 9.1   SAML Requirements

Field	Required Content	Notes	Mitigates
SAML: Assertion			
Version ID	Version 2.0	Required	Prevents SAML 1 vulnerabilities
ID	(Unique value)	Required	Prevents repeat–replay
Issue Instant	Timestamp	Required	Needed for time limits
Issuer	(content)	Required	Trusted token server
Signature	(content)	Required	Prevents modification, identifies trusted source
Subject	(content)	Required—Must contain the X.509 distinguished name	Unambiguous identity for binding to authentication
SAML: Attribute Statement			
Subject	Common Name	For identification in log files	
Claim(s): {parameters]	(content)	Claims may include extended claims for delegation	
End SAML: Attribute Statement			
SAML: Conditions			
NotBefore	(content)	Timestamp – minutes	An appropriate validity period is +/– 5 min The SAML is not involved in authentication Short validity period prevents repeat–replay
NotAfter	(content)	Timestamp + minutes	
Audience	(content)	Target service	Prevents man-in-the middle and re-targeting
End SAML: Conditions			
End SAML: Assertion			

Access is granted when a requester presents an SAML token with an appropriate set of authorization claims to a Java or .NET executable process compiled into the service.

9.3 Establishing Least Privilege

Least privilege is the minimal set of claims that are needed for successful authorization. The requester may or may not need all of the claims that he/she can make. The claims are labeled for the specific service request or for a content access request, and least privilege is established by choosing only those claims.

9.4 Default Values

When no claims or extended claims are present for an active entity, the roles from the role registry (for persons) and the groups from the enterprise group registry are placed in the SAML. All requesters are expected to have at least one claim as defined by the access control requirements in the service registry. An SAML with no claims will not be returned, and an error condition will be set for return to the requester ("Web Service Issue. Please try again. If problems persist you may contact the help desk. Code ####"—where #### is a session attribute for help desk use).

9.5 Creating an SAML Token

An SAML token is created by a trusted STS. An STS is a software service that resides on approved hardware and software, or a combination of hardware and software that meets the requirements for generating and signing specifically configured SAML tokens. Any specific requirements to be met by the underlying software operating system and its hardware are documented and provided with the software. An STS is configured to work with an HSM.

STSs are established throughout the enterprise to issue SAML tokens to requesters as necessary to support authorization to SAML-enabled services and applications. SAML-enabled services within the enterprise support direct PKI-based user authentication. TLS is required for connections to the STS to provide confidentiality, preventing token capture or authentication replay attacks. The STS (see Figure 9.1) accepts requests from authenticated local requesters for SAML services. The STS generates SAML tokens for the local requester by communicating with the EAS ecosystem and placing the requester's claims in the SAML attributes section of the SAML token. The STS reduces these claims to the appropriate set of claims that can be used by the target application. The STS issues an SAML token that is digitally signed and includes an attribute statement (an attribute statement

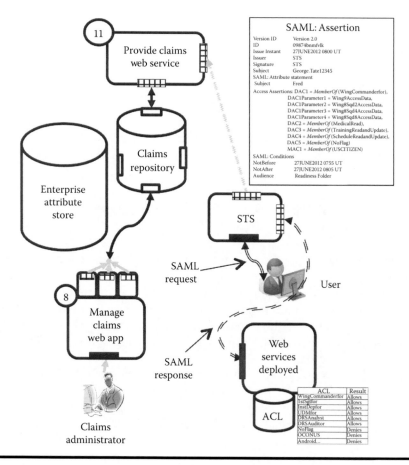

Figure 9.1 **The STS is at the center of access control.**

includes claims needed for access control). The STS is an enterprise trusted software service that meets trust requirements, including software vulnerability analyses and code protection. Providers of commercial-based systems are required to provide additional assurance and certifications. The STS must be Common-Criteria, or other security testing, approved and FIPS-140-certified if the STS performs any encryption functions outside of the HSM.

Service Number 8 is the enterprise claims manager web application that allows the addition/deletion/modification of the claims and triggers a full review of claims expiration dates. Insertion and deletion of claims, while allowed, is not recommended. The preferred method is the import of identity and attributes and computing of claims, but at times even these may be inadequate. Because administrator modifications of claims are not automatically checked, they should be logged and reviewed from time to time for accuracy and currency.

During recomputation, a claim may no longer be valid. As a practical consideration, the claim will be given a grace period. A claim will expire when its grace period has passed. The web application has a full service class of users (enterprise claims administrators).

Service Number 11 supplies claims to the STS. The communication between the STS and the Provide Claims Web Service (Number 11) has an exception to the requirement for a full SAML authorization to prevent thrashing. Access is by identity only. The STS is one of several identities in the EAS ecosystem that allow identity-based access. The identities acceptable are stored in the service ACL.

9.6 Scaling of the STS for High Assurance Architectures

Scale-up to a higher level of users requires a number of different schemes. The most critical, since it involves every request, is the STS. The STS generates SAML tokens for access control. Test data indicates that 100 token requests can be satisfied in 1 second by the current STS combination of STS hardware and software. Improved versions of software or hardware processors may reduce these requirements. The parameters needed for analyzing load-balancing requirements are provided below:

- Initial operational deployment is defined by a requirement for 1000 users in 5 minutes. This corresponds to 4 SAML tokens per second,
    - Need 1 STS (IdP)—based on 100 tokens per second capability.
- Six months after initial operational deployment, the requirement rises to 10,000 users in 5 minutes. This corresponds to 34 SAML tokens per second.
    - Need 1 STS (IdP)—based on 100 tokens per second capability.
- One year after initial operational deployment: the requirement rises to 100,000 users in 5 minutes. This corresponds to 334 SAML tokens per second.
    - Need 5 STS (IdP) cluster—based on 80-tokens-per-second capability, assumes a 20% throughput loss in clustering.
- Two years after initial operational deployment, the requirement reaches and stays at 500,000 users in 5 minutes. This corresponds to a requirement for 1667 SAML tokens per second.
    - Need 23 STS (IdP)—based on 75-tokens-per-second capability, assumes a 25% throughput loss in clustering.

Note that the STS is a trusted component and can be load-balanced in the traditional manner, as shown in Figure 9.2.

In this configuration, the clusters share the same naming, PKI credentials, and end-point identities. This is the only exception to the unique naming, PKI credential, and end-point requirements because the STS is the primary trusted component in the system.

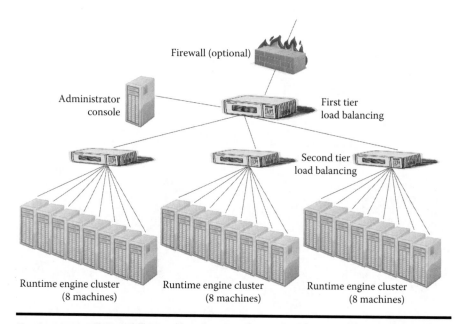

Figure 9.2   STS load balancing.

The second most likely element to need scale-up will be the enterprise's most popular service (MPS). This one is a bit trickier. Schemas that essentially extend the thread capabilities of the application may be employed. When the capacities of the thread architecture are exhausted and independent instance of the application needs to be set up, the process requires care. The application or service is not a trusted element and is not exempt from the unique naming, credentialing, and end-point requirements. Each independent instance must have its own name, URI, and credentials. Further, each independent instance must be provisioned for in the attribute stores if it will make further service calls. Fortunately, all web applications and services can be handled in the same manner, and the process is not dependent on the number of instances needed to handle the user request. A specific (x, where x corresponds to the web application or web service that needs balancing) instance availability service (IAS)x is set up as the end point for a request that needs to be load-balanced. Note that this means that the end point in the MPS must be changed to the specific IASx, and the end point in the widget for the MPS must be changed to the IAS for the MPS. The IASx needs to have the following information available:

- Number of independent instances of the web application
- Unique name of each independent instance of the web application
- Unique end point of each independent instance of the web application
- (OPTIONALLY) Usage and load data for each of the independent instances of the web application

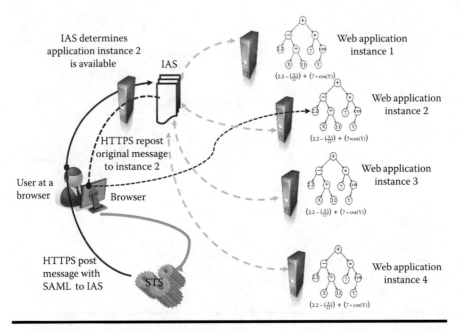

Figure 9.3   High assurance load balancing.

The user goes to the STS with the address of the IAS, which he/she can have stored in his/her favorites, or executed the link. The STS then posts the SAML over HTTPS to the IAS. The IAS doesn't even need to read the SAML (authentication-only or identity-based access control), but would repost the SAML over HTTPS to the independent instance it calculates. It is then completely out of the way, just like the STS is completely out of the way, and the user is in session with the instance of the web application. This process is shown in Figure 9.3.

The IAS (load balancer—or functionality of a load balancer) monitors activity and posts a connection to an available independent instance. Similar to the HTTPS,[*] interface to the STS requires no communication with the user. The determination of an available connection can start on a basic level (initially round robin) and become more sophisticated by monitoring activity at the independent instances and choosing the lowest activity instance. In this case, all of the end-to-end processes work since the new independent instance has a unique name, end point, and credentials with which to proceed. All of this, of course needs to be logged in a standard form and parameters passed to make it easy to reconstruct for forensics.

---

[*] HTTPS ("HTTP over TLS," "HTTP over SSL," or "HTTP Secure") is a communications protocol for secure communication over a computer network, with especially wide deployment on the Internet. Technically, it is not a protocol in and of itself; rather, it is the result of simply layering the hypertext transfer protocol (HTTP) on top of the SSL or TLS protocol, thus adding the security capabilities of SSL/TLS to standard HTTP communications [Wikipedia].

Key management is complex and essential. When a new instance is required it must be built,* and activated (credentials and properties must be placed in the attribute store, as well as end-point assignment). All of these activities must be monitored and logged in a standard format with reference values that make it easy to reassemble the chain of events for forensics. When a current instance is retired, it must be disassembled and deactivated (credentials and properties in the attribute store, as well as end-point assignment). All of these activities must be monitored and logged in a standard format with reference values that make it easy to reassemble the chain of events for forensics.

9.7 Rules for Maintaining High Assurance during Scale-Up

The following are the rules for maintaining high assurance during scale-up:

- Shared identities and credentials break the accountability paradigm.
- Each independent instance of a machine or service must be uniquely named [53] and provided a PKI certificate for authentication. The certificate must be activated while the virtual machine is in being, and deactivated when it is not so as to prevent improper use of the certificate by nefarious entities. The naming and certificates must be pre-issued, and self-certification is not allowed. Each independent instance of a machine or service must have a unique end point. This may take some manipulation through the load-balancing process, but is required by attribution and accountability. This means that simple redirect will not work. The one exception is the STS, which is trusted software. Extending the thread mechanism[†] by assigning resources to the operating system may preserve this functionality. The individual mechanism for virtualization will determine whether this can be accomplished.
- Each independent instance of a service must have an account provisioned with appropriate elements in an attribute store. These must be pre-issued and linked to the unique name for each potential independent instance of a service. This is required for SAML token issuance.
- The importance of cryptography cannot be overstated, and all internal communications as well as external communications should be encrypted to the end point of the communication. Memory and storage should also be encrypted to prevent theft of cached data and security parameters.

---

[*] In a physical environment, this would be the process of standing up another server dedicated to the service. In a virtualized environment, this work is done by the hypervisor.

[†] A server accommodates a number of threads (or execution traces) of a program depending upon the resources assigned to it. If microprocessor speed permits a reasonable service time, adding memory or storage may allow for more threads.

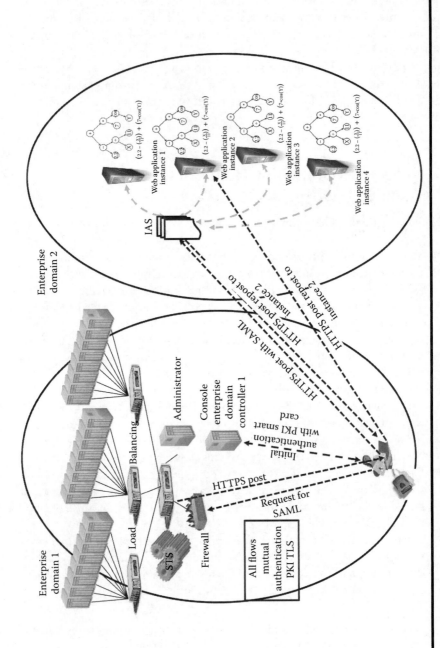

Figure 9.4 Web application access in a scaled-up environment.

- Private keys must reside in HSM. The security of the java software key store does not meet high assurance criteria.
- Stand-up of an independent machine or service must link keys in HSM and activate credentials pre-assigned to the service.
- Stand-down of an independent machine service must delink keys in HSM and deactivate credentials pre-assigned to the service.
- Key management in this environment is a particular concern, and a complete management schema including destruction of session keys must be developed.
- Proxies and redirects break the end-to-end paradigm.
- When end points must be changed,* reposting of the requests is the preferred method. There must be true end-to-end communication with full attribution. This in turn requires communication to be reinitiated from client to the new instance, which must have a unique end point with unique credentials and cryptography keys.
- All activities must be logged in a standard format with reference values that make it easy to reassemble the chain of events for forensics.

Figure 9.4 provides a summary of how a user addresses an individual web application in a scaled-up system.

In the scaled-up system, the user executes the desktop icon or executes a link favorites list. The communication is to the load-balanced STS (IdP), which generates the SAML and does an HTTPS Post to the IAS of the target (load-balanced) web application. (Note that thread extension schemas may have already been employed prior to the standup of independent instances of the application.) Bilateral authentication and TLS session establishment is completed, but the initial package need not be examined further (SAML kept intact), and the initial post is repackaged for the reposting. The IAS determines that instance 3 is available and reposts the HTTPS with the SAML to the third instance of the web application, where bilateral authentication and authorization checks are performed before a session is established. The end-to-end authentication between the user and the third instance of the application is preserved, and the PKI-based TLS ensures that all communications are encrypted to the end points. Similarly, an IAS may be set in place for any subsequent service call that needs multiple independent instantiations. The code for each of the IASs will be essentially the same, with data files and URIs changing for the specific load-balancing task.

---

* End points may need to be changed to another server or instance of a server to maintain the service level (execution times).

Chapter 10

Claims Creation

It took some time to pull together the claims creation process, including the requirements for the enterprise developers and owners of the data. This process finally came together in 2012 [58].

10.1 Access Control Requirements at the Services

For services, access control may include both mandatory and discretionary access. Mandatory takes precedence and access controls that deny in both mandatory and discretionary access take precedence, as discussed below.

10.1.1 Discretionary Access Control List

Each web service is provisioned with a discretionary ACL for DAC and a second ACL for MAC when applicable. DACs are described in Chapter 4.

10.1.2 Mandatory Access Control

Some web services are provisioned with a MAC store for mandatory access control. MACs are developed to allow claim holders access and deny access to those with invalid claims for a specific web service. The initial MACs are specified by the organization that is the owner of the information. MACs are described in Chapter 4.

10.1.3 Access Control Logic

Access control proceeds first with mandatory and then with discretionary access. Mandatory access has both allow and deny access functionality. Deny takes precedence. For example, Non-USCITIZEN may deny access. The access control decision is over and access is denied. It does not matter what is in the rest of the mandatory and discretionary data stores. Any denial terminates the decision. Next, the allow values are evaluated. For mandatory access control, all are needed (they act like a mathematical AND or EACH). For example, if the allow side of the MAC contains Secret and North Atlantic Treaty Organization (NATO), then the claims in the SAML must have both. When both are absent, the access is denied with no need to check discretionary access. Assuming there is no denial of access at this point, we evaluate the discretionary access. Deny takes precedence. For example, Non-Flag may deny access. The access control decision is over and access is denied. It does not matter what is in the rest of the discretionary data stores. Any denial terminates the decision. Assuming there is no denial of access at this point, we evaluate the allow side of discretionary access. Any match allows access (they act like a mathematical OR or ONEOF). Each discretionary control that allows access in the ACL is evaluated, and if the claim is found in the SAML, then access is granted. One match is all that is required.

10.2 Access Control Requirement

The ACR is a formal declaration of what the access requirements are and what data they need. Roles and Permissions define the abilities to access or manipulate information based on a characterization of an individual's role within business processes, organizations, or the overall enterprise and the content of the relevant information assets. This content documents the security requirements for the planned materiel solution that provisions the information addressed by the data owner's project. The Roles and Permissions content should ultimately result in the provisioning of a set of security attributes by enterprise-level security services and implementing the logic for processing them during local authorization checks within the materiel solution. For each information asset, access and authorization rules must be specified. These rules cover the fundamental matters of security levels and information classification, legal and regulatory restrictions (i.e., Privacy Act or Health Insurance Portability and Accountability Act of 1996 [HIPAA] constraints), and restrictions that are derived from the mission processes that scope the data owner's project. As part of the data owner's role in developing detailed information requirements for the implementation of services, these access and authorization rules support the creation and enforcement of roles and permissions within the security infrastructure. The core function of the Roles and Permissions content is to document security requirements that define who should be permitted to perform what actions with the target information assets. These requirements inform a number of downstream activities, in particular the provisioning of security attributes through enterprise-level security services and the implementation of logic to process those attributes when making authorization decisions. The ACR is developed in the basic requirements process, and the data owner has responsibility for it. However, each enterprise security-enabled product requires registration and an ACR, including commercial products. The following format captures the ACR and data to be provided by the EAS. The access checker only evaluates access and does not evaluate privilege. Parameters for privilege may be requested if they are present in the EAS, but the access checker and claims process only passes them along and does not check for their logic or value. The purpose of this exercise is to make a machine-readable ACR.

This first section establishes which service is being documented and where it lives in the ecosystem (the name for the domain naming system and the routers). Each ACR has a name, and there may be more than one access control rule for each service.

☺*ACCESS CONTROL REQUIREMENT: Name of requirement*
Associated Service: Name of Service
   !! (From Associated list of URIs in Enterprise Attribute Store) !!
   !! This is the AUDIENCE RESTRICTION Parameter) !!

The service may have more than one instantiation of the service, and others may be created in a virtual world. This documents the known end points and whether or not other instantiations are anticipated.

▶*Applied Service Endpoints*
   Endpoint1 = www.uri1, PUBLIC KEY1= 1024 bits
   Endpoint2 = www.uri2, PUBLIC KEY2= 1024 bits
   Endpoint 3-n, Dynamic
   ...
◀*End Applied Service Endpoints*

The following sections of the ACR are for resource requirements. Each resource must be in the EAS; otherwise, they do not appear in the ACR and are handled by the service. This is true for both attributes and methods.

▶*Required Resources:*
   !! All must be available in EAS, data outside of EAS may be used for !!
   !! permissions, but not for access and must be obtained by the service !!
      ▶*Attributes:* **!! by type and schema location!!**
         !! data additions to access control may be requested if they reside in EAS !!
      e.g., identity, job title, job role, office symbol, etc.
      ◀*End Attributes*

▶*Methods*   *!! by name from enterprise list of methods available !!*
                e.g., TrustedTime
◀*End Methods*
◀*End Required Resources*

MAC is a list of factors that must be met, and all must be met for access. Any MAC denial will terminate the SAML creation and send an error message back through the system.

▶*MAC List*   *!! must meet each in turn !!*
   MAC1: Example - Classification
      Formulation: *!! True value permits access, sets error and returns message !!*
      Computation: *!! Algorithm or just lookup attribute!!*
   MAC2: Distribution and availability
      Formulation: *!! True value permits access, sets error and returns message !!*
      Computation: *!! Algorithm or just lookup attribute!!*
   …
◀*End Accept MAC List*
▶*Deny MAC List*   *!! may not meet any !!*
   MAC a: Any decline
      Formulation: *!! True value denies access, sets error and returns message !!*
      Message: *!! message returned for denial in lieu of SAML !!*
      Computation: *!! Algorithm or just lookup attribute!!*
   MAC b: Any decline
      Formulation: *!!True value denies access, sets error and returns message !!*
      Message: *!! message returned for denial in lieu of SAML !!*
      Computation: *!! Algorithm or just lookup attribute!!*
   …
◀*End Deny MAC List*

This section provides the name of claims that will deny access. These may include any requirement such as less than 3 years with the company or no affiliation with certain offices. The formulation and computation method are provided (they may be only lookup). They may also be conditional (requiring computation at SAML request time), such as machine type or other real-time computations. This section may be empty (no denial ACLs), or the section may contain many values as needed.

▶*Denial ACL list:*
      !! All must be available in EAS, usually these are real-time computation !!

[-ACL a] Name 1: Description
    Formulation   *!!True value denies access, sets error and returns message !!*
    Message: *!! message returned for denial in lieu of SAML !!*
    Computation: *!! Algorithm !!*
    Associated Parameters: *!! As needed !!*
[-ACL b] Name 2: Description   *!! Access denied example: request from outside the US !!*

    <Conditional>
    Formulation: *!!True value denies access, sets error and returns message !!*
    Message: *!! message returned for denial in lieu of SAML !!*
    Computation: *!! Algorithm !!*
    Associated Parameters: *!! As needed !!*

…

▶*Designated -ACL:*   *!! data owner use for lists without access privileges!!*
    Designation1; Expiration Designation1; data owner List1
    Designation2; Expiration Designation2; data owner List 2
    …
◀*End Designated ACL:*
◀*End Denial ACL List*

This section provides the name of claims that will allow access. These may include any requirement, such as more than 3 years with the company or affiliation with certain offices. The formulation and computation method are provided (they may only be lookup). They may also be conditional (requiring computation at SAML request time), such as machine type or other real-time computations. This section may be empty (no allowed ACLs) or as many values as needed.

▶*Accept ACL list:*
    {ACL1} Name a: Description
        Formulation: *!! includes variables needed from EAS !!*
        Computation: *!! Algorithm !!*
        Associated Parameters: *!! As needed !!*
    {ACL 2} Name b: Description   *!! may be created by delegation !!*
        Formulation: *!! includes variables needed from EAS !!*
        Computation: *!! Algorithm !!*
        Associated Parameters: *!! As needed !!*
    …
▶*Designated ACL:*   *!! data owner use for lists of identities with access privileges!!*

> *Designation a; Expiration Designation1; data owner List1*
> *Designation b; Expiration Designation2; data owner List 2*
> ...

◄*End Designated ACL:*
◄*End Accept ACL List*
☺*END ACCESS CONTROL REQUIREMENT: Name of requirement*

Additional information, including delegation and policy, may also be included in this description.

10.3 Enterprise Service Registry

An ESR is where the details of all the services, the service metadata, are stored. Normally, the service is designed with WSDL, XSD, SOAP messages, and other business-logic-related details. On completion (implying design reviews, test vocabulary for annotation, etc., conducted according to the services design and development process [SDDP]), an enterprise administrator is able to register the web service along with other details in the ESR. These details are provided by the developer and reviewed by the system administrator as part of the registration process. As part of the registration service invocation, an annotation record is generated and stored in the enterprise service metadata repository (ESMR). To facilitate reuse of any web service, the service is registered in the ESMR for discovery. The Registry standard has been the OASIS Universal Description, Discovery and Integration (UDDI) specification, version 3.0.

The services provided by the ESR are the following:

1. Register a web service
2. Add or delete web service instances
3. Obtain web service details
4. Deregister a web service
5. Discover web services
6. Add authorization
   [For a given set of web services]
7. Change authorization
   [For a given set of web services]   Requires changes to
8. Other changes to ACLs   Service Metadata Registry

Before a web service can be used, it is registered in the ESR. The name for the ESR is obtained from appropriate enterprise naming authorities, which must review and provide quality control before registration. The metadata record is updated whenever the web service details are updated.

10.4 Claims Engine

Claims are computed by a web service described as the claims engine. It opens the service registry and reads the access control requirements. It reads the attributes, groups, roles, and other information for each identity and computes the associated claims. Figure 10.1 shows this portion of the EAS ecosystem.

Service Number 5 is the enterprise service registry web application for managing authorized service information and access control requirements. The web application has a full-service class of users (infrastructure administrators) and a read-only class of users.

Service Number 6 is the enterprise claims engine manager for allowing the modification of the claims and the way claims are computed, as well as schedule or demand claims recomputation. The web application has a full-service class of users (Enterprise Claims administrators).

Service Number 7 is the enterprise claims engine that computes claims based upon access requirements stored in the ESR and attributes stored in the EAS (both

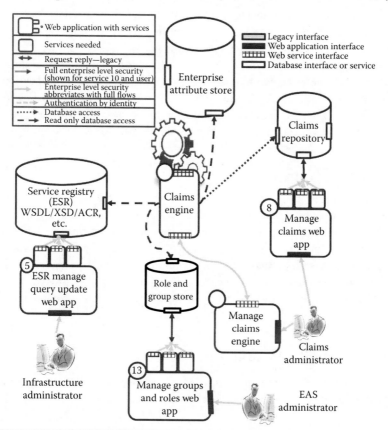

Figure 10.1   Claims building process.

are read-only). It also accesses the groups and roles store as needed. The web application may be triggered by requests from either service 6 or service 4. Each flagged identity (identity that has a change in attributes) triggers a recomputation for all web services. New claims may be created in accordance with changed attributes and the access control requirements of each service. Existing web service access claims may be left in place if access control requirements are still valid, or may be placed in a grace period status, if the access control requirements are no longer met. During the grace period, the entity may continue to access the service. A notification is provided to the entity and a countdown on the grace period begins. If these claims have been delegated, then the extended claims are similarly placed in a grace period with notification.

Service Number 8 is the enterprise claims manager web application for allowing the addition/deletion/modification of the claims and triggering a full review of claims dates of expiration. Insertion and deletion of claims is not the preferred method, which is importing identity and attributes and computing claims. Note that at times, these may be inadequate. Because these are not automatically checked, they should be logged and reviewed from time to time for currency. A claim may expire when a delegation period is complete or the grace period on a claim or extended claim has expired. The claims engine may trigger the grace period when changes to the attributes, as applied to the access control requirements, no longer provide claims. The grace period is extended to all delegatees, and notifications are sent out to these individuals. Grace periods may also apply to the expiration of a delegation period, which triggers a notification to the delegator and delegatee and assignment of the grace period to the claim that has been delegated. Notifications, of course allow those notified to seek additional delegations if desirable. There is no second grace period before expiration. The web application has a full-service class of users (Enterprise Claims administrators).

Service Number 13 is the Enterprise Manager of Groups and Roles. Enterprise-level Roles and Groups, if used as attributes, must be unique over space and time. They must therefore be registered, and uniqueness and membership must be maintained. They may be specified in access control requirements, and the database must be accessible to the claims engine. Roles and Groups that are local to specific services do not require uniqueness (except within the service) and need not be registered. Identities affected by changes in groups and roles must be flagged for claims computation.

10.5 Computed Claims Record*

The claims record has a specific form. It is developed from the service provider access control requirements and policies at the enterprise and service provider level,

---

* The content is provided with examples. However, storage depends on the database, and an XML form would seem appropriate.

and it may include attributes required by access control requirements. The form also includes metadata that indicates how claims are to be handled and to which service provider they apply. The specific form is

(*Note*: The SAML is provided the claims from the claims record—CLAIMS(s) (parameters), MAC(s), AUDIENCE RESTRICTION and PUBLIC KEY (from registry stores). Legacy systems must be accessed through a web service (containing the appliqué) that accepts SAML claims. Nonlegacy systems are expected to deal directly with the SAML-presented claims through either the provided Java or .NET executable package.)

{CLAIMHOLDERDN}, {AUDIENCE}, {CLAIMNAME}, {STATUS
[Time Stamp]},
{NUMBREF, REFDESIGNATION(s)}, {EXPDATE}, {SERVICE NAME},
{NUMBCLAIMS}, {[CLAIMNAME(S), NUMBPARMS (Parameters)]},
{DELSTATUS},
{NUMBMAC, MAC(s)}, {NUMBRECOMPUTATION (method(s) and
message(s))}, {LINK}

CLAIMHOLDERDN—{For example: String (ascii128 padded with trailing blanks if needed)}. The Distinguished Name of the entity for which the ACR has been satisfied.

AUDIENCE—{For example: String (ascii128 padded with trailing blanks if needed)}. Nominally, this is the AUDIENCE RESTRICTION provided by the ACR. This may be the web application or web service DN or another value specified by the data owner in the ACR. It must be enterprise-unique, and DN is recommended.

CLAIMNAME—{For example: String (ascii64 padded with trailing blanks if needed)}. This is the *ClaimName* being satisfied as provided by the data owner in the ACR.

STATUS—{For example: String (ascii9 padded with trailing blanks if needed)} has five values, "Active," "Content," "Designated," "Warning," or "Suspended (date)."

Active is present in all access control requirements generated claims that are not designated. The Time Stamp is the creation date of the claim.

Content—There is one Content claim for each identity, consisting of the identity and enterprise membership in Groups and Roles. Content claims are created in the content management system discussed later.

Designated are individuals who do not otherwise meet the permit access control requirements but have been approved for access by the data owner. There may be several different lists for each service, and these are defined in the access control requirement. These individuals still have the deny claims and the MAC claims computed and included in their claims statement. These have a Time Stamp not to exceed the maximum configured claim period as specified by the data owner. Designated claims may expire with the grace period or may be renewed by the data owner. Warning indicates that a claim is being terminated by the indicated EXPDATE (within the grace period).

Warning applies to claims that have been determined to be within the designated grace period or because of changes to attributes of the entity holding the claim, including Time Stamp expiration. Claims with the status "Warning" are not delegable. The EAS provides a WS-Notification message to the entity, who can request a delegation from their replacement if the claim is needed for continuity.

Suspended (date) is for a claim that has expired on EXPDATE but has not been accessed or recomputed. Date—{For example: String (ascii64 padded with trailing blanks if needed)} the date of status change to suspended.

Time Stamp—{For example: String (ascii64 padded with trailing blanks if needed)}. This is the date the claim was created.

NUMBREF—{For example: Integer between 1 and 256}, Number of reference designations included for the claim. It is incremented each time a reference designation is added to the claim. It has a value of 1 for Content claims. For each of the references:

- REFDESIGNATION—{For example: String (ascii16 padded with trailing blanks if needed)}. This is the unique designator for Content. The ACR ID(s) are generated by the Claims Engine for non-Content. All claims are combined for a given identity and SERVICE NAME.

EXPDATE—{For example: String (ascii64 padded with trailing blanks if needed)}. The expiration date of the claim is set by the claims engine based on the configuration value established for that service (e.g., 80 days) from the date of computation. Each access of the claims record by either the Claims retrieval Service or the Delegation Service resets this value. Inactive claims records will expire after xx days. At the arrival of the grace period before the EXPDATE, the claims record is marked Warning and a WS-Notification is sent to both the delegator and the delegatee. After the arrival of the EXPDATE, the claims record is marked "Suspended" and held for a configured number of days. During this period, an administrator can reset the status and EXPDATE. After this period, the claims are deleted. The claims record can be refreshed (by recomputation) anytime during the configuration-established expiration period (e.g., 87 days) by requesting access to the SERVICE or requesting delegation service action on the SERVICE.

SERVICE NAME—{For example: String (ascii128 padded with trailing blanks if needed)}. Nominally, the AUDIENCE RESTRICTION is provided by the ACR. The service NAME is "CONTENT" for Content status. The NAME parameter reduces the searching by providing claims for the target service request or the target Content. The NAME is derived from the service registry where each active URI for each application name is listed.

NUMBCLAIMS—{For example: Integer between 1 and 256}. The number of claims contained in the claim. This is incremented each time a claim is added. Multiple claims for the same SERVICE NAME and Different REFDESIGNATION may be combined.

For each of the claims specified by NUMBCLAIMS:

- CLAIM—{For example: MemberOf String (ascii16 padded with trailing blanks if needed)}. This provides the claim(s) {may be a role or group as designated in the data owner ACR} specified in the access control requirement for the web service or the author created claim(s) for Content. Claims may be computed (based on ACR requirements) or registered (enterprise group and/or role names with membership in the group or role specified in the ACR).

- NUMBPARMS—{For example: An integer between 0 and 256}. This is the number of parameters requested for the claim.

  Parameters—{For example: MemberOf String (ascii16 padded with trailing blanks if needed). These may have their type modified by service after access decision}. There is one parameter for each value in NUMBPARMS. These claims may have parameters as specified in an access control requirements for the web service.

DELSTATUS—{For example: String (ascii16 padded with trailing blanks if needed)}. This has two values: "delegable" or "notdelegable," and it is based on the access control requirement. Designated claims are not delegable and have "notdelegable" for this parameter. The parameters for claim(s) are the specified delegations in the access control requirement. Content items are not delegable—the claim(s) are provided by the author.

NUMBMAC—{For example: An integer from 0 to 256}. Here, the number represents the number of MAC values.

- MAC—{For example: MemberOf String (ascii16 padded with trailing blanks if needed)}. This may have many values. If the access control requirement does not include MAC data, the value is "NotRequired." If the access control requirement includes MAC, then the first value is the CurrentClearance (Confidential, Secret, Top Secret, [Compartments]), Subsequent Values are NeedToKnow (NATO, FiveEyes, FourEyes, Enterprise, enterprise Only). If the access control requirement requires one or more Code words, the last set of values are Codeword from the EAS.

NUMBRECOMPUTATION—{For example: An integer from 0 to 256}. Here, the number represents the number of parameters that must be recomputed at run time. This parameter concerns the recomputation of claims. For each of the recomputations:

  Method—{For example: String (ascii512 padded with trailing blanks if needed)}. This provides the algorithm for the real-time computation, which resolves to a True or False value. A False value allows the SAML creation to proceed. A True value trips an error sequence with the message that follows.

Message—{For example: String (ascii256 padded with trailing blanks if needed)}. This is an ASCII message returned in the error trip.

LINK—{For example: String (ascii512 padded with trailing blanks if needed)}. The link is compound and includes the appropriate STS, audience end point and the option *ClaimName*.

Chapter 11

Invoking an Application

The secure system started with the standard invocation process. Basically, the requester points a browser at an application, and the application figures out what to do next. It was quickly realized that interfaces that opened up threat surfaces were required. This in turn increased the complexity and reduced security factors. The process for invoking an application that has evolved was first proposed in a pair of short papers presented to a standards body, the W3C [56,59]. Like everything else in this book, it has evolved through pilots and instantiation.

11.1 Active Entities

Entities in the enterprise environment may be active or passive. Passive entities include information packages, static files, and/or reference data structures. Passive entities are the target of activities and do not initiate activities and cannot assume the role of requester or provider. Active entities are entities that change or modify passive entities, request or provide services, or participate in communication flows. Active entities are users, hardware, and services. All active entities in the enterprise have enterprise certificates, and their private keys are stored in tamper-proof, threat-mitigating storage (see Chapter 5). Communication between active entities in the enterprise requires full bilateral, PKI, end-to-end authentication. Active entities must be named in accordance with enterprise Naming instruction. The User naming follows the EDIPI. Nonperson entity naming must be global, unique, and enduring, as spelled out in the standard. Authorization in the operational environment is implemented by a verifiable access control claims-based process. Claims are part of an authorization credential issued by a trusted STS and signed by that entity to preserve integrity. A claims-based credential is sent to the provider with or without

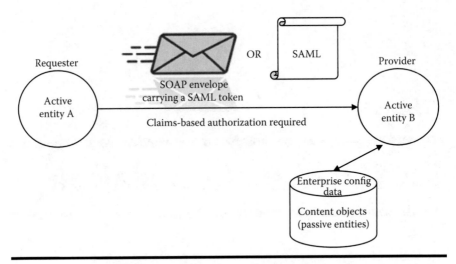

Figure 11.1 Authorization communication between entities.

a SOAP [5g]* envelope. The credential contains a SAML token that includes issuance time and expiration time. Figure 11.1 displays two active entities performing authorization and Active Entity B retrieving content from a passive entity.

11.2 Claims-Based Access Control

11.2.1 *Authorization in the Enterprise Context*

For access control, the required credential is the SAML Token, which is constructed at runtime by an STS that has access to a claims store in an EAS. The SAML may also be created by a trusted federation partner in accordance with federation agreements. In each case, the SAML is provided directly to the service provider after authentication. A software handler, provided by the enterprise as a Java or .NET executable, may be compiled into the software of the web service or web application. This handler (or appliqué) verifies and validates the SAML and extracts the claims.

A request is initiated by an Active Entity for a SAML token to be issued for access to a specific web application or web service. The requester authenticates itself to the STS, and based on the identity established during the authentication process, the STS obtains claims from the EAS for that identity specific to the targeted application or web service. The STS incorporates these claims in a SAML token. The claims include attributes, such as administrator, assigned groups, and organizationally assigned roles that satisfy an access control requirement and policy

---

* SOAP is a requirement anytime the end-to-end communication is broken by a proxy or gateway. Once an end-to-end unbroken TLS connection is established, any valid HTTP protocol may be used for service invocation.

requirements for these web services. The claims can also include delegated responsibilities. The STS signs the SAML credential, indicating to active entities that the claims are from the STS. If the STS is on the trusted list that each service developer is provided, then the service provider can recognize the claims.

If the service provided has been developed by the enterprise, then it may include a Java or .NET executable process that verifies and validates the SAML token. The Java or .NET executable process is also configured to read the ACL and match claims from the SAML to the ACL for completion of a connection to the service provider. The claims included in the SAML token can be used to define the privilege of the access, which is defined in an access control requirement for the service. If the service provided is a commercial software product, then it is preceded by an appliqué process code that serves the same function as the Java or .NET executable. It verifies and validates the SAML. The appliqué process code is also configured to read and decrypt the ACL and the MAC list and match claims from the SAML to the ACL and MAC for completion of a connection to the service provider. There are two possible outcomes: connection is allowed or connection is denied. In the former, a normal session with the software service is established. In the latter, messages are returned and alerts for failed authorization are sent out. The Java or .NET executable process and the appliqué process both provide formatted logs for collection.

11.3 Establishing Least Privilege

Least privilege is the minimal set of claims that are needed for successful authorization. The requester may or may not need all of the claims that he/she can make. The claims are labeled for the specific service request or for a content access request, and least privilege is established by choosing only those claims. An optional parameter for claim limitation is provided as ClaimName, where the claim name is the name of the claim as provided in the data owner ACR. This parameter may be chosen by the requester using the user claim service described in Chapter 16.

11.4 Authorizing the User to the Web Application

Exchange of authentication information uses bilateral TLS. Message flows are configured into the web server and web browser for authenticating the user to a web application and providing SAML tokens for access control decisions. The architectural components include the user, the user browser, a set of enterprise web applications, and the following enterprise web services:

1. STS
2. Identity service provider, which may provide services to the EAS using an LDAPS interface when and if needed (not anticipated)
3. The EAS, which provides services to the STS using an HTTPS interface

The following steps (see Figures 11.1 and 11.2) are followed to allow a user to access a web service using a browser:

1. There are three options (two for the user [a,b] and two for the application [bi,bii] if the user goes directly to the application) for initiation of a session:

   If the user does not have the web application URL or does not want to type it in, he can go to the user query claims service.

   a. The user in a web browser initiates a bilateral TLS connection with the user query claims service. This is an identity-based service that presents to the user the claims he/she has for each of the services for which he/she has claims. The user may select a claim, and the web browser initiates a bilateral TLS connection between the web browser and the federation STS using the certificates of the user and the certificate of the STS. The session is established using the audience and the optional parameter ClaimName establishing least privilege. A message is sent to the STS containing the compound URI, the ClaimName, and a request security token (RST) (the RST may be implied or explicit). The STS now establishes TLS client authentication.

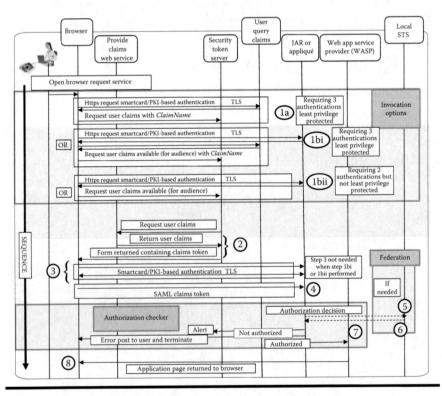

Figure 11.2 User browser authorization to web application.

If the user knows or has cached the URL of the web application, he/she may go directly there. The user in a web browser initiates a bilateral TLS connection with the desired application.

b. If the appliqué is configured to go back to the user query claims service for least privilege, then the appliqué notes that the user has no SAML and posts back the request to the user claims query service with the name of the web application (the audience). If one or more claims exist for the audience, the claim(s) are presented and the user may select one, the web browser initiates a bilateral TLS connection between the web browser and the federation STS using the certificates of the user and the certificate of the STS. The session is established using the audience and the optional parameter ClaimName establishing least privilege. A message is sent to the STS containing the compound URI, the audience, ClaimName, and an RST (the RST may be implied or explicit). The STS now establishes TLS client authentication.

OR

c. If the appliqué is configured to go directly to the STS, the appliqué notes that the user has no SAML and posts back the request to the STS with the name of the web application (the audience). The web browser initiates a bilateral TLS connection between the web browser and the federation STS using the certificates of the user and the certificate of the STS. The session is established using the audience only. A message is sent to the STS containing the compound URI, the audience, and an RST (the RST may be implied or explicit). The STS now establishes TLS client authentication. Multiple claims may be returned.

2. Upon receipt of a successful message from the user's browser and subsequent TLS establishment, the STS establishes a bilateral TLS connection with the EAS and sends a query to look up the user's claims in the EAS or group memberships in the AD. Upon receiving the results, the STS constructs a request security token response (RSTR) message containing a SAML token with authorization claim(s). The token is signed by the issuing STS. The token is returned via an HTTP POST to the targeted web application service provider (WASP).

3. The browser terminates the STS connection and establishes another similar TLS mutual authentication (bilateral TLS) session between the user and the WASP if that session does not already exist. If the user exercises step 1b, then this step is not needed regardless of the option exercised by the web application.

4. The Java or .NET executable process compiled into the WASP or access process fronting the WASP decrypts and examines the authorization token to verify and validate the token. If the user is authorized to access the WASP then the service responds to the request and proceeds to step 8.

   – Verification includes the following:

     a. Checking that the signature block on the SAML is from a trusted STS, if not go to step 6

b. Checking that the SAML token belongs to the entity that authenticated to the service by comparing the Distinguished Name (DN) in the SAML credential to the DN established during authentication

c. Checking the time stamps including notbefore and notafter time stamps

d. Checking the audience for a match to the recipient of the SAML

- Validation includes checking the signature block for integrity and the currency of the STS PKI certificate.

a. The Java or .NET executable process compiled into the WASP or access process fronting the WASP then compares the claims in the SAML token to a service-specific ACL.*

b. If a match is achieved, access to the service is granted (an exception may occur when certain flags are present). The Java or .NET executable process compiled into the WASP forwards the SAML token and the claims to the WASP. If no match is achieved, access is denied. The privilege of the access is determined by the WASP and includes read/write/edit/delete/further distribute/etc.

5. If the authorization token is valid but the signature of the STS is untrusted (each service maintains a trusted STS list), then the Java or .NET executable process compiled into the WASP or access process fronting the WASP establishes a TLS connection to its federation STS and sends a WS-Federation message (with or without a SOAP envelope) containing the SAML token to the trusted STS. When a recognized SAML is returned, the process goes to step 6; otherwise, access is denied (see Chapter 13 for details).

6. The federation STS validates the token and generates a new SAML token. The trusted STS signs the token and sends a WS-Federation message with or without a SOAP envelope containing the encrypted token back to the WASP over the established TLS (see Chapter 13 for details).

7. The Java or .NET executable process compiled into the WASP or access process fronting the WASP decrypts and examines the authorization token to determine whether the token is valid and trusted and the user is authorized to access the WASP and responds to the request. Access is granted when elements in the authorization token match elements in the WASP access control list, which is stored with the service or web application and the MAC matches the MAC requirements. The Java or .NET executable process compiled into the WASP forwards the SAML token and the claims to the WASP. Access is denied when there is no match between SAML token claims and ACLs. An authorization failure message is sent to the requester.

8. The browser receives the results and displays them to the user.

---

* A separate handler written either in Java or .NET will be added to the service before compilation.

11.5 Authorizing a Web Service to a Web Service

A web service may complete the request with or without calls to other web services. The web service includes the WASP and any other web service inside or outside the local domain. Web services may make additional requests of other web services and follow the same authorization process. The following steps are involved with the web service executing the requested web services (see Figure 11.3):

1. The WS-1 may use cached claims tokens. In this case, the WS-1 retrieves the cached token and provides the message in step 4 (start at step 4).
2. The WS-1 establishes a bilateral TLS connection with its federation STS and sends a compound URI with the federation STS and the target web service.

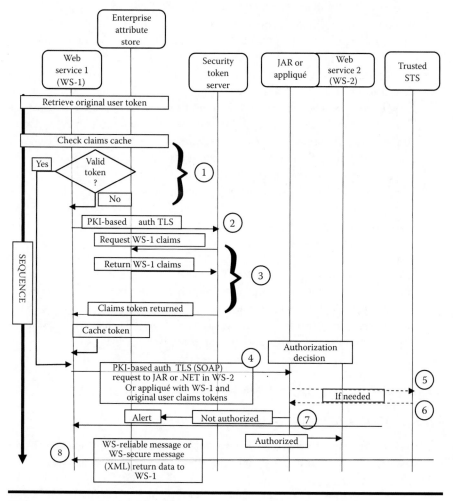

Figure 11.3   Authorization of web service 1 to web service 2.

3. The STS responds with a message containing the claims token. The claims token first time use may be cached at this point.

4. The WS-1 establishes a TLS connection with the WS-2 and sends a WS-SecureConversation or WS-ReliableMessaging message to the WS-2 with or without a SOAP envelope containing the user and WS-1 claims tokens.

5. The Java or .NET executable process compiled into the WS-2 or access process fronting the WS-2 checks the tokens; if they are not from a trusted STS, it establishes a TLS connection to a trusted STS and sends a WS-Federation message with or without a SOAP envelope containing the SAML tokens to the trusted STS (see Chapter 11 for details).

6. The trusted STS verifies and validates each token, checking the federation agreement(s), and translates the claims token to an enterprise claims token. The trusted STS signs the tokens and send a WS-Federation message with or without a SOAP envelope containing the SAML token back to the WS-2 over the established TLS. The Java or .NET executable process compiled into the WS-2 or access process fronting the WS-2 performs verification and validation.

7. The Java or .NET executable process compiles into the WS-2 or access process fronting the WS-2 and then compares the MAC and claims in the SAML token to a service-specific ACL and the service-specific MAC list for WS2 stored in a federation configuration file. If a match is achieved, access to the service is granted. If no match is achieved, access is denied. The claims are provided to WS-2, and the remaining claims can be used to determine privilege (read/write/edit/delete/further distribute/etc.).

8. The Java or .NET executable process compiled into the WS-2 or access process fronting the WS-2 checks the claims in the SAML token. Acceptability is determined by matching the claims in the attribute assertion part of the token to the groups and roles in the ACL of the WS-2.

9. If an acceptable match is present, the WS-2 executes as authorized and sends a WS-SecureConversation or WS-ReliableMessaging* message with or without a SOAP envelope containing the response to the WS-1. The determination of whether WS-SecureConversation of WS-ReliableMessaging is based on the frequency of interaction between services, the choice of messaging type is determined during development of the web service.

11.6 Interaction between Security Components

11.6.1 Access from within the Enterprise

When an enterprise user requests a web application service, seven active and two passive entities in enterprise come into play. Depending upon options for

---

* There is a trade-off between length and number of messages in a session and whether Secure Messaging or Reliable Messaging is used. Either is acceptable at the discretion of the service.

invoking a service, additional services may be used. These are shown in gray and discussed in Figure 11.5, but not elaborated here. If the user is in the enterprise and there are no subsequent service calls, active entities 5 through 7 are not invoked. Details are provided in Figure 11.5, which has labels for the active and passive entities listed below.

Active entities:

1. User's web browser.
2. Security token service (STS 1) in the user's domain.
3. Provide claims web service.
4. WASP.
5. Federation security token service (STS 2) that is trusted by the service. This contains the federation rules to create a set of claims valid for the requester in the enterprise. This may actually be STS 1 or another STS with federation capabilities. If federation is invoked, then the SAML did not come from STS 1 (which is generally in the enterprise user domain).
6. Subsequent web services.
7. Web services required for accessing legacy ACSs (Legacy Wrapper).

Passive entities:

A. Web service ACLs.
B. Enterprise claims store.

The primary message flow sequence is shown in Figure 11.4, together with active and passive entities. Secondary options as described in Figure 11.4 are shown in light gray and are not discussed here.

11.6.2 Disconnected, Intermittent, or Limited Environments

Tactical and commercial mission-critical networks can have disruptions that cause a significant drop in the aggregate data throughput of the network. Problems can take different forms:

- Completely disconnected from all outside networks
- Connected intermittently on a predictable schedule (e.g., only during normal business hours, only when a satellite is overhead)
- Connected intermittently on an unpredictable schedule (e.g., when not being jammed, when mission allows)
- Limited throughput at predictable rate (e.g., 3G link, modem link)
- Limited throughput at unpredictable rate (e.g., congested network shared with others, weather-dependent link)

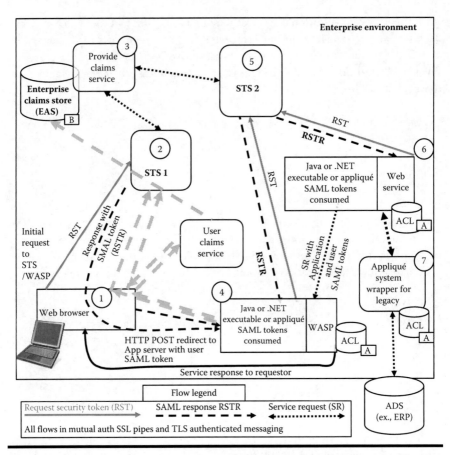

Figure 11.4 General flows during an enterprise user session.

There are many operational solutions for dealing with reduced throughput or capacity. Three of the more common operational solutions are listed below:

■ Prioritization of communications, including channels, packets, and communication types
■ Reduction of the need for capacity by
  – Forward provisioning or
  – Elimination of bandwidth requiring functionality
■ Compression (could be tailored or specialized)

In all cases, compression is assumed. This can be implemented either through existing protocols, such as TLS compression, or through the use of WAN accelerators or other methods to more aggressively compress content over the slow link. Accelerators must be used carefully to ensure that they do not break security or integrity paradigms.

The challenge with disconnected, intermittent, or limited (DIL) environments is to provide applications and services such that performance and security are not adversely affected by the underlying network issues. The first way to address this is by prioritizing communications to make the best use of the available bandwidth. This does not always work, such as with disconnected or intermittent connectivity, but for limited bandwidth, this could be enough to provide the mission-critical services while other noncritical services are simply stopped. Prioritization includes not just throttling of traffic based on its attributes, but also coordination of lower-level protocols to achieve a higher-level objective.

When prioritization is not enough and the critical need for bandwidth exceeds what is available, other measures must be taken to actually reduce bandwidth requirements. The first step is to move the STS and application end points into the DIL environment. This reduces the need for these requests and responses to flow over the network. However, now the STS and applications will call other services over the network, so we must iteratively determine which services are required to implement the full capabilities of the STS and applications. This includes the provide claims service and the claims repository for the STS and any associated services and databases for the application end points.

In some cases, it is difficult to move services into the DIL environment, so services are eliminated and workarounds are used. For example, online certificate status protocol (OCSP) responders are hard to move, but certificate revocation lists (CRL) can be used in the DIL environment instead. This provides a solution to the functional and security problem. CRLs are not used in normal operations for security and scalability reasons, but for a DIL environment where the scope of operations and associated services is limited, CRLs provide a workaround.

11.6.2.1 Prioritization of Communications

A major interoperability problem in the deployment of heterogeneous networks is the coordination of the capacity allocation algorithms associated with, or embedded in, the control of each type of network device. Capacity allocation is an essential underpinning for the proper operation of network-centric services.

In the wired network, capacity allocation is often managed by a single management solution since the underlying technology can be quite homogeneous. For example, the open shortest path first (OSPF) routing protocol or the enhanced interior gateway routing protocol (EIGRP) can determine an optimal mesh of landline links that can range from moderate (1.5 Mbps), to high (100 Mbps to 1 Gbps), to very high (10 Gbps) rates. This mesh typically includes many redundant links that can quickly be employed to support net-centric services by invoking capacity management protocols at the link layer (e.g., Spanning Tree Protocol—IEEE Standard 802.1D) or at the network layer (e.g., OSPF—IETF RFC 2328). In tactical wireless environments, the luxury of link overprovisioning typically does not exist. There are both technical and strategic reasons for limiting the number of links, and the wireless links themselves are subject to environmental (atmospheric, foliage, jamming) effects that are not as prevalent in the wired Internet.

These links can become disconnected when radio frequency (RF) or free space optical (FSO) transmission is blocked, intermittent when connections wax and wane, or frequency-limited when the waveform changes physical layer features such as modulation technique to maintain connection in poor conditions, but at a lower bit rate.

Capacity allocation for satellite communications paths typically uses demand-assigned multiple access (DAMA) and its variants. A DAMA network takes a single 25-kHz channel and breaks it up into time division multiple access formats that allow a number of users onto a single channel simultaneously. Terrestrial line-of-sight (LOS) wireless links have a number of link layers (media-access-control [MAC]) or network layer algorithms that can be used for capacity management. It is imperative that the capacity allocation for all the wired and wireless components in a services-based network be performed according to the same technical pattern. In this way, the constituent element management algorithms will work in cohesion and not inadvertently cancel or contradict each other.

The explicit processes associated with bandwidth and priority management will not be covered in this text.

11.6.2.2 Reduction of the Need for Capacity

Identity and access management can consume a large portion of available network resources when dealing with disadvantaged computer operations. In particular, the reach-back to an attribute ecosystem can consume significant resources and negatively affect latency. The typical response to such elements is to reduce bandwidth requirements by forward provisioning or elimination of required capabilities. The following sections provide the minimum requirements for forward positioning of assets in that ecosystem.

11.6.2.3 Asset Requirements

The attribute ecosystem may be broken into its essential components as follows:

 a. Deployed applications and services as needed
 b. Claims repository
 c. Security token server
 d. Provide claims web service (Service Number 11, see Annex H)

   Since the STS supplies only claims, the attributes, groups, and registries are not required for forward deployment. The claims repository may be tailored for the local operations (e.g., only expected Distinguished Names [DN]).

 For ease of use, additional services may be included:

 e. Claims query (service 17)
 f. Delegation service (service 12)

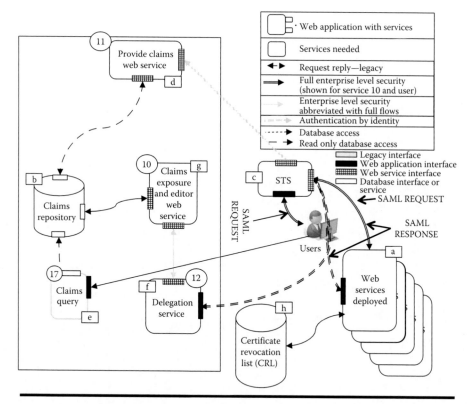

Figure 11.5 DIL reduced EAS ecosystem.

g. Claims exposure web service (service 10)

The claims query is a user convenience service. The delegation service may become important for continuity in the change-out of personnel without an update to the claims repository. Rules for delegation in these circumstances must be carefully constructed. The claims exposure web service is needed by the delegation service.

And to avoid reach-back for certification validation, a CRL may be added. The CRLs may be tailored for the local operations (e.g., only expected DNs). For extended deployments, chronic bandwidth problems, or isolated environments, the checking of credential expiration may also be suspended. Updates for the claims repository and CRLs may occur irregularly and by whatever means are available.

h. CRL repository

A complete example is shown in Figure 11.5.

As shown in the figure, most of the reach-back is eliminated for the access control problem.

Chapter 12

Cascading Authorization

The material that helped shape this chapter was first published in 2010 [57,60].

Providing access and privilege information to a chain of services is subject to the following assumptions:

- User-based requests:
  - A request for service within the enterprise is an implicit request to a service provider to do what the service provider is capable of doing on behalf of the user-based requester to satisfy this request.
  - Claims/attributes definition is fine grained enough to signify access throughout the process.
- Service-based requests:
  - A request for service within the enterprise is an explicit request to a downstream service provider to do what the service provider is capable of doing on behalf of the service requester to satisfy this request.
  - Claims/attributes definition is fine grained enough to signify access throughout the process.
  - Nonaggregation services are atomic.
- Other:
  - For purposes of the examples in this chapter, only web-service calls at or above OSI level 5 are considered.
  - Calls below level 5 on the OSI stack are not made by SAML authorization and do not follow this paradigm.

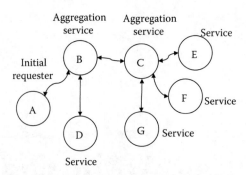

Figure 12.1 Basic use case for cascading authorization.

12.1 Basic Use Case

The basic use case is given in Figure 12.1 and involves an initial requester invoking an aggregation service, which in turn invokes aggregation and other services.

12.2 Standard Communication

Each communication link in Figure 12.1 will be authenticated end-to-end with the X.509 certificates provided for each of the active entities. The attribution and least privilege will be handled by modifications to the SAML token provided by the STS. These modifications need to be handled by the STS for authenticity and integrity. The SAML token for the initial requester A to aggregation Service B is obtained in the normal process described in Chapter 10. A partial representation is provided in Table 12.1.

12.3 Pruning Attributes,* Groups, and Roles

An individual or service request for another service may contain many elements that are not relevant to the service request. This makes the SAML request overly large, increases the cycles for SAML consumption and evaluation, may introduce additional latency, and is a potential source for escalation of privilege. In order to combat these factors, the attribute assertion should be reduced to the minimum required to accomplish the service request.

---

* Since authorization decisions may require any of a combination of attributes, groups, and/or roles, these will be referred to generically as elements in the rest of this chapter.

Table 12.1   SAML 2.0 Format for User to Aggregation Service

Item	Field Usage	Notes
SAML Response		
Version ID	Version 2.0	
ID	(uniquely assigned)	
Issue instant	Timestamp	
Issuer	Yes	STS name
Signature	Yes	STS signature
Subject	Requester A	Must contain the X.509 distinguished name or equivalent
Attribute Assertion		
Subject	Requester A	For attribution
Claims	Requester A	May be pruned for least privilege
Conditions		
NotBefore	Yes	TimeStamp – minutes
NotAfter	Yes	TimeStamp + minutes
Audience	Yes	Mandatory

12.4 Required Escalation of Privilege

Certain services may require privilege beyond that of the original client. Examples include the STS that when called is expected to have access to claims or attribute information, even when the client does not have such privilege. An additional example includes payroll services that can provide average figures without specifics. The service must be able to access all records in the payroll database, even if the client it is acting on behalf of does not have this privilege. For purposes of this methodology, these required elements for escalation will be dealt separately in both data pruning and service-to-service calls. Service developers should take care that the required escalation of privilege is required and that the newly aggregated data do not impose additional access restrictions. The data that has been aggregated and synthesized should be carefully scrutinized for such sensitivities. The process is not unlike combining data from multiple unclassified but sensitive data sources that may rise to a higher classification level when the data are combined.

12.5 Data Requirements for the Pruning of Elements

In order to accomplish the reduction of the SAML assertion, the STS must know the target and the elements that are important to the target. Table 12.2 presents such a data compilation. This table will be used in the subsequent example. An element is an attribute, role, or group used in the authorization decision.

The combing of these elements for least privilege is given by

Let N_{i+1} = new SAML elements for i to call i + 1
Let P_i = prior elements
Let R_{i+1} = service required elements
Let H_i = service held elements
Let E_i = required escalation elements

Table 12.2   Group and Role Pruning Data Requirement

Service	URL	Relevant Claims	Escalation of Privilege Required
...	...	...	
...	...	...	
Personnel30	...//xyz.pers.23	Element 1, Element 3, Element 4, Element 5, Element 6, Identity	Element 6,[a] Identity[b]
PERGeo	...//xyz.perst.45	Element 4, Element 5, Element 6, Identity	Element,[c] Identity
PerReg	...//xyz.persq.45	Element 4	
PerTrans	...//xyz.persaw.45	Element 6	
BarNone	...//xyz.persaxc.45	Element 5	
DimrsEnroll	...//xyz.persws.45	Element 1, Element 3	
...	...	...	
...	...	...	
Endfile			

[a] Element 6 is needed to gather information that will be synthesized and averaged. The average data may be presented to the user even if he or she does not have privilege to access individual data elements.
[b] Identity needed for personalization.
[c] Element 6 and Identity are required escalation elements.

Then,

$$N_{i+1} = (P_i \cap (R_{i+1} \cup H_i)) \cup (E_i \cap R_{i+1}) \qquad (12.1)$$

where
$\cap$ is the intersection of sets
$\cup$ is the union of sets
$\emptyset$ is the empty set (no members)

The formula may be read as the common elements in the prior SAML and the union of the held elements and those required by the next call $((P_i \cap (R_{i+1} \cup H_i))$—normal least privilege). These are added $(\cup)$ to the required escalation elements that are required to be extended by the next call $((E_i \cap R_{i+1})$—extended least privilege by escalation of privilege).

The initial call has no prior elements and P_1 is defined as the initial set of privilege elements.

12.6 Saving of the SAML Assertion

After the SAML is consumed and authorization is granted, the service must retain the SAML attribute assertion (part of the larger SAML token) above—specifically, the subject fields and the elements field to be used in further authorization. The specific instance is shown in Table 12.3.

12.7 SAML Token Modifications for Further Calls

The attribute assertion of Table 12.3 is returned to the STS for modification of the normal SAML token. The SAML token for the unmodified service call is given in Table 12.4.

The attribute assertion is modified in the following way:

The subject is modified to read "Service A OnBehalfOf" the returned SAML subject, which in this case is the identity of the user.

Table 12.3   Retained Portion of SAML Token

Attribute Assertion		
Subject	User A	For attribution
Claims	User A	Mask for follow-on least privilege

Table 12.4   Unmodified SAML for Service B of Use Case

Item	Field Usage	Notes
SAML Response		
Version ID	Version 2.0	
ID	(unique assigned)	
Issue instant	Timestamp	
Issuer	Yes	STS Name
Signature	Yes	STS Signature
Subject	Service B	Must contain the X.509 distinguished name or equivalent
Attribute Assertion		
Subject	Cn for Service B	For attribution
Claims	Service B	$N_{i+1} = (P_i \cap (R_{i+1} \cup H_i)) \cup (E_i \cap R_{i+1})$
Conditions		
NotBefore	Yes	TimeStamp – minutes
NotAfter	Yes	TimeStamp + minutes
Audience	Yes	Mandatory

The attribute, group, and role membership (elements) are modified to include only elements that appear in both the Service B registry and the returned SAML attribute assertion.

The modified SAML token is provided in Table 12.5.

Subsequent calls from Service A would use the modified token. Further, the subsequent service called would save the SAML attribute assertion for its further calls.

12.8 An Annotated Notional Example

A user in the enterprise Forest (Ted.Smith1234567890) through discovery finds the dashboard service on Personnel (Personnel30) that he would like to invoke (Figure 12.2). The discovery has revealed that access is limited to users with Element 1, Element 3, Element 4, Element 5, or Element 6, but that users without

Table 12.5 Modified SAML Attribute Assertion for Further Calls

Item	Field Usage	Notes
SAML Response		
Version ID	Version 2.0	
ID	(uniquely assigned)	
Issue instant	Timestamp	
Issuer	Yes	STS Name
Signature	Yes	STS Signature
Subject	Service B	Must contain the X.509 distinguished name or equivalent
Attribute Assertion		
Subject	Cn B OnBehalfOf Cn A	For attribution
Attributes, claims	Yes B restricted by A	$N_{i+1} = (P_i \cap (R_{i+1} \cup H_i)) \cup (E_i \cap R_{i+1})$
Conditions		
NotBefore	Yes	TimeStamp – minutes
NotAfter	Yes	TimeStamp + minutes
Audience	Yes	Mandatory

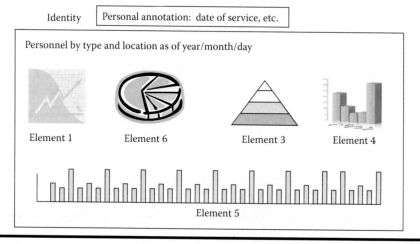

Figure 12.2 Peronnel30 with display and element requirements.

all of these authorizations may not receive all of the requested display. Ted does not have all of the required elements, but is authorized for personnel data restricted to data for personnel currently in the United States and has element membership in Element 1, Element 2, Element 3, Element 4, Element 7, Element 12, and 27 other elements not relevant. The Personnel30 will typically display the dashboard on enterprise personnel provided in Figure 12.2.

The elements required would not typically be displayed. A partial calling tree for Personnel30 is provided in Figure 12.3. The widgets that form the presentation graphics have not been included, but would be part of the calling tree— they do not have access requirements that modify the example and have been deleted to reduce complexity. In Figure 12.3, we show the elements that make up the privilege for each service (holds) and the elements required for access to the service (requires). This data is linked to Table 12.3 and must be synchronized with it. The element privileges for services without subsequent calls are none, and many additional groups may be present but will be pruned on subsequent calls.

Note that each link in the calling graph requires bilateral authentication using certificates provided as credentials to each of the active entities, followed by the

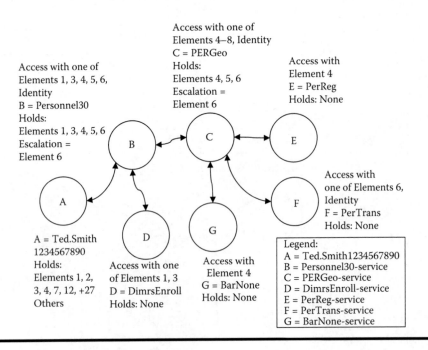

Figure 12.3   Personnel30 calling tree.

push of a SAML token for authorization. The first such token is presented in Table 12.6.

The attribute assertion section is saved for subsequent calls. The call from Personnel30 to service PERGeo will look like Table 12.7.

The SAML attribute assertion is where the work is done. The subject has been modified to include the names of the calling tree, and the elements have been pruned to include only common items between the calling elements in the tree.

Table 12.6   Ted Smith SAML Push to Personnel30

Item	Field Usage
SAML Response	
Version ID	Version 2.0
ID	0qwdrt009kkmn
Issue instant	080820081943
Issuer	Donal STS12345
Signature	Lkhjsfoioiunmclscwl879ooeeujl99vcd78ffgg3422ft...
Subject	CN = TED.SMITH1234567890, OU = CONTRACTOR, OU = PKI, OU = XYZ, O = Commercial
Attribute Assertion	
Subject	TED.SMITH1234567890
Claims	Element1, Element3, Element4[a] $N_1 = (P_1 \cap (R_2 \cup H_2)) \cup (E_1 \cap R_2)$ $= ((1, 2, 3, 4, 7, 12, + 27, \text{Identity}) \cap (1, 3, 4, 5, 6, \text{Identity}) \cup (1, 3, 4, 5, 6)) \cup (\emptyset \cap 1, 3, 4, 5, 6, \text{Identity})$ $= ((1, 2, 3, 4, 7, 12, + 27, \text{Identity}) \cap (1, 3, 4, 5, 6, \text{Identity})) \cup (\emptyset)$ $= ((1, 3, 4, \text{Identity}))$
Conditions	
NotBefore	080820081933
NotAfter	080820081953
Audience	Personnel30

[a] An element is an attribute, role, group, or combination of the previous. Elimination of Element 2, Element 7, Element 12, and 27 other elements based on pruning (see Table 5 under AFPersonnel30).

Table 12.7 Personnel30 SAML Push to PERGeo

Item	Field Usage
SAML Response	
Version ID	Version 2.0
ID	0qwdrt009kkmn
Issue instant	080820081944
Issuer	Donal STS12345
Signature	Lkhjsfoioiunmclscwl879ooeeujl99xfg654bbgg34lli…
Subject	CN = e3893de0-4159-11dd-ae16-0800200c9a66, OU = , OU = Software, OU = XYZ, O = Commercial
Attribute Assertion	
Subject	Personnel30 OnBehalfOf TED.SMITH1234567890
Claims	Group4,[a] Element6[b] $N_{i+1} = (P_i \cap (R_{i+1} \cup H_i)) \cup (E_i \cap R_{i+1})$ $= ((1, 3, 4, \text{Identity}) \cap (4, 5, 6, \text{Identity} \cup 4, 5, 6))$ $\cup (6, \text{Identity} \cap 4, 5, 6, \text{Identity})$ $= ((1, 3, 4, \text{Identity}) \cap (4, 5, 6, \text{Identity})) \cup (6, \text{Identity})$ $= (4, 6, \text{Identity})$
Conditions	
NotBefore	080820081934
NotAfter	080820081954
Audience	PERGeo

[a] An element is an attribute, role, group or combination of the previous. Elimination of Element 1 and Element 3 based on pruning (see Table 5 under PERGeo).
[b] Element 6 and identity are required escalation elements.

Figure 12.4 shows the completion of the calling tree, including only the SAML attribute assertions.

Note that the calls to BarNone in Figure 12.4 (service G in the figures) fails access and while being stealth to the calling routine (which will return with no data after timeout) will trigger alarms to SOA management monitors as follows:

Failed authorization (BarNone) attempt PERGeo on behalf of Personnel30 on behalf of Ted.Smith1234567890 No data returned.

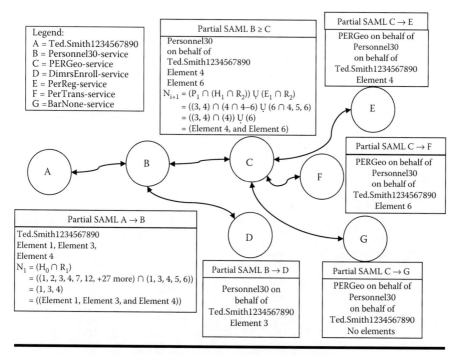

Figure 12.4   SAML attribute assertion for the calling tree.

The returned dashboard (without the annotations) is presented in Figure 12.5. Note that Element 6 privilege was provided by service escalation.

12.9 Additional Requirements

The STS requirements are given in Table 12.8. The additional requirements on the services are given in Table 12.9.

12.10 Service Use Case Summary

The process of using SAML token modification for tracking of delegation, attribution, and least privileges has both advantages and disadvantages.

- Advantages:
  - Use of SAML standard without extension or violation.
  - Full attribution for data analyses and forensics.
  - Least privilege is invoked on service-to-service calls.
  - Aggregation service does not need to filter response to the user based on access credentials.

- — Federation works exactly the same way.
- — Person-to-person delegation compatible.

■ Disadvantages:
- — Use of SAML standard in a way that SAML standard writers did not anticipate.
- — Service must store and convey or forward SAML assertion invoking the thread.
- — STS currently does not process this data.

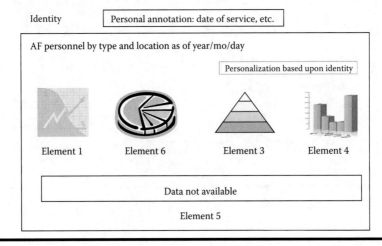

Figure 12.5 Dashboard service Personnel30 case result.

Table 12.8 STS Additional Requirements

Item	Requirement	Data Structure Required
Element pruning by individual service call	Least privilege reduction of attributes, groups, and roles in SAML assertion	Yes, table of service attribute, group, and role requirements for access. Must be synchronized with access managers
Receive prior SAML assertion	Need subject, attributes, groups, and roles for further attribution and group definition	Internal only, no external store required
Apply prior SAML assertion to SAML	Includes modification of subject line in assertion as well as further pruning of elements	Internal only, no external store required

Table 12.9 Service Additional Requirements

Item	Requirement	Data Structure Required
Hold SAML assertion	Required only when subsequent service calls are to be performed on behalf of the requestor	Internal only, no external store required, but must be held on a per thread basis
Send prior SAML assertion	When subsequent service calls are made	Internal only, no external store required, but must be transmitted on a per thread basis
Use subject of SAML assertion in logs	Attribution requirement	Log files in existence
Purge held SAML assertion	When thread is complete	None

Chapter 13

Federation

The material that helped shape this chapter was first published in 2008 in project documentation and in 2009 in the public literature [17]. Two simple forms of delegation include the following:

- Issuing a limited number of credentials and including the individuals in the enterprise attribute stores
- Special delegation as described in Chapter 16

Both forms are meant for either limited numbers or short-duration federation. The material in this chapter covers more permanent or larger federation events.

13.1 Federation

Federation is a joining together of interests. In computing, it means an agreement to share information resources. Examples range from two offices sharing data to work on a proposal to two companies sharing marketing and sales. For an enterprise, it is an agreement to allow individuals not in the enterprise access through acceptance of credentials. The simplest way to federate with a small number of individuals is to issue enterprise credentials to them and include them in enterprise databases. Broader sharing requires a more formal definition of federation and its processes. If we examine the steps in federated communications, we see that they are composed of the basic steps in prior forms of communication.

13.2 Elements of Federated Communication

13.2.1 Naming and Identity

Identity is established by the requesting agency. In an enterprise, this is primarily through the naming scheme adopted by that enterprise, but for other certificate authorities, their naming schemes may or may not be honored. If that naming scheme cannot or will not be honored, then certificate issuance may be by the enterprise. To avoid conflict with the enterprise naming, the identity used by all federated exchanges is the distinguished name (identity) as it appears on the primary credential provided by the certificate authority. The name in association with the certificate authority provides a unique identifier.

13.2.2 Credentials

Credentials are an integral part of the federation schema. Each identity requiring access must be credentialed by a trusted credentialing authority. Part of federation involves examining the credentialing authority and ascertaining whether or not it is trustworthy. Placing the credentialing authority in the trust stores will allow identity federation.

The security token server that will be used for generating SAML tokens must also be credentialed (primarily through the same credentialing authority, although others may be entertained). Within the enterprise, all STSs are directly connected through an out-of-band network for generation of federated credentials.

13.2.3 PKI—X.509 Certificates

The primary exchange medium for setting up authentication of identities and setting up cryptographic flows is the PKI embodied in an X.509 certificate.

13.2.4 Certificate Services

The certificate authority must use known and registered (or in specific cases defined) certificate revocation and currency checking software.

13.2.5 Bilateral Authentication

The requestor will authenticate to the service, and the service will authenticate to the requestor. This two-way authentication avoids a number of threat vulnerabilities and is a direct extension of the identity handling in the enterprise. The requestor and server mutually authenticate and set up a TLS connection to begin communication with the service. The primary method of authentication is through the use of public keys in the X.509 certificate, which can then be used to set up encrypted communications (either by X.509 keys or a generated session key). The preferred method of communication is secure messaging, contained in SOAP envelopes.

13.2.6 Authorization Using SAML Packages

All authorization is done through the use of SAML packages in accordance with the SAML 2.0 specification provided by OASIS [1].

13.2.7 Registration of the STS

All security token servers that create and sign SAML packages must be registered. Information needed for such registration must be provided as part of the federation agreement.

13.2.8 Recognizing STS Signatures

Services only recognize STS signatures for the local STS. Within the enterprise, this is accomplished through the out-of-band network. STS signatures from external entities are recognized only for registered STSs and may be repackaged by the local STS when such registration has been accomplished. Unrecognized signatures are not honored and are logged as a security relevant.

13.2.9 Translation of Properties, Roles, and Groups

Properties, roles, and groups may be translated as indicated in the federation agreement. The STS will keep a record of necessary translations and perform these translations prior to the reissuance of SAML packages.

13.2.10 Other Issues

The registering of recognized STS and role/group translation is not initiated upon ratification of the federation agreement but must be promulgated in an enterprise policy memorandum. The federation agreement may be an attachment to such a policy memorandum. This memorandum must be distributed to the appropriate organization for implementation by the appropriate service administrator. This maintains the lines of authority.

13.3 Example Federation Agreement

The following is an example federation agreement, which may need to be modified for use in any particular enterprise.

Example Federation Agreement

Preamble

This agreement for information sharing is between

The ABC Corporation Enterprise Operations (POC: J. Tenanbaum, New York, john.tennenbaum@ABC.com) and

The XYZ Marketing Company LTD (POC: H. Smythe, London, Henry.smythe@XYZ.co.uk)

An agreement to share marketing and sales recent and current throughout Europe. (It is appropriate to cite rationale for this agreement and any requirements that come from higher authority. The example here is bilateral. Some federations are for unilateral sharing and the agreement must be tailored. This agreement is meant to be a model only; the individual circumstances may change the form and substance of this agreement. The agreement should satisfy both the human-readable needs and the computer information system requirements.)

Duration

This document remains in effect until revoked by either of the authorities cited in this document.

Lines of Authority

Maintenance of this agreement:

The ABC Corporation, Marketing Division, New York, POC: George Wright, george.wright@ABC.com

The XYZ Company LTD, London, POC: Michael Friends, Michael.friends@XYZ.co.uk

Implementation of this agreement:

The ABC Marketing Office, Chicago, POC: Henry Smith, henry.smith@ABC.com

The XYZ Company LTD, London, POC: Michael Friends, Michael.friends@XYZ.co.uk

Responsibility

The ABC Corporation, Marketing Division, New York is responsible for identifying, vetting, credentialing, and training individuals who have access to the information of the ABC Corporation and for the maintenance of this list.

The XYZ Company LTD, Sales Branch, London is responsible for identifying, vetting, credentialing, and training individuals who have access to the information of the XYZ Company LTD and for the maintenance of this list.

Sensitivity

This Document:	Restricted to Joint Executive Committee
ABC Information Shared:	ABC Company Proprietary
XYZ Information Shared:	XYZ Company Proprietary

Credentialing

ABC: Donal certificate authority, PKI issues X.509 certificates (as much detail [but minimal detail] as necessary to provide root authority and validation).

XYZ: Verizon certificate authority, PKI issues X.509 certificates (as much detail [but minimal detail] as necessary to provide root authority and validation).

Identity and Requested Access

(Data in this section may make the agreement at a higher level of sensitivity than the information being shared.) Members of ABC shall be identified by The Distinguished Name on the Donal-issued X.509 certificate, and seeks access from <URL, location, specific enclave within a forest, or other source information pertinent to the requestors of service>. The access is directed to the following services within the Eternal Enterprise XYZ:

1. <Service name, URL for entry, URI, and other information pertinent to access>
2. <Service name, URL for entry, URI, and other information pertinent to access>
3. <Service name, URL for entry, URI, and other information pertinent to access>

   And

4. <Service name, URL for entry, URI, and other information pertinent to access>

The access sought is read-only without edit, modification, or deletion privileges.
The requestor presents a SAML 2.0 package, developed by the following security token server:
<token server name, URL, URI, and other information pertinent to registration>
The X.509 certificate for this server is Donal-issued and is provided electronically.
Members of ABC are identified by The Distinguished Name on the Verizon-issued X.509 certificate, and seek access from <URL, location, specific enclave within a forest, or other source information pertinent to the requestors of service>. The access is directed to the following services within The XYZ Corporation enterprise:

1. <Service name, URL for entry, URI, and other information pertinent to access>
2. <Service name, URL for entry, URI, and other information pertinent to access>
3. <Service name, URL for entry, URI, and other information pertinent to access>
4. <Service name, URL for entry, URI, and other information pertinent to access>
5. <app.xyz.com/ContentRetrievalapplique.asp>

The access sought is read-only without edit, modification, or deletion privileges.

Authorization

The XYZ corporation requestor presents a SAML 2.0 package, developed by the following security token server:

<Token server name, URL, URI, and other information pertinent to registration>

Authorized members have the following groups and roles present in the SAML Assertion:

1. Europe
2. Foxtrot
3. ...

For content associated with this agreement, the token server provides the following claims:

Orange, Blue

Identities may be mapped as necessary to avoid collisions.

And

The ABC Company LTD requestor presents a SAML 2.0 package, developed by the following security token server:

<token server name, URL, URI, and other information pertinent to registration>

The X.509 certificate for this server is Verizon-issued and provided electronically.

Authorized members of the ABC Company LTD have the following groups and roles present in the SAML Assertion:

1. Purple
2. Yellow
3. ...

For content associated with this agreement, the token server provides the following claims:

Navy, Marine

Identities may be mapped as necessary to avoid collisions.

Registration of STS certificates:

Bilateral registration of STS certificates is undertaken and STS databases are updated. Authorization is promulgated by XYZ Enterprise Policy and ABC Enterprise Policy as soon as practical.

Special Considerations

Assistance at interpreting, formatting, displaying, and integrating the information accessed is to be provided bilaterally.

This agreement may be unilaterally revoked by either party with appropriate notice to the POCs above

13.4 Access from Outside the Enterprise

When a federated user makes a request to a web application service or a web service, six active entities (three in enterprise) and three passive entities (each in enterprise) come into play. If there are subsequent web service calls, the flows are the same as in Figure 13.1.

Active entities:

1. The federated user's web browser
2. The federation web service
3. The security token service (STS 1) in the user's domain

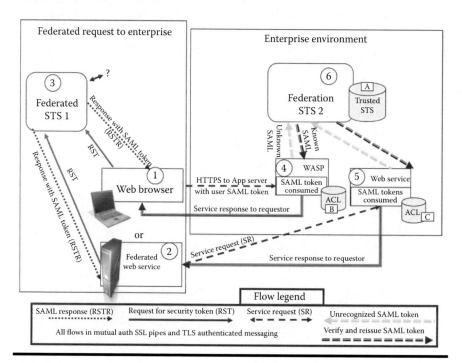

Figure 13.1   Federated requests to enterprise.

4. The enterprise WASP
5. Web service in the enterprise receiving a federated request
6. The security token service (STS 2) trusted by the service. STS 2 contains the federation rules for creating a set of claims valid for the requester in the enterprise. If federation is invoked, then the SAML did not come from STS 1 (which is in the enterprise user domain); federation is invoked

Passive entities:

1. List of trusted STSs
2. Enterprise WASP ACL
3. Enterprise web service ACL

After the SAML is reissued, communications between web services proceed as in normal enterprise operations. The message flow sequences for federated service requests are shown in Figure 13.1, together with active and passive entities.

13.5 Trusted STS Store

Federation is the recognition of entities that are certificated and provide claims from domains that are not recognized by the service. The web service in the enterprise has a limited number of recognized keys stored in the security-related file. Federation applies to any unrecognized signature in the SAML token, whether it is enterprise or not. The federation may be as complicated as sharing information with only partially trusted coalition partners, or as simple as providing information to other enterprise domains. The security model implemented as part of the enterprise implementation requires PKI-based certificates of active entities and relies on details of claims to be incorporated in SAML token assertions to support authorization decisions. Further, a list of trusted STSs is created in a store that is collocated with the STS. This store supports the federation activity. In order to resolve the federation issues, the STS has the following information:

■ Public keys of federated security token servers for resolving signatures in SAML tokens.
■ Recognition of a signature results in an attempted reissuance of the SAML token as outlined below.

Nonrecognition of the signature invalidates the SAML and prompts an invalid SAML return, which causes an authorization failure.

The following data is required for each recognized federated security token server:

■ A set of identity-mapping tuples with the form identity1, indentity2, where * in Table 13.1 indicates no further remapping required. For simple federation,

Table 13.1   Federation Data Requirements

	Original SAML	*New SAML*	
Enterprise STS 1	Enterprise STS Public Key and Distinguished Name, Target URLs		These STS are . recognized
Identity Mapping	*	*	
Claim Mapping	*	*	
Enterprise STS 2	Enterprise STS Public Key and Distinguished Name, Target URLs		
Identity Mapping	*	*	
Claim Mapping	*	*	
Etc.			
End Enterprise STS			
Federation Partner 1	Federation Public Key and Distinguished Name, Target URLs		Each federation partner has its own mapping requirements—in general federation partners are not provided actual ACL claims for authorization
Identity Mapping	Identity 1	Identity 2	
	Identity A	Identity B	
	Identity Q	Identity B	
	Identity r	No change	
	Identity s	No change	
	…	…	
	No further identities accepted		
	*	*	
Claim Mapping	Claim 1 and Claim q	Claim 2	
	Claim A	Null	
	Claim n	Claim z, Claim q	
	Claim y and not Claim r	MAC 2	
	…	…	
	*	*	

(*Continued*)

Table 13.1 (*Continued*) **Federation Data Requirements**

	Original SAML	*New SAML*	
End Federation Partner 1			
Federation Partner 2	Federation Public Key and Distinguished Name, Target URLs		See above
Identity Mapping	Identity x	Identity y	
	Identity Q	Identity R	
	...	...	
	All other identities accepted and not changed		
	*	*	
Claim Mapping Block	Claim n	Claim m	
	Claim o	MAC p	
	...	...	
	*	*	
End Federation Partner 2			
Etc.			
End Federation Partners			

where requests are across enterprise domains, this mapping is "no change," and the names are in the appropriate form already. A null mapping on an identity, upon execution, invalidates the SAML and prompts an invalid SAML return, which causes an authorization failure.

■ A set of mapping n-tuples of the form claim a, claim b, where * in Table 13.1 indicates no further remapping required. For simple federation, where requests are across enterprise domains, this mapping is not required and the claims are in the appropriate form already. Claims may include MAC elements.

■ Mappings may include Boolean operations and may map to multiple alternatives. Boolean operations are not acceptable on the "map to" side. The mapping depends upon the federation agreement.

■ In all mappings, "null" and "no change" mappings are acceptable. "Null" removes the claim or identity, while "no change" leaves the original claim or identity.

- An identity mapping invalidates the HOK on the reissued SAML token. This step is skipped in the verification process.
- The claims that are being mapped must match claims from sources on both sides.
- Claims in the federation partner SAML must match the federation agreement exactly.
- Claims in the reissued enterprise SAML must match enterprise claims for the target service(s).
- Identities and claims are added to the federation store after an amendment to the federation agreement.
- Policy changes for individuals or accesses are implemented by a "null" mapping so that the reissued SAML eliminates the claims.
- Revocation of a federation agreement is accomplished by removing the federation partner from the trusted STS data store.

The basic information is shown in Table 13.1.

13.6 Trusted STS Governance

All services are provided the public key and distinguished name of their local STS and the user forest STS. Any SAML presented that is not signed by one of these two STSs is subject to federation. Federation includes additional enterprise domains, as well as others groups that require information sharing. Table 13.1 must be created and maintained by the enterprise administrator, as either centralized or distributed. An enterprise administrator is responsible for creating the trusted STS store and distributing it to each STS that is used as a federation server. The initial store includes all enterprise domains not in the user forest. These have no mappings, and the federation STS simply reissues the token. The enterprise administrator must be notified whenever a new enterprise domain is added or a federation agreement is put in place (this may be done electronically). The administrator is responsible for adding the new information to the federation table and distributing it throughout the enterprise where it is needed (this may be done by database replication or other means). The enterprise administrator must be notified whenever an enterprise domain is deleted or a federation agreement is modified or deleted (this may be done electronically). The administrator is responsible for adjusting the information in the federation table and distributing it throughout the enterprise where it is needed (this may be done by database replication or other means). While the location of the store within the enterprise and its distribution throughout the enterprise may be accomplished by any approved processes, the store is shown in the EAS for convenience of this document.

Chapter 14

Content Access Control

In the era of WikiLeaks and the sensitivity of documents in an enterprise system at all classification levels, there is a need for assured content delivery. The promise of digital rights management (DRM) has yet to be realized, and knowledgeable analysts opine that it may never be achievable. It will certainly need copious amounts of specialized software—and maybe even specialized hardware before information assurance can be satisfied. We do not rely on DRM technologies at this point, but reserve the right to review future developments in this area. Nonetheless, there is a need for an assured content delivery process for enterprise authoritative documentation. This chapter presents a process of culling the authoritative information and placing it in an authoritative content repository. Content in this repository is available only through a service request, and "browsing" of the content is not permitted. The existence of the document and related documents may be obtained from search engines or other references. The content store has a librarian, which is a collection of software and manual processes, and a retrieval service. These two aspects provide for the authenticity and authority of the content. In an environment of trusted individuals, control is provided in the notification of restrictions and the diligence of the users. However, methods of tracing activities in the use and distribution of the most critical documents are provided as a possible mitigation of insider threats. This enterprise solution is part of a larger enterprise architecture that is web-service-based and driven by commercial standards and includes naming, certificates issuance for identity and PKI, mutual authentication and confidentiality through transport layer security, and digital signatures for integrity. The work on content management has been ongoing since 2004, and it was finally integrated into the SAML approaches in 2011 and published in 2012 [63].

14.1 Authoritative and Nonauthoritative Content

Content includes documents, spreadsheets, web pages, presentations, and other complete or incomplete sets of information. There are two basic types of documentation we consider: authoritative data sources or authoritative content repositories and nonauthoritative content repositories. An example of a nonauthoritative data source (or information repository) is an individual desktop system upon which a number of working papers and works in progress are in use and being developed. Many of these may develop into authoritative content and need to be handled accordingly. Others may never rise to the level of authoritative content. The individual is responsible for restricted distribution, document integrity, and restricting the use of the material for action until it becomes authoritative in accordance with the pedigree of the working material. Nonauthoritative content may be handled in ad hoc fashion through applications that are expressly created for its handling. It may be shared through SharePoint or other content repositories and is indexed and searchable by other processes. Authoritative content, on the other hand, must only be realized through a content delivery service that assures its integrity, sharing restrictions, access control, and verifiable content. This discussion concerns authoritative content because this level of control is currently impractical for all content. Before discussing the details of distributing assured content, the following sections review several concepts that apply to content delivery:

1. Digital rights management
2. Mandatory access control
3. Metadata and metacards
4. Creation of an information asset in an authoritative data store

14.2 Content Delivery Digital Rights Management

DRM technologies attempt to control the use of digital media by preventing unauthorized access and authorized end users from copying or converting it to other formats. Long before the arrival of digital or even electronic media, copyright holders, content producers, and other financially or artistically interested parties had business and legal objections to copying technologies. Examples include player piano rolls early in the twentieth century, audio tape recording, and video tape recording. The advent of digital media and analog/digital conversion technologies, especially those that are usable on mass-market general-purpose personal computers, has vastly increased the concerns of copyright-dependent individuals and organizations, especially within the music and movie industries, because these individuals and organizations are partly or wholly dependent on the revenue generated from such works. While analog media inevitably loses quality with each copy generation, and in some cases even during normal use, digital media files may be duplicated an unlimited number of times with no degradation in the quality of subsequent copies. The advent of personal computers as household appliances has made it convenient for consumers to convert media (which may or may not be copyrighted) originally in a physical/analog form or a broadcast form into a universal, digital form (this process is called ripping) for moving the information to other locations or viewing the content at a later time. This, combined with the Internet and popular file-sharing tools, has made unauthorized distribution of copies of copyrighted digital media (digital piracy) much easier. DRM technologies have enabled publishers to enforce access policies that not only disallow copyright infringements, but also prevent lawful fair use of copyrighted works, or even implement use constraints on noncopyrighted works they distribute; examples include the placement of DRM on certain public-domain or open-licensed e-books, or DRM included in consumer electronic devices that time-shift (and apply DRM to) both copyrighted and noncopyrighted works. DRM is most commonly used by the entertainment industry (e.g., film and recording). Many online music stores, such as Apple Inc.'s iTunes Store, and many e-book publishers have implemented DRM. In recent years, a number of television producers have implemented DRM on consumer electronic devices to control access to the freely broadcast content of their shows, in response to the rising popularity of time-shifting digital video recorder systems such as TiVo.

Common DRM techniques include the following:

- Encryption
- Scrambling of expressive material
- Embedding of a tag(s) (this technology is designed to control access, distribution, and reproduction of accessed information)

Many DRM approaches use encrypted media, which requires purpose-built hardware to hear or see the content. This appears to ensure that only authorized users (those with the hardware) can access the content. Additionally, purpose-built hardware for the content can enforce restrictions on saving or modifying content, dates of applicable use, etc. It also tries to protect a secret decryption key from the users of the system. While this in principle can work, it is extremely difficult to build the hardware to protect the secret key against a sufficiently determined adversary. Many such systems have failed in the field. Once the secret key is known, building a version of the hardware that performs no checks is often relatively straightforward. In addition, user verification provisions are often subject to attack, pirate decryption being among the most frequent. A common real-world example can be found in commercial direct broadcast satellite television systems such as DirecTV and Malaysia's Astro. These companies use tamper-resistant smart cards to store decryption keys so that they are hidden from the user and the satellite receiver. However, the system has been compromised in the past, and DirecTV has been forced to roll out periodic updates and replacements for its smart cards.

There is considerable discussion in the technical literature [64] over whether digital rights management works, or even can work. There is certainly contention over whether it should be allowed. The most workable solution seems to be targeted machinery with DRM root kits, and even these are leaky and not foolproof. The approaches, presented here, dismiss the idea of full DRM for the enterprise application and rely on "vetted" trusted users.

In a "compliant" environment where the content is delivered safely to an enterprise machine under the control of a trusted individual, it may be sufficient to notify the trusted individual of the restrictions placed upon the material. While this does not protect against the malicious insider, it simplifies the problem by eliminating the need for purpose-built hardware and software.

14.3 Mandatory Access Control

MAC is a system of access control that assigns security labels or classifications to system resources and allows access only to entities (people, processes, and devices) with distinct levels of authorization or clearance. These controls are enforced by the content delivery system. For example, the delivery system should not deliver a NATO-only document to a requester without NATO claims. These principles also apply to the delivery of classified documents to holders of the appropriate security clearances. With content delivery, changes to authoritative data are not allowed and MAC consists of four basic elements:

1. Enforcing access control, including read/copy/print/store/, etc.
2. Labeling the document and content parts and restrictions within an information asset
3. Conveying the restrictions to the requestor, including screen displays where appropriate
4. Enforcing restrictions or obtaining acknowledgment of these restrictions from the requestor

14.4 Access Control Content Management System

Entities in the enterprise environment may be active or passive. Passive entities include information packages, static files, and/or reference data structures. Passive entities are the target of activities, do not initiate activities, and cannot assume the role of requester or provider. Active entities are those entities that change or modify passive entities, request or provide services, or participate in communication flows. The active entities discussed in this section include the content management system and the content development applications. All active entities in the enterprise have enterprise certificates, and their private keys are stored in tamper-proof, threat-mitigating storage. Active elements (content development applications) on the user end devices act in the security context of the user. If the user is on a thin client, the content development applications are web services and have their own certificates and identities. Communication between

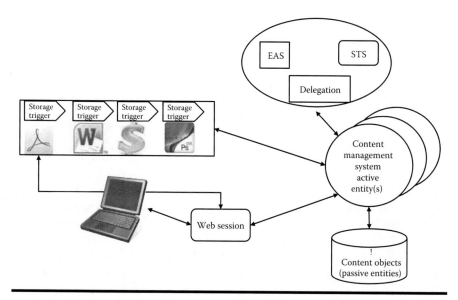

Figure 14.1   Communication between entities.

active entities in the enterprise requires full bilateral, PKI, end-to-end authentication. Authorization in the operational environment is implemented by a verifiable access control claims-based process. Claims are part of an authorization credential issued by a trusted STS and signed by that entity to preserve integrity. A claims-based credential is sent to the provider with or without a SOAP envelope containing a SAML token that includes issuance time and expiration time. Figure 14.1 displays a user interacting with the content management system through the content developing application on the user end device. Authorization for the content and the content management system for retrieving content (passive entity) from an enterprise content store is in accordance with the access control requirements in this document.

14.5   Enforcing Access Control

Enforcing both mandatory and discretionary access control is through the discretionary access control process. The information asset is encrypted and provides an extension that takes the request to open the file to the appliqué for enforcing access. The claims are used to limit the authority over the data as shown in the following list:

a. Claim 1: read, copy, and retain the information asset.
b. Claim 2: read-only on screen, may print the information asset but not cut and paste any parts of the information asset, cannot save to user environment in electronic form, read-only on screen. With MAC displays, it presents no other privileges.

The details of these claims and their names are presented in access control requirements as discussed in Chapter 10, Section 10.5. However, some additional considerations for the MAC control include hardware and software compatibility.

14.6 Labeling of Content and Information Assets

Labeling, when combined with ACLs based upon access control requirements and claims presented by requesters, provides a tightly coupled combination of mandatory access control and discretionary access control. Since labeling is the basis for access, the labeling system must be uniform and trusted. Uniformity is achieved by standardized approaches and criteria. Standards exist for use by enterprises [2m,65,66].

The labeling also carries restrictions for reproduction or usage of portions of the material provided and what attributions and labeling must be made upon such usage, if permitted.

14.7 Conveying Restrictions to the Requester

Depending upon the level of access granted, there are multiple ways to convey the restrictions to the requester. Restrictions include modification (any modification causes the signature check to fail), reproduction and storage (including which stores are appropriate), distribution restrictions, required receipts (if any), and reuse of content in whole or in part. These restrictions are stored with the MAC displays. The following factors apply:

- If the requester is an individual viewing the document without the ability to save or extract information, the display can be tailored to provide the restrictions in prominent form (usually banners at the top and/or bottom of the screen). Classified banners are red with white lettering; unclassified banners are blue with white lettering.
- If the requestor is an individual with the permission to store and save the information, or the requester is not an individual, the entity must be provided the restrictions placed upon the material.
- Requesters who are individuals may get the banners when the information is displayed, and they get the restrictions again when storing or saving the information.

In any of these scenarios, the labeling must stay with the document and the document may not be edited and returned to the authoritative content store, except by changing the version number and submitting it to the librarian for rework.

14.8 Enforcing/Obtaining Acknowledgment of Restrictions

Information sharing must be logged as an event in the logging format of the enterprise web services and periodically reviewed. Abuse of such sharing is treated as a disciplinary problem and suspension of access is possible. Saving of the file and printing or cutting segments to memory can only be done by authorized individuals and does not proceed until an acknowledgment of the distribution and access restrictions is obtained. These acknowledgments must be logged as a special event in the logging format of the enterprise web services, and they are periodically reviewed.

14.9 Metadata

Metadata (metacontent) is traditionally found in the card catalogs of libraries. Metadata is also used to describe digital data using metadata standards specific to a particular discipline. By describing the contents, key words, concepts, and context of the information, the quality of the original information is greatly increased. For example, an information asset's metadata may include the key words, concepts, language, and even tools/systems that were used to create it. This metadata is used by a search engine to discover which information assets relate to a specific subject or concept. A metacard is used to hold all of the metadata content and its reference data for a subject information asset. The actual web service/application (URI) used to acquire the information asset is included in the metacard. For example, if aircraft parts delivery information is required, the search engine queries the metacard directory based on logistics-related concepts/key words and provides a means (e.g., web service/app/office app) for information retrieval/presentation. This information can be a browser-displayed mash-up of extracts from several data stores accessed via web services, a document (presentation, spreadsheet, text) that meets the search results, etc. When an information asset is created and placed in a content store, a number of actions must take place before adding the information asset to the content store, as discussed below.

14.10 Content Management Function

Content management is a collective concept that includes the automated and manual processes to accomplish the following steps:

1. The information asset must be labeled for access and distribution; this is done by the author. Defaults may be assigned absent author input and are defaulted to the most restrictive case. Such labeling may include classification,

availability, and distribution such as Nonsensitive Employee only or Company Confidential. Data owners develop standard access control requirements to compute claims, while others, such as Executive ONLY, require access control requirements to be developed and provided to the EAS. If a standard access control requirement is not available, an access control requirement is dynamically generated based on defaults and user specifications. The information asset is also labeled by the author as "draft" or "final." When more than one signature is appended, this label can be changed to "approved" by the user if this is an officially approved/sanctioned information asset. These tags are part of the metadata that is recorded for the information asset.

2. Signed by the author for content integrity (additional signatures may be affixed for authority; see section below).
3. Generation of associated metadata.
4. Assignment of an identity (name)—defaulted by the system but can be changed by the user.
5. Author assignment of the actual storage location on the network and filing of the cross-reference between the location and the identity of the asset. The information asset is stored in an enterprise location and/or a personal location for author retrieval and further work.
6. Presentation of a privilege information request page (defaulted to read/write/delete privileges to the creator and read/delete privileges to all others and signature. If additional group-level privileges are required (e.g., data owner group, special-access group), these are specified at this time. Content-related groups are enterprise level, are subject to the rules of uniqueness over time and space, and are registered in the group registry. The privileges information is stored in the ACL headers and is available in the EAS.
7. Examination of the MAC labels and
   - For information assets that are not available to all (internal/external enterprise).
   - Encryption of the information asset.
   - Attachment to the information asset of an ACL that is used to allow access control. If the information asset is not MAC-labeled and is available to all internal and external to enterprise, the information asset is not encrypted.
8. Both encrypted and unencrypted assets may be further distributed without consequence.

To access an information asset, an appliqué is the default process for the information asset. The appliqué performs identical functions of the Java or .NET executable process or appliqué process fronting a commercial program. It examines the information asset, and if it is encrypted, retrieves the SAML of the requester, acquires the ACLs of the document, and matches the SAML claims to the ACL; once a match is achieved, the document is decrypted.

14.11 Components of a Stored Information Asset

The components of a stored information asset are provided in Figure 14.2 and are created in the steps described below.

14.11.1 Information Asset, Section A: ACL, MAC, and Data

The primary ACL is provided by the author (e.g., "MyGroup" appended by common name for uniqueness). Once the label is chosen, the content manager adds this as an ACL of the author. The group registry is invoked to meet enterprise naming requirements where necessary. The author may also designate roles in the ACL. If the document contains MAC requirements, they are included as an AND function (MyGroup and Executive ONLY). The ACL is stored in the header and separately encrypted, and the encryption key is accessible to the appliqué that processes the request for access (shared secret encrypted header, or known location, etc.). The header is not added where no MAC or DAC is indicated, and the extension is provided for the content application.

14.11.2 Information Asset, Section B: Information Asset as Labeled

This is provided by the content management software, with defaults based upon user data owner memberships or by a user from the approved list. It also includes

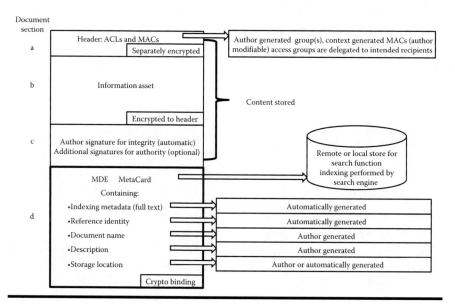

Figure 14.2 Authoritative content information asset format.

"*draft,*" "*final,*" or *Approved*, as previously described. Labels may be reviewed and modified by the author.

14.11.3 Information Asset, Section C: Information Asset Signature(s)

The author signatures (and others) are added, and further changes to the information asset at this point are prohibited. Revisions are treated as a new information asset and are either renamed or the version is changed. Implementing any changes required to get additional signatures involves starting the same process over again. The information asset may be retrieved (using the appliqué) by authorized users and additional signatures applied, as long as the information asset is not revised.

14.11.4 Information Asset, Section D: MDE Metacard

The meta data environment (MDE) metacard is prepared. This involves a number of items described below. Note that most information assets are not directly retrievable and must be retrieved by the content appliqué for checking of ACLs, MAC issues, and restricted authorities. The exception is nonsensitive, unlimited distribution.

14.12 Additional Elements for Stored Information Assets

Some additional considerations are provided below.

14.12.1 Key Words

The key words either are developed from a full information asset text scan or can be manually entered.

14.12.2 Storage Location(s) of Key Word Metadata

Storage location is the actual reference location of the information asset in a network asset store. Each time an unmodified copy of the information asset is stored in a different location, the storage process provides that location and the unique ID of the information asset to the content manager for updating the metacard. The metacard may contain any number of storage locations. This latter allows cleanup when archiving old content.

14.12.3 Reference Identity and Information Asset Description

This is the mechanism for discovery and retrieval. The content manager software defines the identity to prevent duplication, ambiguity, or confusion in the information asset file-keeping system.

14.12.4 Information Asset Name

The content management software provides a default name. It may be modified by the author.

14.12.5 Information Asset Description

The content management software suggests a description based upon a title or lead heading. It may be modified by the author.

The content is encrypted (except when there is no MAC requirement with no distribution limitations), with key management maintained by the content manager and available to the retrieval appliqué software.

Figure 14.3 shows the two cases for content creation and entry into the content management system.

As shown in Figure 14.3, the creator of the document, upon save, triggers the content manager that sets up a web session and allows tagging and definition of ACL requirements before the encrypted content is stored (may be distributed). The encrypted file is given a .cntz extension (for example). This extension is linked to the content appliqué on the user's desktop. The appliqué is operating in the user's security context.

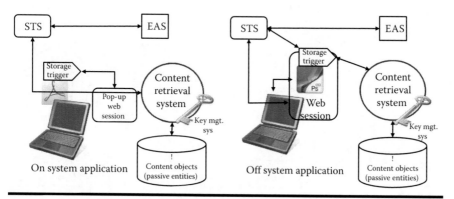

Figure 14.3   Content creation on save.

14.13 Key Management Simplification

Key management may be simplified by using a key that is computed based upon the access control requirements. This requires a significantly robust algorithm for key computation. In this case, return to the content manager is not needed for decryption of the content, only a match between the claims in the SAML token and the access requirements in the header of the document. The access requirements are the encryption key, and a match assures decryption. In this case, the appliqué is essentially the Java ARchive (JAR) or Microsoft Developer Network (.NET) software that performs this work or an access process (appliqué) matching the SAML claims to the ACLs of the document (access to the ACLs for the document may be by secure communication to the content manager or by a shared secret for decryption of the header that contains the ACLs). The ACLs map to the decryption key. Decryption is the final step. Key management is still needed for the ACLs associated with each content object; however, these do not need separate encryption keys for each content object. A copy of the encrypted content may, under this process, be stored anywhere. If the information asset is distributed, attempting to view the content will trigger the appliqué. When the information asset is encrypted (an unencrypted document indicated no distribution or viewing restrictions), the credentials/access of the user are checked before decrypting and providing the content. Sets of documents may be encrypted to the same key in this fashion by stating identical access requirements (e.g., Enterprise Merger Study Group, Company Executive Only, all nonsensitive documents of the environment). This can simplify federated processing. Figure 14.4 and Table 14.1 show the retrieval process.

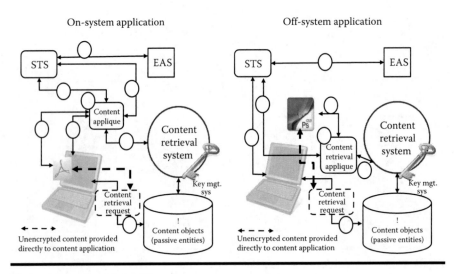

Figure 14.4   Content retrieval.

Table 14.1 Steps in Retrieval

Thin Client Off-System Application	On-System Application
1. Content selection	1. Content selection
2. Request for SAML for content appliqué service	2. Picked up by content appliqué 3. Request for SAML
3. STS asks EAS for content claims	4. STS asks EAS for content claims
4. SAML returned to appliqué service (through user)	5. SAML returned to appliqué
5. Key retrieval (or shared secret) decrypt header	6. Key retrieval (or shared secret) decrypt header
6. Access control decision	7. Access control decision
7. Decryption and content provided to application service—session setup (or denied access)	8. Decryption and content provided to application (or denied access)

14.13.1 Information Asset

Distribution may be done in the following ways:

1. The information asset may be sent by anyone in an email to anyone, but only members of the groups indicated in the ACLs and MACs may decrypt controlled information assets. Any changes to the information asset are stored under a new name or version, and under the signature of the individual who changed the content. If the information asset is encrypted it invokes the appliqué. If the information asset is not encrypted, it is simply displayed for the user.
2. The creator of the content may also provide the reference location. The reference location is used in a normal method to retrieve the data, but if it is encrypted, the appliqué checks credentials whenever the content is requested for viewing.
3. An individual may have discovered the information asset by search, and the individual can request access to the content as in item 2. Any attempt to open the information asset triggers the appliqué.
4. Unauthorized users have an encrypted package of no value. There are two exceptions:
   – Nonsensitive unlimited distribution packages have no encryption and may be opened by anyone.
   – Federated partners (other agencies, coalition partners, etc.) that have included specific content in their federation agreement may have their

claims verified by a federation STS in the enterprise portal area and decrypt the content based on that SAML,* its claims, and the appliqué. It is important to realize that any document provided to a federation partner is practically out of enterprise control and essentially loses its distribution restrictions. However, all security events (including content access) are logged by the web service providing the access. While this may be impractical, the content may be provided with a unique fingerprint that is logged for use in case future forensics are needed. If a document is found released where it should not have been, its fingerprints can be evaluated and traced back to the access that first released the document from enterprise control.

14.14 Import or Export of Information Assets

Imported/exported information assets are processed through the content management service. When information assets are imported into the enterprise enclave, saving the assets triggers the content management system as described above. The source of imported information assets can be the email (or similar communication) system or a removable storage device.

For exported information assets, the appliqué is needed to open the encrypted information asset and the appliqué provides decryption keys based upon the verified and validated SAML token. If the information asset can be accessed outside of the enterprise domain, the asset is decrypted and made available to the recipient; if not, a rejection notice is displayed. In order to support external accessing of information assets, an instance of the appliqué may be located within the enterprise portal area. A soft cert (software X.509) may be used for coalition and other federated partners.† The enterprise portal area must also contain a federation server for remapping as required.

---

* SAML claims are normally pruned for the minimum required by the target service. This principle is called least privilege, and it mitigates one aspect of intrusions, which is privilege escalation. These SAMLs are unpruned because we cannot anticipate which claims will be needed.

† The requester and the service provider mutually authenticate using the PKI certificates provided for each, along with TLS mutual authentication. SAML is passed from the requester to the provider and is verified and validated before the requested retrieval can take place.

Chapter 15

Delegation

The material that helped shape this chapter was first published as early as 2010 [61] and 2011 [62].

15.1 Delegation Service

Delegation is the process by which Active Entity B can use a claim that is owned by Active Entity A. If the entity is a person, then delegation is described as providing the claims that a user (Active Entity A) has been issued to a second user (Active Entity B). These claims are used for the purpose of access to information and services. If the claims have temporal data, the claims are marked temporal and must be computed in real time. Delegated claims are stored in the EAS and are reflected in the SAML claims. A delegation service allows authorized users to delegate their claims on behalf of the user to an identified delegate. These delegated claims will be referred to as extended claims. Delegated or extended claims retain the delegator, date of delegation, and life of delegation parameters. This delegation activity is shown in Figure 15.1. The delegator must be authorized to use the delegation service, and the delegator can only delegate claims that he or she possesses and is allowed to delegate in accordance with access control requirements. There may be rules for acceptable delegation, such as clearances or other activities (the classic example is that of a purchaser not be allowed to sign the purchase check). The delegation has a finite life chosen by the delegator not to exceed 1 year. If the delegated claims have changed, then the extended claims of delegation are invalidated. Delegation claims are renewable through the delegation service to the extent that they meet delegation restrictions.

The right to delegate is defined by the owner of the data, as defined in Chapter 10 ACR. Certain claims cannot be delegated (they are called MAC in the ACR and

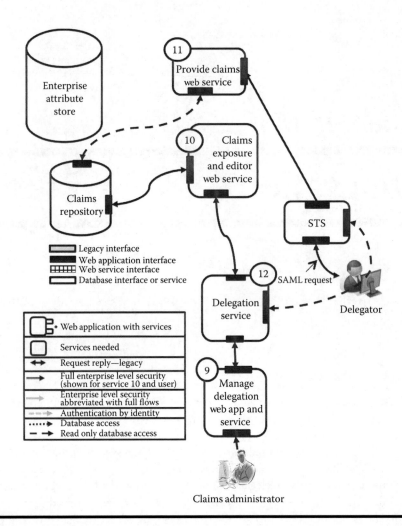

Figure 15.1   Delegation mechanics.

must be met by the individual—US CITIZEN is one. Delegations are revoked by the delegator at any time. Delegators cannot delegate extended claims that they possess (no second-order delegation), and designated claims are not delegable. There is a loss of attribution in multilevel delegation, and some insiders may use this for privilege acquisition and escalation. Multiple delegations can be made by one delegator to the multiple users. The enterprise process is shown in Figure 15.1.

The delegation service is an enterprise trusted software service, and it must meet all enterprise security requirements, as well as trust requirements, including software vulnerability analyses and code protection. Providers of commercial systems are required to provide additional assurance and certifications. The delegation service may be a commercial system but it must be certified, preferably by a standard approach such as

Common Criteria [3]. It must be additionally crypto certified, such as FIPS 140˚ [2h], if the delegation service performs any encryption functions outside of an HSM.

15.2 Service Description for Delegation

Service Number 9 is the enterprise delegation service manager for allowing modification of the way delegation is provided, the way extended claims are stored and dated, grace periods for expiration, etc. Modification of expiration and grace periods on individual claims must be carefully considered. The web application has a full-service class of users (Enterprise Claims administrators).

Service Number 10 is the enterprise claims exposure service for use by the delegation service and other authorized users. It has read-only privilege for claims and read/write for extended claims.

Service Number 11 supplies claims to the STS. It has an exception to ELS to prevent thrashing, and in that access is by identity only. The acceptable identities are stored in the service ACL. This service is part of the SAML process and is discussed in Chapter 9.

Service Number 12 has a service interface for the content manager program and a web application interface for authorized users. The service supplies extended claims where appropriate delegation has been assigned as authorized. The service will also delete or mark for deletion any delegations that have expired. Any user with a computed claim that is delegable may use the service.

15.3 Form of Extended Claims Record

The extended claims record has the same specific form that is based upon the access control requirement(s) and attributes required by the access control requirement(s), present enforcement of policy, and access control policies. Certain variables in the claims record are different for delegated claims. The specific form is identical to the designated claims record for database compatibility:

{CLAIMHOLDERDN}, {AUDIENCE}, {CLAIMNAME}, {STATUS [Time Stamp]}, {NUMBREF, REFDESIGNATION(s)}, {SERVICE NAME}, {DELEGATOR}, {DATEOFDELEGATION}, {EXPDATE}, {NUMBCLAIMS}, {[CLAIM(S), NUMBPARMS (Parameters)]}, {DELSTATUS}, {NUMBMAC, MAC(s)}, {NUMBRECOMPUTATION (methods and messages)}, {LINK}

- CLAIMHOLDERDN—{For example: String (ascii128 padded with trailing blanks if needed)}. This is the Distinguished Name of the entity for which the Access Control has been delegated.

˚ FIPS 140 is a standard for the certification of crypto algorithms. NIST certifies commercial laboratories to do this certification.

■ AUDIENCE—{For example: String (ascii128 padded with trailing blanks if needed)}. Nominally, the AUDIENCE RESTRICTION provided by the ACR. This may be the web application or web service DN, or another value specified by the data owner in the ACR. It must be enterprise-unique, and DN is recommended.

■ CLAIMNAME—{For example: String (ascii64 padded with trailing blanks if needed)}. This is the *ClaimName* being satisfied as provided by the data owner in the ACR for the delegated claim.

■ STATUS—{For example: String (ascii9 padded with trailing blanks if needed)} has three values, "Active," "Warning," or "Suspended (date)."
  – There are no extended content claims.
  – Active is present in other initial delegations. The TIMESTAMP is the creation date of the extended claim. It is also present in extended claims that have not been modified by status changes of the issuer of the extended claim or by the expiration of the delegated claims.
  – Warning indicates that a delegation of an extended claim is being suspended by the indicated EXPDATE (default is 7 days).
  – Suspended (date) is for an extended claim that has expired on EXPDATE, but has not been accessed or recomputed. Date—{For example: String (ascii64 padded with trailing blanks if needed)} the date of status change to suspended.
  – Time Stamp—{For example: String (ascii64 padded with trailing blanks if needed)}.

■ SERVICE NAME—{For example: String (ascii128 padded with trailing blanks if needed)}. This is the AUDIENCE RESTRICTION parameter inherited from the delegator's claims.

■ DELEGATOR—{For example: String (ascii256 padded with trailing blanks if needed)}. The identity of the delegator for updating the claim when claims of the delegator change.

■ DATEOFDELEGATION—{For example: String (ascii64 padded with trailing blanks if needed)}. The date when the delegation was put into effect.

■ EXPDATE—{For example: String (ascii64 padded with trailing blanks if needed)}. The expiration date of the delegation that is set by the delegator not to exceed the value configured by the data owner. At the arrival of the EXPDATE minus the grace period, the claim is marked Warning and WS-Notification is sent to both the delegator and the designate. At the arrival of the EXPDATE, the claim is marked Suspended (date) and WS-Notification is sent to both the delegator and the designate.

■ SERVICE NAME—{For example: String (ascii128 padded with trailing blanks if needed)}. Nominally the AUDIENCE RESTRICTION is provided by the ACR. The NAME parameter reduces the searching by providing claims for the target service request. The NAME is derived from the service registry, where each active URI for each application name is listed.

- NUMBCLAIMS—{For example: Integer between 1 and 256}. The number of claims contained in the claim. This is incremented each time a claim is added. Multiple claims for the same SERVICE NAME and Different delegations may be combined. For NUMBCLAIMS claims:
    - CLAIM—{For example: MemberOf String (ascii16 padded with trailing blanks if needed)}. This provides the claim(s) specified in the access control requirement for the web service.
    - NUMBPARMS—An integer between 0 and 256.
    - Parameters— {For example: MemberOf String (ascii16 padded with trailing blanks if needed)}. NUMBPARMS parameters are present. These claims may have parameters as specified in a delegation (must be present in the computed or designated claim being delegated for the web service).
- DELSTATUS—{For example: String (ascii16 padded with trailing blanks if needed)}. "notdelegable" for delegated claims.
- NUMBMAC—{For example: An integer from 0 to 256} where the number represents the number of MAC values.
    - MAC—{For example: MemberOf String (ascii16 padded with trailing blanks if needed)}. Not subject to delegation and must be computed for the recipient of the extended claim. May have many values. If the access control requirement does not include MAC data, the value is "NotRequired." If the access control requirement includes MAC, then the first values are the CurrentClearance (Confidential, Secret, Top Secret, [Compartments], Subsequent Values are NeedToKnow (NATO, FiveEyes, FourEyes, Enterprise, enterprise Only), if the access control requirement require one or more Code words, the last set of values is Codeword from the EAS.
- NUMBRECOMPUTATION—{For example: An integer from 0 to 256} where the number represents the number of parameters that must be recomputed. Recomputed data is not delegable and must be computed for the recipient of a delegation at runtime. This parameter concerns the recomputation of claims. For each of the recomputations:
    - Method—{For example: String (ascii512 padded with trailing blanks if needed)}. This provides the algorithm for the real-time computation, which resolves to a True or False value. A False value allows the SAML creation to proceed. A True value trips an error sequence with the message that follows.
    - Message—{For example: String (ascii256 padded with trailing blanks if needed)}. An ASCII message is returned in the error trip.
- LINK—{For example: String (ascii512 padded with trailing blanks if needed)}. The link is compound and includes the appropriate STS, audience end point, and the option ClaimName.

15.4 Special Delegation Service

The special delegation is not intended for normal federation. Normal federation is treated in Chapter 13 and is for longer-term relationships. The special delegation is intended for short-term access in the case of emergency responders or similar activities. The claims store is independent of the attribute store, allowing the creation of claims for anyone with a trusted authentication credential. The creation of this claim is through a special delegation service. Delegation is the process by which

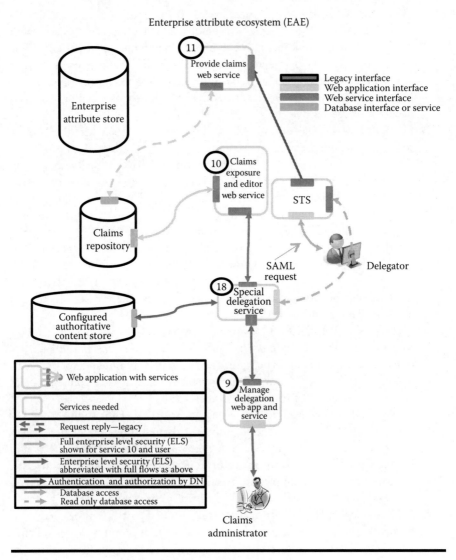

Figure 15.2   Special delegation service.

Active Entity B can make a claim about owning a claim that normally is owned by Active Entity A. If the entity is a person, then delegation is providing the claims that a user (Active Entity A) has been issued to a second user (Active Entity B) for the purpose of the second user making claims for access. In the case of special delegation, Active Entity B will not reside in the EAE attribute store but must reside in a preconfigured authoritative content store such as first responders (see Figure 15.2). Specially delegated claims may be further delegated if the data owner specifies this. Delegated claims are stored in the EAE in the claims repository and are reflected in the SAML claims. Since the user claim service is identity-based, the user may request that service directly. The user is returned any delegated claims, with a link to get the process started. The link will go to the STS, which is identity-based, and the STS will go to the claims retrieval service, which will fetch the delegated claims from the claims store. The STS fashions these claims into a SAML, and normal processing ensues.

Chapter 16

The Enterprise Attribute Ecosystem

Chapter 15 mostly completes the enterprise attribute ecosystem that was begun in Figures 9.1 and 10.1. Note that all of the services are expected to meet the enterprise requirements for security, including bilateral PKI authentication and SAML authorization. There is an exception for the STS and a few other utility services that use identity-based access control. The AE consists of a number of information services and stores as listed below:

- Services:
    1. Authoritative content import service (multiples)
    2. Manage import and aggregation web application
    3. Manual entry web application for attributes
    4. AE data import service (aggregation and mediation)
    5. Enterprise service registry web application
    6. Manage claims engine service
    7. Claims engine application
    8. Manage claims web application
    9. Manage delegation web application and service
    10. Claims exposure and editor web service
    11. Provide claims web service
    12. Delegation service and web application
    13. Manage groups and roles web application
    14. Auto registration web service
    15. Write attribute list
    16. Attribute query
    17. Claims query
    18. Special delegation service

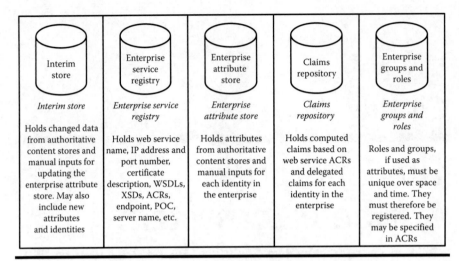

Figure 16.1 Enterprise attribute ecosystem content repositories.

- Stores:
    1. Interim store
    2. Service registry
    3. Enterprise attribute store
    4. Claims repository
    5. Enterprise groups and roles store

The relationship between these services and stores is shown in Figure 16.1, and the attribute ecosystem is shown in Figure 16.2. This chapter discusses each of the services and stores, as well as several use cases for the AE. We start with use cases. Attack surfaces are kept to a minimum by having the attribute store with a minimum number of interfaces and only one write-authorized interface.

16.1 User and Data Owner Convenience Functions

A number of convenience functions will be included, as listed below:

1. Limited self-registration
2. User attribute service
3. User claims service
4. Trusted delegation service

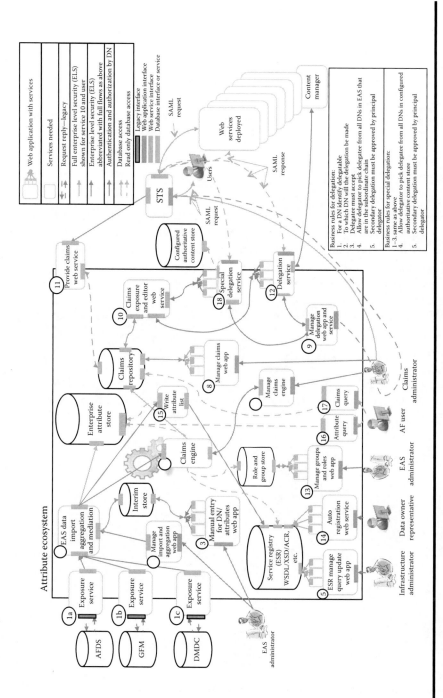

Figure 16.2 Enterprise attribute ecosystem.

16.1.1 Self-Registration (Partial)

A web service may be provided to provide partial self-registration. The service must define access and privilege in the normal fashion, and the data owner may delegate authority to an individual whom he may trust. The web service will assist in developing ACRs based upon the current schema with the EAS and allow upload of WSDLs, XSDs, and other registration data. All uploads, including the ACR, will be signed for integrity by the individual registering the service. Registration does not constitute authority to operate—that is obtained through normal processes.

16.1.2 User Attribute Service

The user attribute service will allow any individual with an enterprise PKI certificate to check his own attribute—it is an identity access service, and SAML is optional. The service will return a web page with the attribute present in the EAS, together with information about correcting errors in each of the attribute types. The page may be blank for individuals with no entries in the EAS. The connection is broken after the page is returned. The user attribute and user claims functions are shown in Figure 16.3.

The numbers on the services are related to functional breakdown.

16.1.3 Service Discovery

For ELS, services are registered in the registry and in the claims store. Discovery of available services for which the user has claims can be obtained from the claims store using a service that provides these claims, described in the next section.

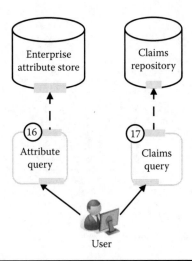

Figure 16.3 Attribute and claims services.

Discovery can be initiated by any entity with computed or delegated claims, even when that entity is not in the enterprise attribute store.

Service discovery can be initiated locally for DIL environments with a local cache of the claims repository and EAS services. For mobile devices that are provided network connectivity to the primary EAS instance, no cache is required and a normal request is sent. Discovery may be accomplished initially using the claims query service as described in the next section. The initial handshake is bilateral PKI mutual authentication, as described in Chapter 8. This service is identity-based and returns links to claims for service that the requester has. The requester must know the local URL for that service in the connected network.

16.1.4 User Claim Query Service

Because of the complex calling sequence, a service is provided that allows a user to obtain his or her claims of record and the link for requesting that service (user claims query service). The user claims query service will allow any individual with a PKI certificate to check his own claims. It is an identity-only access service, and SAML is not required. The service will return a web page with a linked list of claims by type for each service for which the individual has claims present in the claims store. The page may be blank for individuals with no claims. Each claim will have a click-on link that will post a request for service back through the user's web browser to the appropriate STS for SAML processing. A convenience feature for services is the ability to request claims for a specific audience. If the request is for a specific audience (audience value is included in the request), then the claims provided back will be limited to that audience, and if a single claim exists for that audience, then the link is automatically executed. If multiple claims exist, the user is offered a choice for least privilege. If no claim exists, an error is created and an error message is provided back to the requester. The section below describes using this feature to allow direct user request to a service or web application. The connection is broken after the page is returned and before a page link is executed.

16.1.5 Direct Service/Application Invocation

The availability of the user claims query service will allow a direct invocation of a web application or service even when the service is not aware of the STS portion of the rest link. In this instance, the user provides the URL in the window of the browser by either typing the link or selecting a link from favorites. Under previous methods, the link would be severed after bilateral authentication because a SAML is not present. However, the web application may be configured to post a request back through the browser to either the STS or the user claims query service described in Section 4.3.3 with the specific audience requested. The primary difference is web application awareness of the STS location (which may change) or the user claims query service location (which is unlikely to change).

For the User Claims Query Option:

The post back is to the user claims query service with the audience specified. The user claims query service will restrict the claims returned to the audience, and if one or more exists, the user may select one, and a link to the STS for that audience will be invoked. The STS in turn will post a SAML back through the browser to the application or service. The result is that the user will have access with a direct invocation of the service. Note that each authentication is done separately in that proxies and single sign-on are not part of ELS. If no claim exists for the audience, the access will be denied. The direct invocation process for this option involves four separate pieces, as shown in Figure 16.4.

For the STS Option:

The post back is to the STS, with the audience specified. The STS in turn will post a SAML back through the browser to the application or service. The result is that the user will have access with a direct invocation of the service. Note that each authentication is done separately in that proxies and single sign-on are not part of ELS. If no claim exists for the audience, the access will be denied. The direct invocation process for this option involves three separate pieces, as shown in Figure 16.4.

The numbers on the services are related to functional breakdown of services provided in the next chapter.

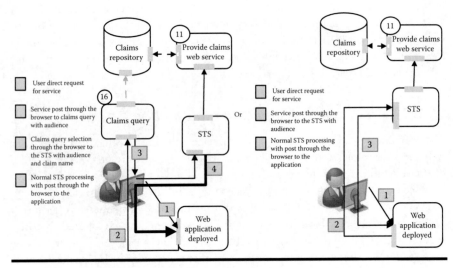

Figure 16.4   Direct web application or service access.

16.1.6 Trusted Delegation Service

Delegation is the process by which Active Entity B can make a claim about owning a claim that normally is owned by Active Entity A. This process is treated in detail in Chapter 15.

The delegation service is an enterprise trusted software service, and it must meet all enterprise security requirements and trust requirements, including software vulnerability analyses and code protection. Providers of COTS-based systems are required to provide additional assurance and certifications. The delegation service, if it is procured COTS, must be Common Criteria-approved and also FIPS-140-certified if the delegation service performs any encryption functions outside of an HSM.

16.1.7 Special Delegation Service

The special delegation is intended for short-term access in the case of emergency responders or similar activities. This process is treated in detail in Chapter 15.

16.2 Attribute Ecosystems Use Cases

Use cases are used to provide guidance in operations and to shape the capabilities of the enterprise services. There are seven use cases considered.

16.2.1 Process Flows Related to Security for Each Service

The process flow for all services is described below:

- Authentication provided by DoD-issued PKI TLS 1.2 Mutual Authentication
- Authentication identity provided out-of-band to access control handler
- Access control handler:
  - Inputs:
    - Requester SAML
    - Requester identity
  - Actions
    - Well-formed input checks
  - Collective handler exceptions (where applicable)
    - Invalid SOAP: <invalid SOAP> exception, log event, notify security administrator, fail silently
    - Unknown operation on known service: <unknown operation> exception, fail silently
    - No SAML: <no saml> POST request back to the user claims query, log event

- SAML signature invalid: <invalid SAML signature> exception, log event, notify security administrator, fail silently
- SAML signature certificate expired: <expired SAML signing cert> exception, log event, notify security administrator, fail silently
- SAML signature certificate revoked: <revoked SAML signing cert> exception, log event, notify security administrator
- SAML signature cert revocation check timeout: <The Online Certificate Status Protocol (OCSP) timeout> exception returned, log event, notify security administrator
- SAML signature cert revocation check bad response: <OCSP failure> exception returned, log event, notify security administrator
- Request message signature invalid: <invalid request signature> exception, fail silently, log event, notify security administrator
- Request message cert issues (expired, revoked, OCSP timeout, bad response): same as above but <request [exception name]> exception, fail silently, log event, notify security administrator
- Request cert chain issue (issuing, intermediate, or root CA cert issue): <request [issuing/intermediate/root CA] [exception name]> exception, fail silently, log event, notify security administrator
- Request cert not trusted (chains to untrusted root): <request cert not trusted> exception, fail silently, log event, notify security administrator
- SAML subject does not match identity of signing cert: <SAML identity mismatch> exception, fail silently, log event, notify security administrator
- Claims insufficient for access: <access denied> exception returned, log event
  - Outputs
    - SAML for requester
    - List of claims
- Log handler:
  - Inputs:
    - Information to be logged
  - Actions
    - Creation of entry into log file
  - Exceptions
    - Poorly formed request exception, log event, notify security administrator, fail silently
    - Unknown operation on known service: <unknown operation> exception, fail silently
  - Outputs
    - Log file entry
- Other handlers may exist

16.2.2 Updating Claims

While claims are mainly static, persons and nonperson entities change position, location, and other attributes. Keeping the claims current is a necessity. The steps for these are listed below:

- Exposure services periodically (by configuration) or on-demand (by administrator inputs) bring authoritative content updates into the interim store.
- These data are uploaded to the AE, tagging all changes periodically (by configuration) or on-demand (by administrator inputs)
- These trigger the claims engine to review and modify all claims based upon these changes either automatically or manually by the administrator.
- The claims engine goes through each new attribute and when a claim (computed or delegated) is affected, it gets the access control requirement and then computes the claim over again.
- When an existing claim is no longer valid, it sets a timestamp to the default grace period and notifies the identity (WS-Notification).
- If a delegation of an claim that is expired, the claims engine sets an expiration timestamp to the default grace period and notifies the delegatee (WS-Notification).
- Periodically, the claims are reviewed for expiration and updated as delineated in the bullets above.
- The UploadIntoEAS service is the only entity in the AF that has authn/authz rights to modify the EAS data store. One other entity has the ability to get to the EADS without coming through the service gateway and that is the claims engine and it is read-only.

16.2.3 Adding a New Identity

Adding a new entity to the enterprise is a provisioning exercise and triggers the below steps:

- The claims engine is triggered as in updating claims.
- A new identity is added to the schema.
- The data for the new identity are uploaded to the EAS.
- This triggers the claims engine to review claims for all services.
- The claims engine goes through each service from the access control requirement and computes the claim for that service.
- The claims engine stores the resultant claims in the claims store.

16.2.4 Adding a Service

Services are a special case of a new identity and start with enterprise registration. From that point, the following steps are taken:

- The claims engine is manually triggered following registration.
- The claims engine goes through every identity and computes claims for each identity using the access control requirements provided at registration.

16.2.5 Accessing Services

Service access requires both authentication and authorization as described below:

- The requestor requests an SAML for the desired service (audience) from the STS. This request may come from the claims query service or as a targeted service through the web browser. The authentication is the normal bilateral mutual authentication TLS1.2, but the STS uses identity only as a basis for authorization (identity-based authorization).
- The STS requests SAML assertions for the identity and web service (audience) from the provide-claims web service, the authentication is the normal bilateral mutual authentication TLS1.2, but the authorization is using identity only and the ACL for the provide-claims service includes all valid STS identities.
- The provide-claims web service opens the claims store and finds all claims pertinent to the web service (audience) for the given identity.
- The provide-claims web service may compute some dynamic information based upon the embedded data from the access control requirements for the service.
- The provide-claims web service then strips all metadata from the claim and provides a list of claims for the SAML assertion for a specific audience to the STS.
- The STS creates the SAML and posts it through the browser to the originally requested service (audience).
- This process applies to all service invocation within the AE except the STS to provide claims as noted above, the claims query service, and the attribute query and claims query services, which are all identity-based access control.

16.2.6 Providing Delegation

The delegation has the security requirements of any other service and provides the following:

- A requestor accesses the delegation service.
- The delegation service accesses the claims exposure and modification service and reviews the requestor's claims for possible delegations and offers the requestor choices based upon this review. Each service determines what is delegable.

- The requester chooses the service he wishes to make a delegation for and identifies the delegatee by identity.
- The delegation service creates an extended claim for the delegatee and provides it to the claims exposure and modification service to place it in the claims store. This service allows read-only on claims and read/write on extended claims to the delegation service.
- Elements of the extended claim are not provided in the attribute store at this time, but they could be. It raises the complication of removing them when the delegation expires.
- Extended claims are not delegable, and expire either at the delegated expiration time or when the delegator no longer has the claim to delegate.

16.2.7 Providing Special Delegation

The special delegation has the security requirements of any other service and provides the following:

- A requestor (usually the data owner or his appointee) accesses the special delegation service.
- The special delegation service accesses the claims exposure and modification service and reviews the requestor's claims for possible delegations and offers the requestor choices based upon this review. Each service determines what is delegable.
- The requester chooses the service he wishes to make a delegation for and identifies the delegatee by identity. The identity is not in the attribute store but in a specially configured authoritative content store (such as first responders with a personal identity verification (PIV) identity. If the identity is trusted for authentication, this will provide a delegated claim for SAML.
- The delegation service creates an extended claim for the delegatee and provides it to the claims exposure and modification service to place it in the claims store. This service allows read-only on claims and read/write on extended claims to the delegation service.
- Elements of the extended claim are not provided in the attribute store.
- Extended claims are may be delegable (delegator choice), and expire either at the delegated expiration time or when the delegator no longer has the claim to delegate.

16.3 Attribute Ecosystem Services

There are a total of 18 services in Figure 16.2. Brief descriptions of each service are provided below. The section number corresponds to the service number in Figure 16.2.

16.3.1 Authoritative Content Import Service(s)

Service Number 1 is an exposure service to draw attributes from the authoritative content store. Each exposure service is triggered by a call from the AE Data Import Aggregation and Mediation Service (Service Number 4). The call may be scheduled or triggered by a system administrator who requests the schedule or demand through the Manage Import and Aggregation Web App (Service Number 2). The purpose is to bring information into the AE, mediate and sanitize as appropriate, and place it into the interim store for later upload to the EAS. There are similar services (1b, 1c, …) for other authoritative content stores. At present, all are assumed to be legacy and the exposure service must conform to the legacy process. In the future, they may become web service and ELS enabled.

16.3.2 Manage Import and Aggregation Web Application

Service Number 2 is an AE service to manage import of data from the authoritative content stores for later dissemination to the EAS. The call for attribute updates may be scheduled or triggered by a system administrator. The purpose is to bring information into the AE, mediate and sanitize as appropriate, and place it into the interim store for later upload to the EAS. A second purpose is to schedule or demand an upload of sanitized and mediated information to the EAS and to trigger the claims engine for recomputing the claims.

16.3.3 Manual Entry Web Application for Attributes

Service Number 3 is a web application that allows manual entry of attributes and distinguished names by the EAS administrator. This is not the preferred method, which is the import of identity and attributes. It is noted that times exist when these may be inadequate. Because these are not automatically checked, they should be logged and reviewed from time to time for currency. The changes are placed in the interim store for upload later as described in Service Number 2.

16.3.4 AE Import Service

Service Number 4 is an enterprise attribute store service to request authoritative content store updates, and sanitize and hold attributes from the authoritative content store for later dissemination to the EAS. The call for attribute updates may be scheduled or triggered by a system administrator who requests the schedule or demand through the Manage Import and Aggregation Web App (Service Number 2). The purpose is to bring information into the AE, mediate and sanitize as appropriate, and place it into the interim store for later upload to the EAS. A second purpose is to upload sanitized mediated information to the EAS. The call for AE updates may be scheduled or triggered by a system administrator who requests the schedule or demand through the Manage Import and Aggregation Web App (Service Number 2). A third purpose is to trigger the claims engine for recomputing the claims. The call for AE update may be scheduled or triggered by a system administrator who requests the schedule or demand through the Manage Import and Aggregation Web App (Service Number 2). This service creates a tagged list of identities where one or more attributes have changed (for a new identity, all attributes are tagged new), and sends it to the claims engine where information for an identity has changed.

16.3.5 Enterprise Service Registry Web Application

Service Number 5 is the enterprise service registry web application to manage authorized service information and access control requirements. The web application has a full-service class of users (infrastructure administrators) and a read-only class of users.

16.3.6 Manage Claims Engine Web Application

Service Number 6 is the enterprise claims engine manager to allow the modification of the claims and the way claims are computed as well as schedule or demand claims recomputation. The web application has a full-service class of users (enterprise claims administrators)

16.3.7 Claims Engine

Service Number 7 is the enterprise claims engine that computes claims based upon access requirements stored in the ESR and attributes stored in the EAS (both are read-only). It also accesses the groups and roles store. The web application may be triggered by requests from either Service Number 6 or Service Number 4. Each flagged identity triggers a recomputation for all web services. New claims may be created in accordance with changed attributes and the access control requirements of each service. Existing web service access claims may be left in place if access control requirements are still valid, or may be placed in a grace period status if the access control requirements are no longer met. The grace period is for the entity to take action. A notification is provided to the entity and a countdown on grace period begins. If these claims have been delegated, then the extended claims are similarly placed in a grace period with notification.

16.3.8 Manage Claims Web Application

Service Number 8 is the enterprise claims manager web application to allow the addition/deletion/modification of the claims and to trigger a full review of claims dates of expiration. Insertion and deletion of claims is not the preferred method, which is the import of identity and attributes and computing of claims. It is noted that times exist when these may be inadequate. Because these are not automatically checked, they should be logged and reviewed from time to time for currency. A claim expires when a delegation period is complete or the grace period on a claim or extended claim has passed. The claims engine may trigger the grace period when changes to the attributes, as applied to the access control requirements, no longer provide claims. The grace period is extended to all delegatees, and notifications are sent out to these individuals. The delegation period expiration triggers a notification to the delegator and a delegatee and assignment of the grace period as expiration. There is no second grace period before expiration. The web application has a full-service class of users.

16.3.9 Manage Delegation Web Application and Service

Service Number 9 is the enterprise delegation service manager to allow the modification of the way delegation is provided and extended claims are stored, dated, provided grace periods for expiration, etc. Modification of expiration and grace periods on individual claims must be carefully considered and not as a way of business. The web application has a full-service class of users.

16.3.10 Claims Exposure and Editor Web Service

Service Number 10 is the enterprise claims exposure service for use by the delegation service and other authorized users. It has read-only privilege for claims and read/write for extended claims.

16.3.11 Provide Claims Web Service

Service Number 11 supplies claims to the STS. It has an exception to ELS to prevent thrashing in that access is by identity only. The identities acceptable are stored in the service ACL.

16.3.12 Delegation Web Application and Web Service

Service Number 12 has a service interface for the content manager program and a web application interface for authorized users. The service supplies extended claims requested by the user and where the are delegatable, and may delete or mark for deletion after a grace period the delegated claims as requested by the user. Any user with a computed claim that is delegable may use the service.

16.3.13 Manage Groups and Roles Web App

Service Number 13 is a management interface for enterprise-level roles and groups. If roles and groups are used as attributes, they must be unique over space and time. They must therefore be registered, and uniqueness and membership must be maintained. They may be specified in access control requirements and the database must be accessible to the claims engine. Roles and groups that are local to specific services do not require uniqueness (except within the service) and need not be registered. Identities affected by changes in groups and roles must be flagged for claims computation.

16.3.14 Autoregistration Web App

Service Number 14 is a web service to provide self-registration of services and information assets to data owners. The service defines access and privilege in the normal fashion, and the data owner may delegate authority to an individual whom he may trust. The web service assists in developing ACRs based upon the current schema with the EAS, and allows upload of WSDLs, XSDs, and other registration data. All uploads, including the ACR, will be signed for integrity by the individual registering the service. Registration does not constitute authority to operate, which is obtained through normal processes.

16.3.15 Write Attribute List

Service Number 15 is an EAS service that writes the list of available attributes to the ACR for use by other services. The write function will be triggered by the EAS Import Aggregation and Mediation, periodically or on demand at the same time as invocation of the claims engine. It has no subservices.

16.3.16 User Query Attributes

Service Number 16 is an EAS service that provides a list of attribute values for the requesting individual only. Personally identifiable information (PII) values may be withheld. The authorization is identity based and ELS authentication is required, but use of SAML is not. A chart with attributes is provided. The session is then terminated. Contact information for correction of errors is provided as part of the list. It has no sub services.

16.3.17 User Query Claims

Service number 17 is a web service which provides a list of claims for the requesting individual only. The authorization is identity based and ELS authentication is required, but use of SAML is not. A chart with claims is provided. The session is only open for a requested link. After return to the browser of claims with links, the session is terminated. Links are included in the list that will invoke an ELS session by posting a properly formatted request through the browser to the appropriate STS for the service requested. If the initial request includes an audience, and one or more claims exist, the user may execute a link for least privilege. It has no sub services.

16.3.18 Special Delegation Web Application and Web Service

Service Number 18 has a web application interface for the data owner and authorized users. The service supplies extended claims for entities that are not in the enterprise attribute store. These entities possess an identity credential that is accepted as evidenced by their identities occurring in a preconfigured authoritative content store. Only the data owner or users with a computed claim that is provided by the data owner may use the service.

Chapter 17

Database Access

The material that helped shape this chapter was first published in 2013 in project documentation and in 2015 in the public literature [67]. A *database* is a collection of data. Database systems provide an abstraction layer that allows this data set to be accessed using a standard query language. Many query languages have useful properties that can be used to provide functionality and security guarantees at an abstract level. The actual storage implementation for the data is typically optimized for performance, subject to the constraints of the query language. One common query language is Structured Query Language (SQL), which is based on relational algebra. Each set of data is a "relation," which has an associated schema, and each query takes one or more relations as input and produces a relation as output. The processing is described by the rules of the algebra. This is a highly structured database system with tight restrictions and formal guarantees.

Standard references for database applications are available [6,68–74]. Additional readings on databases are provided in References 75–81.

17.1 Database Models

A database model is a type of data model that determines the logical structure of a database and fundamentally determines in which manner data can be stored, organized, and manipulated.

Database models come in many forms, and a few are listed below:

- Flat model: This may not strictly qualify as a database model. The flat (or table) model consists of a single, two-dimensional array of data elements, where all members of a given column are assumed to be similar values, and all members of a row are assumed to be related to one another.

- Hierarchical model: In this model, the database is organized into a tree-like structure, implying a single, upward link in each record to describe the nesting, and a sort field to keep the records in a particular order in each same-level list.
- Network model: This model organizes data using two fundamental constructs, called records and sets. Records contain fields, and sets define one-to-many relationships between records: one owner, many members.
- Relational model: This database model is based on first-order predicate logic. Its core idea is to describe a database as a collection of predicates over a finite set of predicate variables, describing constraints on the possible values and combinations of values.
- Entity relationship model: This is a special case of the network model in which elements are entities and the connections have a value or semantics as well as a direction.
- Object-relational model: This is similar to a relational database model, but objects, classes, and inheritance are directly supported in database schemas and in the query language.
- Star schema: This is the simplest style of database warehouse schema. The star schema consists of a few "fact tables" (possibly only one, justifying the name) referencing any number of "dimension tables." The star schema is considered an important special case of the snowflake schema.

A structural representation is shown in Figure 17.1.

The most popular example of a database model is the relational model, which uses a table-based format, shown in Figure 17.2. The choice of pivot values and tables entries is called a schema.

Databases all satisfy some basic properties for data storage and access, but they use different underlying models. The type of database used is based on the mission

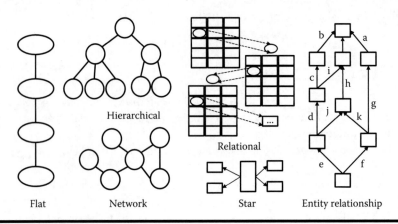

Figure 17.1 Database models.

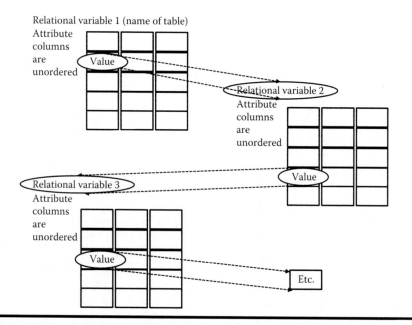

Figure 17.2   Relational database layouts.

requirements and the needs of those mission requirements. The ACID properties are satisfied by all databases:

- Atomicity
- Consistency
- Isolation
- Durability

The entity relationship (ER) model structures data as tables with rows and columns. Each column has a name and properties. Each row contains data in cells, where each cell corresponds to one column.

The object model uses objects instead of tables to store data. Objects closely match the concept as defined in object-oriented programming, and these databases can be tightly integrated with object-oriented languages to produce tighter couplings between the data and the programs that access the data.

An XML database is structured through XML tags, which use a hierarchical nesting structure. The XML can be serialized as text with nested tags or represented internally through data structures with references. XML databases offer XPath, XQuery, and XSLT as processing options, and these are closely tied to the hierarchical XML structure of the data model.

A triplestore is a type of database optimized to store triples that consist of a subject, predicate, and object. These triples are often related to real-world relations such as "Bob knows Fred" or "Fido is a dog." The Resource Description Framework (RDF) format can be used to represent these relations and provide an input format for data into such a triplestore.

Google Maps uses its own database model, which maintains properties of locality using tiles of map images at different resolutions. When loading a particular map, the surrounding tiles at the same resolution are returned in order to form an entire picture. This type of storage lends itself naturally to distributed processing, since different tiles can be retrieved in parallel and integrated by the requester in the browser. This type of storage also provides an API through which users can add their own content to maps, including imagery, routes, points of interest, or other structures.

The protein structure database is a collection of experimentally determined protein structures. The primary information is the three-dimensional structure of a protein, including coordinates of each component of the structure. Secondary information can include experimental information, protein sequence information, size, or other information related to the protein. The data model is designed so that queries can be made for similarly structured proteins, specific gene sequences, or other queries useful to this field of work.

A distributed database model treats a database as a collection of independent nodes that together provide the functionality of a single database. The individual nodes can be homogeneous or heterogeneous. The heterogeneous nodes can use different types of underlying databases, or they may have only small differences. Key issues to consider are communication and synchronization of nodes. One approach is a client-server model in which the communication has an inherent structure. Another model allows any node to request services from any other node as needed. The individual nodes could simply store replicas of the same data, or different parts of a single data set, or a combination of these. The data to be divided can be broken down by rows or columns (assuming an ER* database structure). To manage where data is stored, a catalog is used, which can be a global lookup as well as local information stored on each node that is relevant to the data stored on that node and its replica locations. This catalog itself is replicated to prevent a single point of failure. An issue unique to a distributed database is deadlock between the different nodes. There are different mechanisms to either detect or mitigate deadlock conditions, such as centralized dependency analysis, hierarchical analysis, or a fixed timeout at each node.

Large-scale databases allow operations on data sets that are prohibitively large for the models listed above. For example, Hadoop and other map–reduce implementations provide a distributed computation approach to working with large data sets. They provide two operations, map and reduce, which are run across many compute nodes. The map operation performs an operation on different pieces of

---

* Entity relationship structure is defined in Section 17.1.

a large data set. The reduce operation combines these results. A single query often takes a long time to complete, so these database systems are not well suited to dynamic queries from requesters. However, they provide a scalable approach for queries that may run periodically on very large data sets that other database models are not able to handle.

17.2 Database Interfaces and Protocols

Databases provide interfaces and use protocols to enable automated access to the data they store. These database-level interfaces and protocols are specific to the data store and generally are not portable to other databases. To provide portability, higher-level interfaces and protocols have been developed, which allow a single set of commands to work across many different implementations that support the interface or protocol.

The ER model is often used with some variant of SQL. SQL is a language that allows a requester to describe actions to be performed on database. The SQL commands are translated to storage-specific instructions for execution on the data store.

Open Database Connectivity (ODBC) and Java Database Connectivity (JDBC) are two standard APIs for accessing databases from C or Java code, respectively. There are also ODBC-to-JDBC and JDBC-to-ODBC "bridges" that translate between these APIs. These provide standard APIs to be invoked from code, so that code can be reused with any database that supports these APIs.

Standard query languages and APIs are also available for XML databases. XQuery is a language for XML database queries. XPath provides a standard way to search the tree structure based on node names, attributes, and text values. XSLT provides a way to transform XML data, either to other XML structures or to other representations such as HTML.

XML can be parsed using Document Object Model (DOM) and Simple API for XML (SAX). SAX uses event-based parsing, indicating which tags it encounters as it traverses the document linearly. This requires no internal state and saves on resources. DOM uses a tree structure to represent and parse the document. This requires additional resources but allows rapid arbitrary access to the document contents.

Large-scale databases have multiple interfaces. The user interface defines queries that can be run by the distributed system. For the compute nodes, there are interfaces that describe communications between distributed compute nodes for both data and control. For map–reduce, a simple user interface allows the choice of map and reduce algorithms. The interface can also include the choice of how many or which nodes are used in the computation.

Geographic database interfaces provide functions that add, update, retrieve, and delete information relevant to a defined geographic area, map data, and other geospecific data. They may also allow functionality to increase or decrease the size of the geographic area of interest while decreasing or increasing the level of detail, respectively. Retrievals that are "close" to previous retrievals, such as neighboring geographic regions or similar levels of detail in the same region, are optimized for low latency because these are often executed sequentially.

17.2.1 SQL Databases

SQL databases use tables to store data. Schemas describe the data in these tables, and each row consists of data that has some type, such as string or integer. A set of columns can be a "key" for a table, meaning that the same combination of values can only occur once in the table for those columns. Sometimes these keys consist of multiple columns of data, such as name, address, and date of birth (DOB), and other times they are a single column of unique values, such as an employee ID.

Rows can be added or removed dynamically through queries. These additions and deletions are fast, so changes to content can be handled without hurting the latency of associated services. The queries to the database do not change its values and typically represent most of the activity of a database, so these also have low latency as well as high throughput.

In order to maintain consistency of the database, transactional behavior is required. This means that certain sequences of actions are not allowed to be interleaved with other sequences. They start and end in a time period where no other conflicting actions take place. The contents of a transaction are configurable so that the owner of the content can define what is and is not allowed.

17.2.2 XML Databases

XML databases use a different underlying structure than SQL (or relational databases). XML is essentially tagged text, much like HTML. However, XML's rules are stricter in that each opening tag has a corresponding closing tag and the properties of the tags are precisely defined. The rules are defined in an XSD. This defines what tags can be subtags of other tags, what attributes a tag can have, how many subtags can exist, what data types can be present at different tags, and other properties.

XPath is a language used to find nodes in an XML tree. An XPath query lists a sequence of nodes or attributes, and the request is completed by searching the XML tree for a matching sequence, either from the root of the tree, the current position, or any other position. Wildcards can be used to represent any tag value, any attribute value, or a sequence of any number of arbitrary subtags. Operations like "and" and "or" are also allowed, making these queries potentially complicated and rich in expressiveness.

XQuery is a method of not only searching, using XPath-like queries, but also returning data according to a set of rules. The rules are essentially a simple functional programming language that allows loops and variable assignments.

The output is based on the original file, but modified by the XQuery rules to produce a new XML structure.

XSLT is another more powerful method of querying XML databases. The XSLT query describes a transformation to do on the XML file. This could be a conversion to a new XML file, like an XQuery request, or it could convert XML to HTML or any other format according to XSLT rules. XSLT is typically more difficult than XQuery, especially for simpler queries that XQuery can handle. However, it is more general and has the property that XSLT queries are defined as XML files, which can help with automation.

17.2.3 Large-Scale Databases

Methods of processing very large data sets typically focus more on parallelism and performance than on accuracy of results. For large data sets, the data often changes rapidly, so perfect accuracy is not important, since in a microsecond the result would be different anyway. This model works well when aggregating results across large amounts of data, where exclusion of a few random entries affects the outcome in a minimal way. In some sense, the output results are "smooth" with respect to the input data.

Methods such as map–reduce are useful for processing data in these scenarios, since the map and reduce are done in a highly parallelizable way and perform fairly simple operations with low latency. The map step takes the entire data set and recursively divides it into smaller data sets. Different worker nodes then process the smaller sets in parallel. The reduce step combines the results of multiple workers into a single result, which satisfies the original query when done at the initial (root) node. The result is typically a one-time analysis that is done periodically, which is different than SQL or XML, which continuously query.

17.2.4 Geospatial Databases

Geographic databases provide a way to store information that is related to geography. They can be organized as different layers that are overlaid on a map based on a geographic positioning scheme. Items in such databases can consist of points, lines, or regions, as well as combinations of these. In some cases, one layer depends on, or is closely related to, another layer, such as watershed regions and topography.

The geospatial database may offer the ability to do the following:

■ Store a rich collection of spatial data in a centralized location
■ Apply sophisticated rules and relationships to the data
■ Define advanced geospatial relational models (e.g., topologies and networks)
■ Maintain the integrity of spatial data with a consistent, accurate database
■ Work within a multiuser access and editing environment
■ Integrate spatial data with other IT databases

■ Easily scale a storage solution
■ Support custom features and behavior

Geospatial databases are different in the types of data and optimizations they contain and use. The types of data are related to geographic regions, paths, or points. These can also extend into the third dimension, either through altitude information or through a native three-dimensional representation. A two-dimensional representation is often sufficient for simple mapping applications, but for military applications that involve ground and air forces, as well as satellites and other space assets, a three-dimensional representation is essential. Also, mappings between different coordinate systems are essential, since raw data can come in different representations from different sources, and the data in the database should be raw to preserve fidelity.

The geospatial database stores entities such as geographic regions, paths, and points, along with information about them. Often different types of information are separated into different layers that can be turned on and off in a visualization tool. In many cases, information in one layer depends on information in another layer. For example, national boundaries often depend on the path of a river or the ridge of a mountain range. Road locations often depend on the location of bridges. Geospatial databases provide mechanisms to support these links between different but related layers.

Queries to a geospatial database consist of bulk data additions, deletions, or updates. These queries occur infrequently, such as when new information is available, related information is retrieved, and/or scrolling through geospatial references. The bulk uploads are optimized for throughput because the goal is to replace the old data with the new data as quickly as possible. Retrieval sequences occur when a user is scanning a visualization tool and panning, zooming, rotating, or making other adjustments to the information viewed in a way that preserves the notion of closeness of data. The geospatial database anticipates that the next query is close to the previous sequence and optimizes performance for these close queries. Sequences of uploads, such as periodic fixed sensor readings or streaming data from a moving sensor, also have a notion of closeness and are optimized for performance.

17.3 Overall Database Considerations

Both SQL and XML database systems were designed for precise processing of data sets. Formal rules define how operations are conducted, and well-defined outputs are produced for any given input state. This works well for traditional data models, where the requester wants the correct results for a given query at that particular time. However, these database systems only scale to certain sizes, based on their inherent architectural structures. For example, parallelism is difficult to provide while maintaining all the guarantees of SQL or XML databases. This makes it difficult to process very large data sets with reasonable performance.

Owing to the important role database systems serve in the enterprise, they are protected from failures. This includes redundancy of hardware and software instances. The data itself is stored on multiple different hardware instances. These are part of different logical and software database system instances. The hardware redundancy protects against disk failures. The logical redundancy protects against software bugs or failures. Another type of redundancy related to physical redundancy is geographic distribution. Since some failures, such as electricity or natural disasters are regional, there is at least one instance of the data being stored in a different region. This could be, different bases, Eastern United States and Western United States, or North America and Europe, for example.

The important concept is to meet continuity of operations (COOP) requirements for continuous operations in the event of failure of the main operational system. In addition to redundancy, extra copies are generated, maintained, and synchronized and available in standby mode so that the switch can be made automatically to promote the backup to the live operational system. The backup is updated by transaction with the primary instance to ensure consistency. When the primary data is destroyed or corrupted, some method of determining which transactions—if any—are rolled back when invoking backup data, is provided. There might be a time lag between the primary and backup data sources. Ideally, the transaction would involve the backup copies so that when a transaction is complete it is also backed up; but if performance limits this capability, a method to maintain consistency when promoting the backup to primary is provided.

Serializability is a property of a database such that there is a valid sequence of events that could have resulted in the database state for all externally visible states of the database. In particular, intermediate internal states involved in transactions are not accessible to external entities. This ensures that actions are taken in the correct order. In some cases, the database manager reorders requests for performance or other reasons. However, this can result in inconsistencies. For example, if one application queries the value of two cells and another application increments their values, the query of the first cell might get the updated value while the second cell gets the old value, which could violate assumptions about the underlying content. Different guarantees on serializability are possible in database systems. Stricter guarantees limit optimizations, and looser guarantees allow more optimization.

Triggers are actions taken within a database system based on changes that take place to its data. These are useful to maintain internal consistency. Instead of writing complex applications to scan the data after each operation to check consistency and take appropriate actions, triggers can be used to automatically do this whenever a change is made to a database.

Indexes allow faster querying. They provide a different way to organize data: one that allows queries to be processed faster than if searching an entire table. Instead of using a search that looks through the table entries to find values that match a query, the index is used to directly point to the rows in the table that have that value. One implementation involves a binary tree to search for the value in logarithmic time instead of linear time.

Data cubes and data grids are a way to use a database to store aggregate information across multiple categories. For example, if a database keeps track of sales, with attributes for location, date, and type, a data cube would include automatically generated entries that sum across all locations, all dates, all types, any combination of two categories, and a grand total across all data. This makes aggregating queries fast since it involves a single lookup instead of aggregating across large numbers of entries. Other variations of cubes allow different dimensionality (e.g., two-dimensional) or aggregation functions (e.g., average or max), but the same concepts apply.

Checkpointing is a method of periodically saving the database state. The challenge is to do this in a consistent way while updates and queries are being run on the database. Saving the entire state of a database is a time-consuming activity, so shutting down other activity while this is done is not an acceptable solution for performance reasons. The goal of checkpointing is to save the current state in such a way that as far as all requesters can tell the state was saved at a given point in time.

Logging captures the time and nature of all requests to the database system, as described in CEIT Provide Web Services. When combined with checkpointing, logging allows reconstruction of a "broken" database. The last checkpointed version can be loaded, and then the history in the log files can be repeated starting at the time of the checkpoint. This requires checkpointing information to be included in the log files.

Databases can allow or deny actions to different users based on authorization rules. In ELS systems, services are the front end of all databases, so these rules are not needed for individual web browser requesters. However, for an exposure service that reads only from a database, it would be beneficial to allow read-only permission for that service, so database authorization rules are important for ELS systems even though the database authorization is not strictly part of the ELS security model.

Although the underlying data structures are not always made available at the database service layer of abstraction, certain common patterns should be made available or used, such as B-Trees and hash tables. A B-Tree provides a balanced tree structure to optimize query performance, and a hash table provides a constant time lookup for arbitrary data sets.

Recent news reports are replete with instances of database compromises, theft of data, and other incursions. To understand the vulnerabilities, we should first examine how database applications are currently organized.

17.4 Enterprise Resource Planning Business Software

Access to a database is normally organized along the lines of a business software solution. Enterprise resource planning (ERP) is business management software—typically a suite of integrated applications—that a company can use to collect,

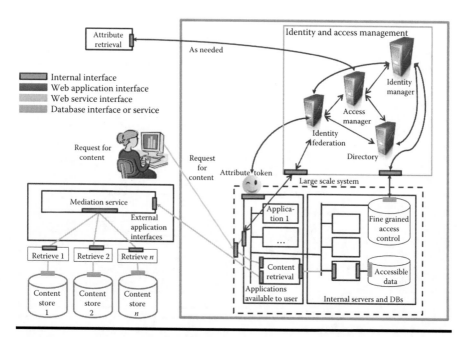

Figure 17.3   ERP overall organization.

store, manage, and interpret data from many business activities, including product planning, cost, manufacturing, service delivery marketing, and sales. The form is complex and involves self-sufficiency on everything from security to external interfaces. The basic form is shown in Figure 17.3.

The complexities associated with ERP are due, in part, to control of security and other aspects. However, since the ERP does not use web-service approaches (end-to-end approaches with distributed authentication, and authorization), they must be treated as legacy and untrusted from the high assurance standpoint.

17.5 ERP as a Legacy System

There are two aspects of interfacing with a legacy system. The first is control of the attributes associated with an identity, and the second is the sanitization and checking of communications and data that an untrusted system provides. Figure 17.4 shows a somewhat simplified version of the ERP with the security interfaces in place. In the figure, external interfaces have been removed since they will not be discussed.

17.5.1 ERP Attribute System Synchronization

Large-scale legacy systems (such as the ERP) maintain their own attributes for users and establish roles and privileges based upon those attributes. Current updating

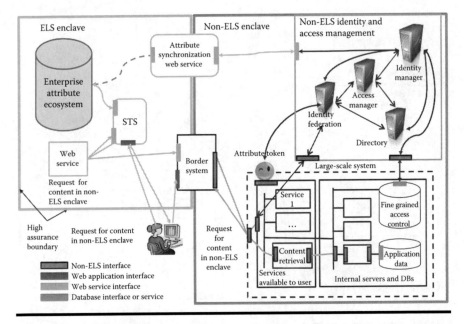

Figure 17.4   ERP as a legacy system.

may or may not happen based upon manual input. Notifications of changes within the enterprise are not uniform (and often not in a form easily used by legacy system administrators), and updating may or may not occur. This leads to an unacceptable delay in adjusting to changes within the enterprise. Attribute synchronization between the legacy system and the EAS may be undertaken to allow a more automated adjustment to the tempo of operations. This requires a synchronization system and changes to the legacy system for compatibility in definitions of roles, etc.

The synchronization system described above must meet the following considerations:

■ Not all EAS entities will be in legacy databases. However, all legacy identities should be in the EAS.
■ Each identity in a legacy database has roles and privileges based upon attributes.
■ Each identity in the legacy has enterprise-level attributes.
■ Maps must be established between the EAS attributes and the legacy roles and privileges.
■ Local naming may differ from that for enterprise DN, but it can be mapped to the enterprise identity.
■ Some EAS attributes currently map to legacy roles and privileges.
■ The enterprise must add and maintain other attributes in the EAS that are needed to establish legacy roles and privileges.

- For identities that occur in both, EAS contains attributes (for each identity) that can map to legacy roles and privileges.
- EAS will be maintained and reflect the current attributes of all its active entities, including those attributes added for legacy mappings.
- The legacy (Access Manager Interface) will import (periodically or on demand) changes to attributes of identities in its stores as reflected by changes in EAS identity attributes.
- The legacy will remap its roles and privileges based upon updated attributes.
- The legacy roles and privileges will be harmonized with the roles and privileges in the EAS. This will allow a synchronization between the EAS and legacy roles and privileges.

17.5.2 ERP Border System

The extent to which the border system must translate/mediate communications depends on the Non-ELS system. The border system is in the ELS enclave unless the particular Non-ELS enclave opts to provide some of the functionality in its environment, preferable for PKI-enabled Non-ELS enclaves, should synchronize access and privilege attributes with the EAS to simplify the process. However, the main assumption is that Non-ELS systems do not change. Access and privilege resides with the Non-ELS enclave identity and access management (IDAM). For Figure 17.5, the communication flows are the following:

0. Standard ELS flows for browser SAML request to STS, with call to EAS for claims. Browser window info includes the STS name, application name, border service name, and content object name.
1. The browser calls border system service (BSS) using standard ELS AuthN and AuthZ.
2. The trusted application within BSS creates new TRUSTED APPLICATION for specific user call, NEW trusted application calls Non-ELS IDAM with its own credentials (if IDAM is DN-enabled and PKI-enabled—else has an account with IDAM and AuthN credential recognized by IDAM) with request for local ID and AuthN credentials based on DN of original requester.
3. The trusted application fork/execs untrusted application and passes local ID, AuthN credential, and APPLICATION name/content object name to untrusted application via local IPC.
4. The untrusted application establishes connection to Non-ELS application using local ID and AuthN credentials.
5. The untrusted application sends request to Non-ELS application of content object name.
6. The Non-ELS application sends request to IDAM with local ID of untrusted application for AuthZ credentials.

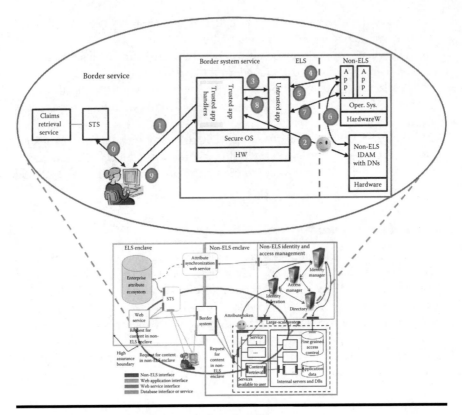

Figure 17.5   Legacy border system functionality.

7. The Non-ELS application determines access, retrieves content from store, and sends response(s) to untrusted application.
8. The untrusted application passes response to trusted application (at session close untrusted application terminates), Special Handling including sanitization—offline.
9. The new trusted application sends content to browser (on session close NEW trusted application terminates and clears state). Note that these can also be threads of a single process.

17.6 Hardening of ERP Database Systems

ERPs contain a number of applications (for specific functionality), and a back-end that will provide attributes related to identities. These applications are normally identity-based and often username/password-enabled. The sources of attributes may contain local stores that need to be maintained for the specific database, and of course, all of the interfaces need to be secured. To discuss the hardening of the ERP, we have further simplified the diagram, as shown in Figure 17.6.

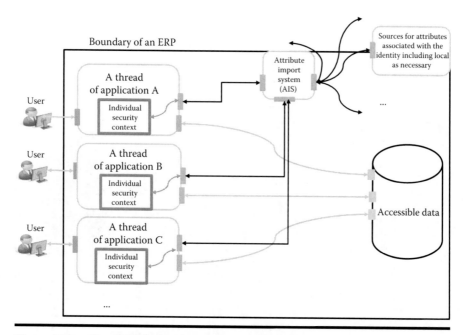

Figure 17.6   The simplified organization of an ERP.

Hardening will occur in five stages, discussed below:

1. Encryption of data at rest
2. Encryption of data in transit
3. Claims-based identity, access, and privilege
4. Hardening the application for accessing databases
5. Applying homomorphic encryption processes to the database

17.6.1 Hardening Stage One: Encryption of Data at Rest

Figure 17.7 shows the basic idea. All data within the database is encrypted as it sits in storage. This stops any threats that are present from benefitting from picking up the entire stored database and exporting it. Many database systems already do this. It should be automatic and built in to the storage system.

17.6.2 Hardening Stage Two: Encryption of Data in Transit

Although this may seem obvious, many of the implementations have not encrypted all of the links. Links within the spaces considered to be the ERP are often considered trusted, but as we have seen again and again, such spaces may contain threats, at least for a while. The preferred process for ELS is TLA-based bilateral authentication (Figure 17.8).

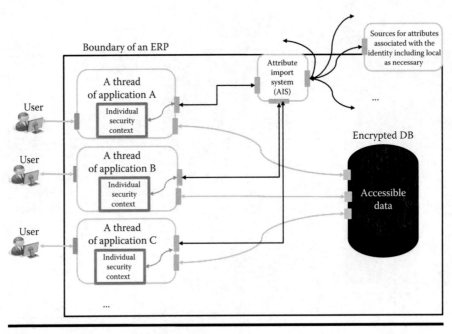

Figure 17.7 Encryption of data at rest.

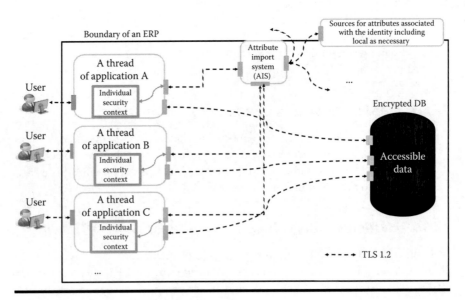

Figure 17.8 Encryption of data in transit.

17.6.3 Hardening Stage Three: Claims Identity, Access, and Privilege

This stage is more difficult, but much more rewarding. Figure 17.9 shows that a number of interfaces are completely eliminated and their vulnerabilities are no longer a problem. Many of these old software interfaces went outside of the ERP system. The claims-based system is the one discussed in earlier chapters and will be assumed from this point forward. The hardening does not stop here, however, and the fourth stage is discussed in the next few sections.

17.6.4 Hardening Stage Four: Least Privilege for Application

We will proceed from the position that the databases are claims-driven as opposed to account-driven. Most database systems maintain accounts for users. These accounts have privileges and status for each individual, are expensive to maintain, and are error-prone. With ELS we have two basic credentials: the PKI for identity and SAML for access and privilege. The basic security model indicates that all functionality is realized by web services. This precludes database grazing, which is a situation in which the requester can peruse most of the database at once. This is to be preceded by PKI-based mutual authentication and a TLS pipeline and followed by a SAML token for access and privilege. However, that still leaves two paradigms for database operations (application-driven and data-driven). To illustrate the

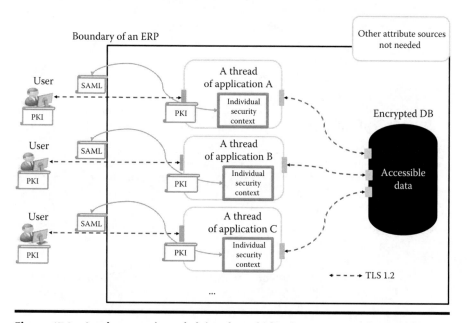

Figure 17.9   Implementation of claims-based identity, access, and privilege.

difference, the following section contains a notional example whereby a financial database is accessed by an individual who has the credentials of a financial analyst.

17.6.4.1 Financial Roles

The enterprise financial database (EFD) has many predefined roles. These are determined by the data owner and placed in the format of an ACR for storage in the enterprise service registry. They may be arbitrarily complex since the claims engine will only sort through their satisfaction and provide any variables or restrictions requested. A few are defined below:

1. Financial analyst is determined by position, training, and job identifier.
   Financial Analyst =>
   a. manager and above, AND
   b. job identifier = xxx12, AND
   c. training = [basic finance (within last 5 years) + Financial Analysis (within last 5 years)] OR [BS, Accounting or finance (within last 10 years)] OR waiver.
   RESTRICT
   a. subarea q unless supervisor is corporate director or above.
   b. Data restricted to location code. AND
   c. Cannot update any project over $5M UNLESS memberof $5Mupdatewaiver
   d. Additional restriction may be included.
2. Financial analyst is determined by position, training, and job identifier.
   Financial Supervisor =>
   a. manager and above, AND
   b. job identifier = xxx14, AND
   c. training = [basic finance (within last 5 years) + Financial Analysis (within last 5 years)] OR [BS, Accounting or finance (within last 10 years)] or waiver.
   RESTRICT
   a. Cannot update any project over $5M until he has been using the system 6 months, unless memberof $5Mupdatewaiver (include 5Munresolved).
3. Financial auditor is determined by training and job identifier.
   Financial auditor =>
   a. job identifier = xx316, AND
   b. training = [basic finance (within last 5 years) AND Financial Analysis (within last 3 years) AND Financial Audit (within last 3 years)] OR (MS, Accounting or finance (within last 15 years)) OR waiver.
   RESTRICT
   a. Data restricted to audit location code. …

4. Bookkeeper ...
5. Quality Control Specialist ...
6. Administrator ...
7. ...

17.6.4.2 Application-Driven Database Operations

Each of the roles must be coded for operations. For illustration, we will deal only with the financial analyst in this example. Who, in this case, is Fred2345432, or just Fred. The evolution is the normal preparation for the access and privilege associated with an application or service. Figures 17.10 through 17.15 show the evolution of the access control, which involve most of the services in the enterprise attribute ecosystem.

The process has seven steps, as explained below:

1. Access control requirement: The administrator or data owner enters ACR into the system for each of the roles he defines. We understand he will need help through tools or assistance to get it in computer terms. It may take a couple of iterations. Basic training will help all make the right decisions when the checklists do not work (Figure 17.10).
2. Claims engine computation: The claims engine will activate either periodically or on demand, gathering the required information from the ACR. It will cycle through all of the identities and compute claims for the new ACR. It will cycle through all of the identities that have had attribute changes since the last update and calculate claims for all of the ACRs in the registry. It will provide warnings for those claims that are expiring and suspend those that have expired. It will terminate claims that have been suspended for some time (Figure 17.11).

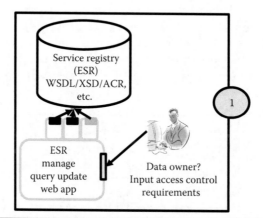

Figure 17.10 Data owner develops access control requirements.

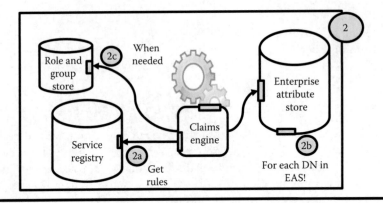

Figure 17.11   Claims engine computation.

3. Claims stored in the claims repository: The claims engine computes and stores the claims, tags things that need further computing, adds creation dates, expiration dates, delegation that is allowed, and any unresolved claims that need to be determined locally (Figure 17.12).

4. User request to STS: There are three ways to invoke an application. All end with the user making a request (either purposefully, or as part of a process) to the STS. Chapter 11 reviews all of these methods in detail. A user makes a request to the trusted STS for his SAML to be used in a specified application. He starts with a bilateral PKI authentication with the STS. The STS is configured so that no one else can request his SAML. The STS will generate a SAML only for the authenticated requester (Figure 17.13).

5. STS claims retrieval: The STS bilaterally authenticates with the Provide Claims service, which goes to the Claims Repository and retrieves the claims for the specific identity and the application. The Provide Claims service resolves those claims that need to be resolved at runtime, and passes the claims and unresolved claims to the STS (Figure 17.14).

6. Return of the SAML: The STS builds, signs, and passes the SAML through the user to the requested service. This is done by using the HTTPS POST protocol. Chapter 11 reviews all of these methods in detail. The user

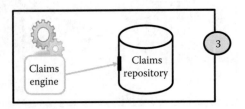

Figure 17.12   Claims storage.

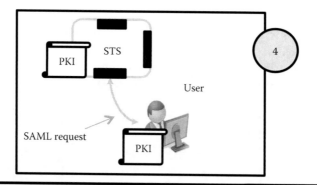

Figure 17.13   User request.

bilaterally authenticates with the requested service (if he has not already done so) and presents its SAML credential. Each service or application within the enterprise is provided software that perform various functions such as logging, inspection, and signature data so that end points can be relatively self-sufficient. Software that can be compiled in-line for added functionality are termed handlers. These handlers are discussed in Chapter 17. One of the handlers is a SAML Validation Handler that will parse the SAML and retrieve access and privilege data. The SAML contains all of the claims and required data in a form that can be verified and validated for that user/application pair. Note that the SAML does not contain the usual database privilege parameters of Create, Read, Update, and Delete (CRUD) for each individual data element (Figure 17.15 and Table 17.1).

7. Application Receipt of SAML: The handler in the specified application verifies and validates the SAML. It then separates the claims and provides the claims to the application. If additional EAS data is needed, it is because the ACR was not explicit enough and it should be rewritten. No entity outside of the EAS ecosystem has access to the EAS. Claims are provided only by a SAML created by the STS and only for the user/application pair. If the

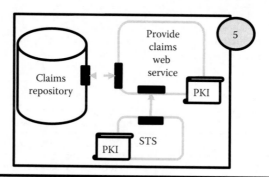

Figure 17.14   STS gathers claims.

application still needs to derive additional information for privilege determination, it must do so from its own stores of information (an example might be a specialized training database that deals with the software or methods of the database system). When these steps are completed, the application will have a complete security context for the requester (Figure 17.16).

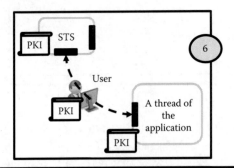

Figure 17.15 SAML is pushed to application.

Table 17.1 Basic SAML Format

SAML: Assertion		
Version ID	Version 2.0	Required
ID	SAML ID	Required
Issue Instant	Timestamp	Required
Issuer	(content)	Required
Signature	(content)	Required
Subject	User	Required—X.509 Identity
SAML: Attribute Statement		
Subject	User	For local use
Claims (stored and runtime): Roles: included data: restrictions, unresolved claims	(content)	May include parameters
SAML: Conditions		
NotBefore	(content)	Timestamp
NotAfter	(content)	Timestamp
Audience	(content)	Target Service

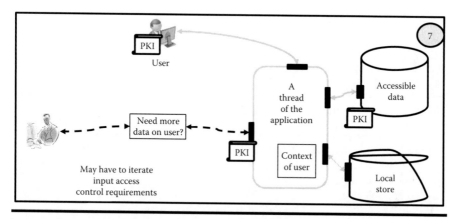

Figure 17.16 SAML receipt and context development.

17.6.4.3 Application-Driven Annotated Example

The definitions of the various roles are added to the ESR, and the claims engine is invoked to compute claims for all identities and the financial database service.

Fred is evaluated by the claims engine, and based upon the enterprise data, he is provided a claim of financial analyst with some restrictions, as shown in Table 17.2.

For databases, the service-driven approach has the following advantages and disadvantages:

Advantages

1. The data owner does not have to know the database schema in order to specify access and privilege.
2. The service controls Fred's interaction with the database.
3. Database administrators may or may not establish CRUDs for the role in question.

Disadvantages

1. The service developer must know the database specifics.
2. The service is granted full access to the database (to accommodate the different users).
3. The service computes what is allowable (CRUD) and send computed SQL for what it believes are reasonable requests consistent with Fred's authorities.

Table 17.2 Evaluation of Fred's Claims Financial System

Financial Analyst Implies	Fred	Claims Engine for Fred
Manager and above, AND	Chicago Branch Manger	True
Job identifier = xxx12, AND	Job code = 43212	True
Training = [basic finance (within last 5 years) AND (Financial Analysis within last 5 years)] OR [BS, Accounting or finance (within last 10 years)] OR waiver.)	Training = training on basic AND finance(8/4/2012), AND (Financial Analysis (6/5/2010, BS Mathematics Purdue (6/1/2000)) OR On the enterprise Training Waiver list group for Financial Analysts (TWFIN)	True AND True AND (False or True) = True
Bottom Line		Overall Fred = Financial Analyst
Restrictions		
Subarea q unless supervisor is corporate director or above.	Supervisor (all billets report to 43200 or 43201) is Field Office Manager	False Supply Notq token to application
Data restricted to location code. AND	Location Code = Chicago	Supply Chicago token to application
Cannot update any project over $5M UNLESS *memberof* $5Mupdatewaiver	Not in enterprise group for ($5Mupdatewaiver)	False supply Not$5M+ token to application

17.6.4.4 Data-Driven Database Operations

A number of additional requirements are needed for data-driven applications:

1. Database schema must be known to the developer of the access control requirements. For illustration, we assume column-authorization-defined CRUDs.
2. Elements in the database (when they represent the same thing in the EAS) must be identical to the elements in the EAS. (Example: location code in the

database is a three-character code. It must be the same code in the EAS—when multiple databases use the same value, they must all have the same representation as the EAS).

3. The database must be prepared: The column CRUD permissions are set in the database for each role (Figure 17.17).
4. CRUD by role is shown in Figure 17.17.
5. View Template (see Figure 17.18) by Role shows all columns that a role can view.
6. Creation of a stored program provides a tailored view for each role as tailored by the individual attributes in the CRUD security of the role [82,86].
7. This view can only be restricted—not enhanced. If enhancement is desired, a new role must be created in the ACR and database.
8. View restrictions are by column but apply to rows (Example: Project Location = "Chicago").
9. When more than one role is in SAML, the application must ask the requester which role is being exercised for the appropriate view to be computed.

For illustration, we will assume for this example a column-organized relational database; however, the claims can be built for any database. For this database, permissions are usually given in terms of CRUD, normally by columns as we have described above. The database also applies these CRUD elements to the role

	Project	Total value	Initial entry date	Current expense entry date	Project lead	Project financial officer	Project lead e-mail	Current expense	Project location	Comments	etc.
Financial analyst	R	R	R	RU	R		R	RUD	R	RU	
Financial auditor	CRUD	CRUD	CRUD	CRUD	R	R	R	CRUD	CRUD	RU	
Project leader	CRUD	CRUD	CRUD	CRUD	R	CRUD	CRUD	CRUD	CRUD	RU	
Financial analyst2	R	R	R	CRUD	R		R	CRUD	CRUD	RU	
Financial analyst3	CRUD	R	CRUD	CRUD	R		R	CRUD	CRUD	RU	
Project leader2	CRUD	CRUD	CRUD	CRUD	CRUD	CRUD	CRUD	CRUD	CRUD	RU	
Administrator	CRUD	CRUD	CRUD	CRUD	CRUD	CRUD	CRUD	CRUD	CRUD	CRUD	CRUD
User	R	R	R	R	R	R	R	R	R	R	R
...											

The leftmost label reads "Security context of financial analyst" and the rightmost label reads "Security context of financial analyst".

Figure 17.17   CRUD by role.

Security context of financial analyst

View template for financial analyst with no restrictions

Project	Total value	Initial entry date	Current expense entry date	Project lead	Project lead e-mail	Current expense	Project location	Comments
CRUD	R	R	R	RU	R	R	RUD	RU
123400r	5,500,000	12/11/2013	02/04/2014	George Henry	ghenry345@ent.org	3,450,000	Chicago	Initial contracts provided on 02/04/2014
137800q	2,500,000	08/02/2012	02/04/2014	Helmut Smith	hsmith123@ent.org	2,450,000	Chicago	Initial contracts provided on 10/01/2012 Awaiting final deliverable sign off on 02/04/2014
567400r	4,500,000	09/10/2013	12/06/2013	Rita Jones	rjones345@ent.org	3,450,000	Chicago	Initial contracts provided on 12/06/2013
713200q	3,000,000	08/02/2012	02/04/2014	Janet Smith	jsmith456@ent.org	2,450,000	Chicago	Initial contracts provided on 10/01/2012 Awaiting final deliverable sign off on 02/04/2014
456200r	4,500,000	12/11/2013	02/04/2014	George Henry	ghenry222@rb.com	2,450,000	Chicago	Initial contracts provided on 02/04/2014
912400t	3,500,000	08/06/2011	02/04/2014	Mike Frank	hmfrank199@fnc.itl	2,450,000	New York	Initial contracts provided on 10/01/2012 Awaiting final deliverable sign off on 02/04/2014
778800r	4,500,000	09/10/2013	12/06/2013	Harry Ga	hga778@chi.com	3,450,000	Chicago	Initial contracts provided on 12/06/2013
657800s	3,000,000	08/02/2012	02/04/2014	Jim Rich	jrich657@fnl.net	2,450,000	Chicago	Initial contracts provided on 10/01/2012 Awaiting final deliverable sign off on 02/04/2014
...								

Security context of financial analyst

Figure 17.18 View template for financial analyst.

described above. In an identity-based access control system, they would be written for each identity. The use of roles and restrictions simplifies the definitions. The process now involves nine steps to replace the seven needed for application-driven access control.

Transfer of the SAML and the local data to a stored program (to be developed) in the database to set the view for the role as limited by other factors. Example— Columns and their CRUDs are set in the stored view for the role. Each role has one such view. Rows are restricted by setting acceptable values in various columns. The stored program validates the SAML, resolves the role, and sets the view in the security context of the role (for application of CRUDs to be transferred to the application for further transmittal to the user). The application must have at least four SQL queries programmed in. These include the following:

- Execute stored program for view and security context
- Create—New entry in the stored view and security context
- Update—(column, row) in the stored view and security context
- Delete—(column, row) in the stored view and security context

Any violation of the CRUD for the context view should return an error.

17.6.4.5 Data-Driven Annotated Example

Fred is evaluated by the claims engine, and claims are slightly modified based upon the database schema and the instructions to the stored program, as shown in Table 17.3.

At this point, the application must ask which role is being exercised if more than one role is in the revised SAML. The revised SAML for Fred is shown in Table 17.4.

The application authenticates itself to the database and triggers the stored program with the SAML for Fred, as shown in Figure 17.19.

The stored program verifies and validates the SAML, pulls up the view template stored in the permissions for financial analyst, and applies the restrictions to the view. This view is provided for action. The stored program modifies the view as shown in Figures 17.20 and 17.21.

The handoff between the application and the stored program in the database is shown in Figure 17.22.

The CRUDs in the database will be enforced for the restricted view.

Figure 17.23 shows the exchange with the user. Only accessible data leaves the database.

Communications shown in Figure 17.23 and labeled as A in the figure: Scripted exchange with application about user request related to tailored view (requests are not filtered)

Table 17.3   Reevaluation of Fred for Data-Driven Access

Financial Analyst =>	Fred	Claims Engine for Fred
Manager and above, AND	Chicago Branch Manger	True
Job identifier = xxx12, AND	Job code = 43212	True
Training = [basic finance (within last 5 years) AND (Financial Analysis (within last 5 years)] OR [BS, Accounting or finance (within last 10 years)] OR (waiver)	Training = training on basic AND finance(8/4/2012), AND (Financial Analysis (6/5/2010, BS Mathematics Purdue (6/1/2000)) OR On the enterprise Training Waiver list group for Financial Analysts (TWFIN)	True AND True AND (False or True) = True
	Overall Fred = Financial Analyst	
Restrictions		
Subarea q unless supervisor is corporate director or above	Supervisor (all billets report to 43200 or 43201) is Field Office Manager	False Restrict: Project ≠ ??????q
Data restricted to location code. AND	Location Code = Chicago	Restrict: Project Location = Chicago
Cannot update any project over $5M UNLESS *memberof* $5Mupdatewaiver	Not in enterprise group for ($5Mupdatewaiver)	False Restrict: Total Value <= 5,000,000

Communications shown in Figure 17.23 and labeled as B in the figure:

- SQL Requests (Read is assumed in the view)
- Create—New entry in the stored view and security context
- Update—(column, row) in the stored view and security context
- Delete—(column, row) in the stored view and security context
- No other SQL requests allowed

Table 17.4   Rework of Fred SAML

SAML: Assertion		
Version ID	Version 2.0	Required
ID	SAML ID	Required
Issue Instant	Timestamp	Required
Issuer	(content)	Required
Signature	(content)	Required
Subject	Fred	Required—X.509 Identity
SAML: Attribute Statement		
Subject	Fred	For local use
Claims: Role = Financial Analyst Restrict: "Project" ≠ ??????q Restrict: "Project Location"= "Chicago" Restrict: "Total Value" >= 5,000,000	(content)	May include parameters
SAML: Conditions		
NotBefore	(content)	Timestamp
NotAfter	(content)	Timestamp
Audience	(content)	Target Service

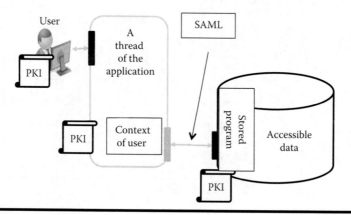

Figure 17.19   Posting SAML to stored program.

View template for Fred financial analyst

Security context of financial analyst

Security context of financial analyst

Project	Total value	Initial entry date	Current expense entry date	Project lead	Project lead e-mail	Current expense	Project location	Comments
CRUD	R	R	R	RU	R	R	RUD	RU
123400r	5,500,000	12/11/2013	02/04/2	Further restrict: total value <= 5,000,000		3,450,000	Chicago	Initial contracts provided on 02/04/2014
137800q	2,500,000	08/02/2012	02/04/201	Restricted by project ≠ ??????q	nt.org	2,450,000	Chicago	Awaiting final deliverable sign off on 02/04/2014
567400r	4,500,000	09/10/2013	12/06/2013	Rita Jones	rjones345@ent.org	3,450,000	Chicago	Initial contracts provided on 12/06/2013
713200q	3,000,000	08/02/2012	02/04/2014	Janet Smith	jsmith456@ent.org	2,450,000	Chicago	Awaiting final deliverable sign off on 02/04/2014
456200r	4,500,000	12/11/2013	02/04/	Restricted by project ≠ 456???	???@rb.com	2,450,000	Chicago	Initial contracts provided on 02/04/2014
912400t	3,500,000	08/06/2011	02/04/	Restricted by project location = Chicago		2,450,000	New York	Awaiting final deliverable sign off on 02/04/2014
778800r	4,500,000	09/10/2013	12/06/2013	Harry Ga	hga778@chi.com	3,450,000	Chicago	Initial contracts provided on 12/06/2013
657800s	3,000,000	08/02/2012	02/04/2014	Jim Rich	jrich657@fnl.net	2,450,000	Chicago	Awaiting final deliverable sign off on 02/04/2014
...								

Rows eliminated based upon Fred's restrictions

Figure 17.20 Tailoring the view for data-driven data base operations (shaded rows are eliminated in the tailored view for the circled restricted values).

Restricted view for Fred financial analyst

Security context of financial analyst

Project	Total value	Initial entry date	Current expense entry date	Project lead	Project lead e-mail	Current expense	Project location	Comments
CRUD	R	R	R	RU	R	R	RUD	RU
567400r	4,500,000	09/10/2013	12/06/2013	Rita Jones	rjones345@ent.org	3,450,000	JBWRight	Initial contracts provided on 12/06/2013
713200q	3,000,000	08/02/2012	02/04/2014	Janet Smith	jsmith456@ent.org	2,450,000	JBWRight	Initial contracts provided on 10/01/2012 Awaiting final deliverable sign off on 02/04/2014
778800r	4,500,000	09/10/2013	12/06/2013	Harry Ga	hga778@chi.com	3,450,000	JBWRight	Initial contracts provided on 12/06/2013
657800s	3,000,000	08/02/2012	02/04/2014	Jim Rich	jrich657@fnl.net	2,450,000	JBWRight	Initial contracts provided on 10/01/2012 Awaiting final deliverable sign off on 02/04/2014
...								

Security context of financial analyst

Figure 17.21 Tailored view.

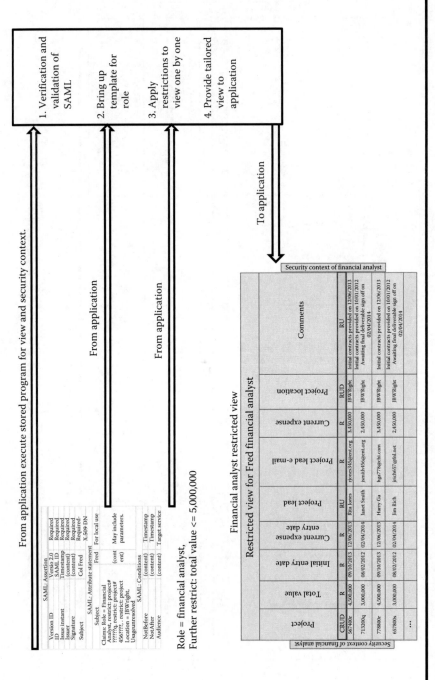

Figure 17.22 Stored program to application flow.

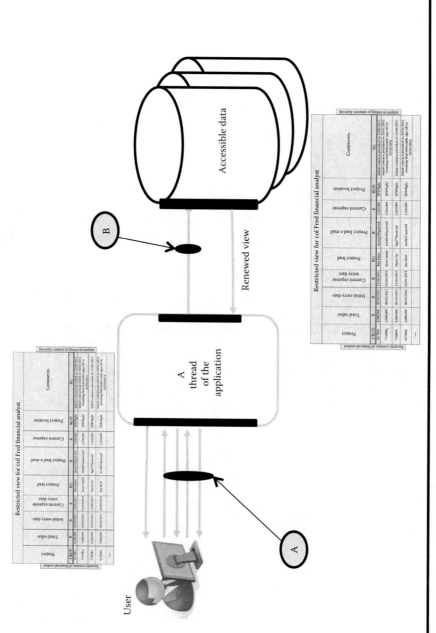

Figure 17.23   Data-driven exchange with the user.

Any violation of the CRUD for the context view will return an error.

For databases, the data-driven approach has the following advantages and disadvantages:

Advantages

1. The service has limited access to the database.
2. The database controls Fred's interaction with the database based upon Fred's credentials.
3. Database administrators *must* establish CRUDs for the role in question.
4. The SQL authority of the service is limited and verified by the database.

Disadvantages

1. The data owner does have to know the database schema in order to specify access and privilege.
2. Views are moved multiple times.
3. The service computes what is allowable (CRUD) and send computed SQL for what it believes are reasonable requests.

17.6.5 Hardening Stage Five: Homomorphic Encryption

Homomorphic techniques allow encrypted queries of encrypted data. The techniques have been proven in the lab, but are currently impractical. Of current concern is partial homomorphic encryption of databases, which may be practically applied to SQL database queries. The details of their application will await future editions of this book; further reading in References 112–116.

Chapter 18

Building Enterprise Software

Web services provide the current best form of enterprise services, allowing the reuse of software modules and the protection of information at layers 6 and 7 of the OSI protocol. The development of web services is based upon a separation of security (through handlers) and functionality to provide a seamless user experience while maintaining the required level of protections for sensitive information.

18.1 Services Types

Within the enterprise there are three basic types of services:

- Web application service provider (WASP)—differs from a normal web service only in that it exchanges HTML with a human user
- Aggregation services
- Exposure services

The web application is set up to communicate with a user's browser in HTML. It may call aggregation services or exposure services. Each of these communicates using SOAP/XML over HTTPS or other protocols after authentication and authorization. Services may use SOAP web services or Representational State Transfer (REST), JavaScript Object Notation (JSON), or Asynchronous Java and XML (AJAX). The services may not use these for authentication or authorization for security reasons. For the purposes of this discussion, the web application is treated as an aggregation service. An aggregation service is defined as a service whose function is to provide data to the user from a number of ACS using a series of exposure services or aggregation services and may include a number of widgets or other display code segments. An exposure service is defined as a service whose primary function is to provide synthesized data to the user from one or more authoritative content sources, and this service may not call other exposure services or aggregation services, but it may directly interface with one or more ACSs.

18.2 Functionality of All Services

The following are required for all services.

18.2.1 Evaluating Inputs

Once authentication and authorization are complete, communications between requester and provider should be evaluated. Each web service is required to have an XSD for each interface, to be filed in the ESR. An example of an XSD is provided in Table 18.1.

18.2.1.1 Extensible Markup Language

XML is a markup language that defines a set of rules for encoding documents in a format that is both human-readable and machine-readable. It is defined in the XML 1.0 specification produced by the W3C [5a]. It is a textual data format with strong support via Unicode. Although the design of XML focuses on documents, it is widely used for the representation of arbitrary data structures in web services. XSD, a recommendation of the W3C, specifies how to formally describe the elements in an XML document [5a]. This description can be used to verify that each item of content in a document adheres to the description of the element in which the content is to be placed. A schema is an abstract representation of an object's characteristics and relationship to other objects. An XML schema represents the interrelationship between the attributes and elements of an XML object (e.g., a document or a portion of a document). XSD has several advantages such as document type definition (DTD) [5e,5f] or Simple Object XML (SOX). XSD is written in XML, and hence does not require intermediary processing by a parser. Benefits include self-documentation, automatic schema creation, and the ability to be queried through XML transformations (XSLT), which is used for discovering services. An example of an XSD file is provided in Table 18.1.

As shown, the XSD has the type and expected range of values for each element in the API. All inputs in the dialogue should be reviewed by the requester, for correctness, formatting, and other considerations before passing them on to other code processors. The provider should again check for correctness, formatting, and

Table 18.1   XSD Example

```
<?xml version="1.0" encoding="UTF-8"?>
<xsd:schema targetNamespace="http://com.ibm.wbit.comptest.
controller"
    xmlns:Q1="http://com.ibm.wbit.comptest.controller"
    xmlns:xsd= "http://www.w3.org/2001/XMLSchema">
    <xsd:complexType name="TestResults">
        <xsd:sequence>
            <xsd:element maxOccurs="unbounded"
            minOccurs="0"
            name="testSuites" type="Q1:TestSuiteRun"/>
        </xsd:sequence>
            <xsd:attribute name="testProject"
            type="xsd:string"/>
    </xsd:complexType>
        <xsd:complexType name="TestSuiteRun">
            <xsd:complexContent>
                    <xsd:extension base="Q1:TestRun">
                                <xsd:sequence>
                    <xsd:element maxOccurs="unbounded"
            minOccurs="0" name="testCases"
            type="Q1:TestCaseRun">
                                        </xsd:element>
                                </xsd:sequence>
                    <xsd:attribute name="tests"
                    type="xsd:int"/>
                    </xsd:extension>
                </xsd:complexContent>
        </xsd:complexType>
    <xsd:complexType name="TestCaseRun">
        <xsd:complexContent>
                <xsd:extension base="Q1:TestRun">
                    <xsd:sequence>
<xsd:element name="result" type="Q1:Severity"/>
        <xsd:element maxOccurs="unbounded" minOccurs="0"
        name="variations"
        type="Q1:VariationRun">
                </xsd:element>
                </xsd:sequence>
                <xsd:attribute name="variationCount"
                type="xsd:int"/>
            </xsd:extension>
        </xsd:complexContent>
        </xsd:complexType>
```

(*Continued*)

Table 18.1 (*Continued*)   XSD Example

```
            <xsd:complexType name="VariationRun">
            <xsd:complexContent>
                   <xsd:extension base="Q1:TestRun">
                   <xsd:sequence>
      <xsd:element name="result" type="Q1:Severity"/>
      <xsd:element name="exception" nillable="true"
      type="xsd:string">
                                         <xsd:annotation>
                                             <xsd:documentation>
<<THIS ELEMENT IS USED TO DISPLAY THE EXCEPTION OF A FAILURE
OR ERROR.>>
                                             </xsd:documentation>
                                         </xsd:annotation>
                   </xsd:element>
                         </xsd:sequence>
                   </xsd:extension>
            </xsd:complexContent>
      </xsd:complexType>
   <xsd:simpleType name="Severity">
            <xsd:restriction base="xsd:string">
                   <xsd:enumeration value="pass"/>
                   <xsd:enumeration value="fail"/>
                   <xsd:enumeration value="error"/>
            </xsd:restriction>
      </xsd:simpleType>
   <xsd:complexType name="TestRun">
      <xsd:attribute name="name" type="xsd:string"/>
            <xsd:attribute name="startTime"
            type="xsd:dateTime"/>
            <xsd:attribute name="endTime"
            type="xsd:dateTime"/>
            <xsd:attribute name="result"
            type="xsd:string"/>
      </xsd:complexType>
   </xsd:schema>
```

other considerations before acting upon the data. Vulnerabilities occur with malformed inputs. The "well-formed" checks avoid many attacks, including buffer overflow. All inputs should be read as general or strongly typed variables, tested for correctness, and reformatted into the required API response when expected characteristics are verified. Malformed and malicious inputs are tested by the software before it accepts them for action. Unrecognizable, uncorrectable, or improper inputs result in an error code, and return with the error. These events are logged and possibly alerted.

18.2.2 Credentials

Credentials are an integral part of the schema. Each service requiring access is credentialed by a trusted credentialing authority. Further, the security token server that is used for generating security assertion tokens is also credentialed (primarily through the same credentialing authority, although others may be possible). For aggregation services, the credentialing includes not only registration with the identity provider, but also the population of attributes with the groups and roles necessary to access the exposure services. This can be done only by enterprise operations administrators; however, the developer should ensure this step is complete, so close coordination with operations administrators is required. Chapter 8 deals with credentialing in more detail.

18.2.3 PKI Required: X.509 Certificates

The primary exchange medium for setting up authentication of identities and setting up cryptographic flows is the PKI embodied in an X.509 certificate. All web services must be issued these credentials.

18.2.4 PKI Bilateral Authentication

The requester authenticates to the service, and the service authenticates to the requester. This two-way authentication eliminates a number of threat vulnerabilities. The requester initially authenticates to the server and sets up a TLS connection to begin communication with the service. The primary method of authentication is through the use of public keys in the X.509 certificate, which can then be used to set up encrypted communications, either by X.509 keys or a generated session key. The preferred method of communication is secure messaging, contained in SOAP envelopes.

18.2.5 Authorization Using Authorization Handlers

All authorizations are through the use of authorization handlers in accordance with the SAML 2.0 specification provided by OASIS [1] and customized by the enterprise developers. Because of the critical requirements associated with authorization, the code to accomplish this should be provided in the Java 2 Enterprise Edition (J2EE) [112–114] or .NET executable files [115] for use in implementations [116]. Code developers use these code elements without modification. In fact, handlers may be used for many functions. The basic handler architecture is shown

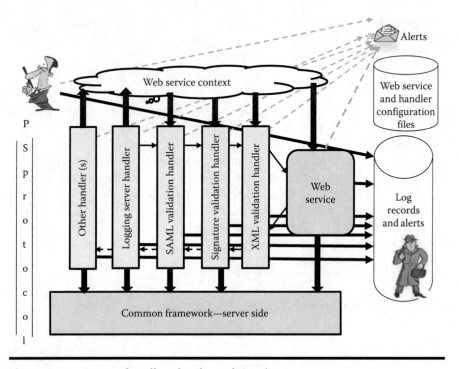

Figure 18.1 Context handlers for the web service.

in Figure 18.1. Chapter 21 discusses additional use of handlers to help maintain the end-to-end communication approach.

18.2.6 Agents in the Enterprise

Two of the agents are introduced in Figure 18.1. Agents provide utility and monitoring data throughout the enterprise, and these are introduced briefly below. They will be discussed more in Chapter 19. Agents are of five types: self-help, embedded, monitor sweep, import, and self-protection. Each fulfills a different function in the architecture. Although they are referred to as agents, they are full web services and must meet ELS requirements.

18.2.6.1 Self-Help Agents

Self-help agents are provided on the standard desktop and provide the user with a tool to examine configuration and software conflicts. They also allow support personnel at the enterprise help desk to take over the desktop or device for diagnosis and repair of common software problems.

18.2.6.2 Embedded Agents

The embedded agent sits on the J2EE or .NET stacks and monitors the performance of the server and its threads. It should be configured to provide performance, connectivity, and anomaly data to the log file for the service. It is unaware of sequence numbers or events transpiring within the service itself. It is also configured to provide alert data as discussed below.

18.2.6.3 Monitor Sweep Agents

Monitor sweep agents are placed throughout the enterprise, even though they may reach outside the enterprise on external calls. It is the job of the monitor sweep agents to read, translate, and submit monitor records to the centralized database. There is no translation for enterprise-developed services, and translation is minimal when commercial products allow for log4j configurations. They may be extensive for other types of monitor data in external sources.

18.2.6.4 Import Agents

Import agents are used by the EAS to refresh data from ACSs. The agents pull data through a guard for integrity and accuracy checking. These agents were first introduced in Chapter 3, Section 3.2.

18.2.6.5 Self-Protection Agents

All devices in the enterprise have software agents that are configurable to protect against improper use of communication ports, obvious intrusions and viruses, policy specific to the device, and blocking of unwanted communications through black lists or white lists. They may also have other functionality.

18.2.7 Data Keeping and Correlation

The web application is responsible for creating or acquiring a sequence number or identifier for each new session. This sequence number or identifier must be unique over all applications and sessions. The web application initializes and increments a record number counter for each sequence number for the life of the associated session. These numbers allow easy search and recovery of session data across machines and services. These two identifiers are passed to all subsequent

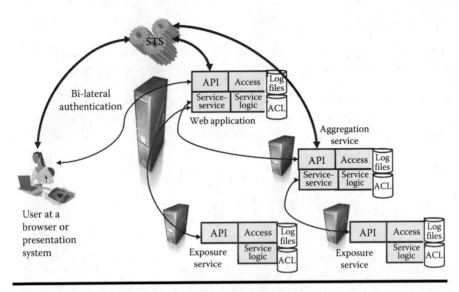

Figure 18.2 Web service flow for a notional application.

service requests and are used for every monitor entry of all web applications, exposure services, and aggregation services. The sequence number remains the same throughout the requesters' session; the record number is incremented for a given sequence number each time a log record is written. Missing log records are an indication of malicious behavior.

There are many development environments and approaches. The current research has been limited to either a .NET environment or a Java J2EE environment. Some environments such as C and C ++ may be considered conformant to Java. Additional formulations may be developed in the future. Each has specific requirements as noted below. Development of security aspects is handled last and close to the time of registration and certification. The web service flow for a notional application is presented in Figure 18.2.

18.3 Service Model

The web application, aggregation service, and exposure service are similar in their security, as shown in Figure 18.2. The service model can be applied to legacy systems by applying ELS appliques or wrapper services as described in Chapter 11. Access to ACS may be through database services (see Chapter 16). From a technical point of view, web services are a set of application-level standards built on top of TCP/IP. The web services standards for WSDL [5g] describe, precisely, how to discover and then invoke a web service. Other systems interact with the web service in a manner prescribed by its description using SOAP messages, typically conveyed using HTTP with an XML serialization in conjunction with other W3C [5] and IETF [4] standards as shown in the references at the end of this book.

Web services semantically encapsulate discrete functionality, in the same way that objects encapsulate functionality in an object-oriented system. This notion of encapsulation is an important element of thinking about modularity. Creating "atomic" services that can be reused by other projects is preferred. For example, Parnas discusses the advantages of designing a module "to reveal as little as possible about its inner workings" [84]. Encapsulating specific process knowledge within a discrete object is also a key element of sharing that capability within the framework of modular design.

To put a web service model together for the enterprise, the services are structurally similar, with registered and accessible details for use by other services. Encapsulation is encouraged, and the elements that are registered include the following:

- *Web Service Description Language [5h,5i,5j].* WSDL, an Interface Definition Language (IDL), is the standard to describe web services. WSDL is defined with XML. WSDL describes everything needed to use the web service, as well as what to expect back from the service. This information includes what protocol is used to transport the SOAP message (HTTP, SMTP, or FTP), how the data passed between client and server is structured, what it means, and the URI by which the service is accessed. Web services can exist without a WSDL description, but without this description, clients cannot figure out, in an unambiguous manner, how to access the desired web service. All enterprise services have a WSDL description.
- *Access control requirements.* ACR is needed to register a service in the registry for computing of claims in the EAS. The format of the ACR is provided in Annex B of CEIT *Control Access.* The ACR is used to compute claims and is the basis for the ACL resident with the service and used to match the claims presented in a SAML token. The entire process, together with examples, is given in Chapters 9 through 11.
- *Process for registry in an enterprise service registry.* The initial registry will be manual, but it is expected that tools will be quickly developed to facilitate and audit the registry process.
- *Naming conventions.* Each application has a root name from which other names are derived. The root name should be reflective of the application and include within it a unique identification of the original applications for which the code was initially developed.

18.4 Enterprise Services Checklist

Servers have properly configured operating systems and network interfaces and are configured for TLS 1.2 with mutual authentication. The checklist in Table 18.2 is for standing up the service within an enterprise.

Table 18.2 Enterprise Services Checklist

Step	Enterprise Developed	Commercially Developed	Legacy Systems That Cannot Be Adapted
1.	Discover similar services for reuse	Discover similar services for reuse	Discover similar services for reuse
2.	Integrate with ELS handlers	Integrate with ELS handlers. If unable, front with wrapper service	Front with wrapper service
3.	Establish access control requirements (see Chapters 10 through 12)	Establish access control requirements for either service or wrapper service (see Chapters 10 through 12)	Establish access control requirements for wrapper service (see Chapters 10 through 12)
4.	Generate PKI key pairs in hardware security module (HSM) for each web server and instance of web service	Generate PKI key pairs in HSM for each web server and instance of web service	Generate PKI key pairs in HSM for each web server and instance of web service
5.	Request PKI certificates for each web server and instance of web service	Request PKI certificates for each web server and instance of web service	Request PKI certificates for each web server and instance of web service
6.	Register web server and configure it with PKI and TLS 1.2. If more than one web server is involved, register each separately	Register web server and configure it with PKI and TLS 1.2. If more than one web server is involved, register each separately	Register web server and configure it with PKI and TLS 1.2. If more than one web server is involved register each separately
7.	Set up web server and publish web services [83]	Set up web server and publish web services	Set up web server and publish web services
8.	Verify that web services are working correctly [86]	Verify that web services are working correctly	Verify that web services are working correctly

(Continued)

Table 18.2 (*Continued*) Enterprise Services Checklist

Step	Enterprise Developed	Commercially Developed	Legacy Systems That Cannot Be Adapted
9.	Lock down web server(s) and web services [87]	Lock down web server(s) and web services	Lock down web server(s) and web services
10.	Turn off the debug switches [88]	Turn off the debug switches	Turn off the debug switches
11.	Configure each web service for monitoring, security events provided by contract. Configure monitoring information and monitor records and events	Configure wrapper web service and commercial product for monitoring, security events provided by the enterprise system engineering. Configure monitoring information and monitor records and events	Configure wrapper web and legacy service for monitoring, security events provided by the enterprise system engineering. Configure monitoring information and monitor records and events
12.	Configure load balancing if needed [89]	Configure load balancing if needed	Configure load balancing if needed
13.	Complete configuration of web server(s) for web hosting	Complete configuration of web server(s) for web hosting	Complete configuration of web server(s) for web hosting
14.	Complete web services ACL for accepting specific remote connections	Complete web services ACL for accepting specific remote connections	Complete web services ACL for accepting specific remote connections
15.	Complete specification of web service	Complete specification of wrapper web service and commercial product	Complete specification of wrapper web service and legacy product

(*Continued*)

Table 18.2 (*Continued*)   Enterprise Services Checklist

Step	Enterprise Developed	Commercially Developed	Legacy Systems That Cannot Be Adapted
16.	Publish all web services with all relevant details in enterprise service registry (ESR)	Publish all web services with all relevant details in ESR	Publish all web services with all relevant details in ESR
17.	If the service also faces the Internet, then configure additional protection as required by enterprise policies	If the service also faces the Internet, then configure additional protection as required by enterprise policies	If the service also faces the Internet, then configure additional protection as required by enterprise policies

18.5 Enterprise Service Registry

The ESR was first discussed in Chapter 10. An ESR is where the details of all the services, the service metadata, are stored. Normally, the service is designed with WSDL, XSD, SOAP messages, and other business-logic-related details. On completion (implying design reviews, test vocabulary for annotation, etc.), an enterprise administrator is able to register the web service along with other details in the ESR. These details are provided by the developer and reviewed by the system administrator as part of the registration process. As part of the registration service invocation, an annotation record is generated and stored in the ESMR (see Chapters 10 through 12). To facilitate reuse of any web service, the service is registered in the ESMR for discovery. The Registry standard has been the OASIS Universal Description, Discovery, and Integration (UDDI) [1n] specification, version 3.0.

Before a web service can be used, it is registered in the ESR. The name for the ESR is obtained from appropriate enterprise naming authorities, which must review and provide quality control before registration. The metadata record is updated whenever the web service details are updated.

18.6 Service Discovery: Manual and Automated

Requestor engagement methods with a web service and secure discovery are provided below:

The engagement by which a requestor finds out about a provider is captured below: [5p]

1. The requester and provider entities "become known to each other," in the sense that whichever party initiates the interaction becomes aware of the other party.
   a. If the discovery service is implemented as a registry (such as UDDI), then the provider entity publishes the service description and functional description directly to the discovery service.
      i. In a typical case, the requester agent is the initiator. The requester entity supplies criteria to the discovery service to select a web service description based on its associated functional description, capabilities, and potentially other characteristics. One might locate a service having certain desired functionality or semantics.
      ii. The discovery service returns one or more web service descriptions (or references to them) that meet the specified criteria. If multiple service descriptions are returned, the requester entity selects one, perhaps using additional criteria.
2. The requester entity and provider entity agree on the service description (a WSDL document) and semantics that govern the interaction between the requester agent and the provider agent (in automated systems, a match must be defined by relevant terms; in manual systems, agreement between the agents is required.) *The requester and provider entities may communicate directly with each other, to explicitly agree on the service description and semantics.*
3. The provider entity may publish and offer both the service description and semantics as take-it-or-leave-it "contracts" that the requester entity accepts unmodified as conditions of use.
4. The service description and semantics (excepting the network address of the particular service) may be defined as a standard by an industry organization and used by many requester and provider entities. In this case, the act of the requester and provider entities reaching agreement is accomplished by both parties independently conforming to the same standard (see Figure 18.3).

Web services involve different models depending on different aspects of the interoperability issues between web service agents. The message-oriented model focuses on how web service agents (requester and provider agents) may interact with each other using a message-oriented communication model.

The service-oriented model builds on the basics of message communication by adding the concept of action and service. Essentially, the service model allows us to interpret messages as requests for actions and as responses to those requests. Furthermore, it allows an interpretation of the different aspects of messages to be expressed in terms of different expectations

In order for this process to work, the WSDL, functional descriptions and descriptors, as well as service-level information, must be precise and complete. It is

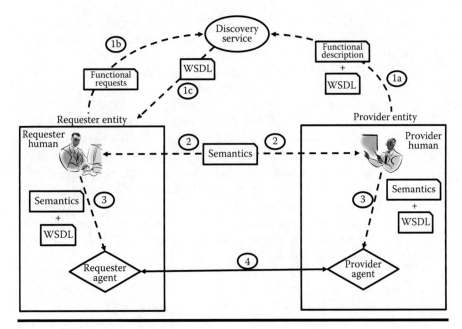

Figure 18.3 Service discovery.

initially provided by the developer and reviewed and possibly modified by the COI before registration.

Relevant tags need to be created and processed for entering the information into the metadata repository.

18.7 Additional Considerations

Authentication is performed as usual via two-way authentication at the TLS 1.2 layer between the end points. For details, refer to Chapters 8, 10 through 12.

Each web service generates a number of messages that provide information pertaining to the web service behavior. Why they are needed, what the messages are, under what conditions they are to be generated, and where they are to be sent are described below.

18.7.1 Agents in the Enterprise Environment

A brief explanation of agents as they are used in the enterprise environment is provided in Chapter 19. There is no direct interaction between the enterprise web services and the agents.

18.7.2 Code Elements of a Service

Figure 18.4 shows a code block development used in the infrastructure build-compatible web services software. The code blocks are provided by the enterprise. The code blocks are functional and not literal, and the code may be developed in any fashion that meets the functional representation. The names are functional designations and apply to both .NET and J2EE applications.

The block marked "web service" contains the service logic, if any. This block is the responsibility of the developer. It contains an error handling routine for healing errors or posting monitor records and preparing return messages. It also contains an exit routine for normal and abnormal exits. This routine creates monitor files and alerts as needed and formulates return messages when needed. Each service has a management interface for setting the monitoring level as "Basic," "Security," and "Enhanced." The levels are hierarchical in that "Security" records only those events marked "Security," "Basic" records those events marked "Basic" plus "Security." "Enhanced" includes all events. Monitor sweep agents read, translate, and submit monitor records to a relational database for recording, and they clean monitor records periodically or on demand. Monitor sweep agents may also request external monitor files, translate them, and submit them to a relational database for recording periodically or on demand. The agents are covered in Chapter 19 and do not interact directly with the web services.

Additional code element details are included in Figure 18.4.

18.7.3 Anatomy of a Service

The basic service elements are given below.

18.7.3.1 Commercial Off-the-Shelf and Legacy Software

Since the enterprise does not have control over these interfaces, all commercial off-the-shelf (COTS) and legacy systems are fronted by an application wrapper or configurable web service. The application wrapper is a full web service or web application that is provided to the code developer and uses the above paradigm. The body of the service then performs whatever translations are necessary to invoke the COTS or legacy system. To the extent possible, the logs are generated in accordance with Log4j and contain the elements specified Chapter 19. In all events, the logs are swept by the log sweep agent and modified to the extent possible for compatibility.

18.7.3.2 Load Balancing Applications

For certain legacy and other applications, access to the service may be through a load balancer. Many applications are amenable to end-point balancing, and end points

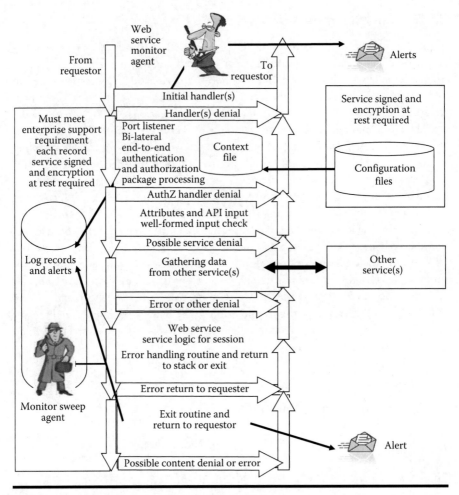

Figure 18.4   Anatomy of a web service.

in these cases are the instances of the application. In some of these applications, the load balancer becomes the target end point and is fronted by application wrapper. The load balancer in certain instances terminates the TLS session from the requester; however, TLS must be reestablished with the specific instance of the application.

18.7.3.3 Web Service Monitor Activities

Security, health, and execution monitors involve several categories of information as follows:

- Data generation
- Automatic response

- Records analysis
- Records review
- Event selection
- Record storage

These are used for the following:

- Security analysis
- Health state monitoring
- Maintenance activities
- Historical record keeping
- Post incident forensics

A specific set of events in the categories above are the responsibility of the web service. These events are enumerated below. For web services, we discuss the following:

- Data storage architecture
- Monitor files
- Developer debug files
- Data generation
- Required monitor records
- Alerts and automatic responses

Other elements such as web servers and agents also contribute to these files; their requirements are given in Chapter 19.

18.8 Orchestration

An orchestration engine is used to encapsulate and execute business process logic. A process can introduce complex rules and workflows that often contain new business rules, exception handling, and transaction management features, involving a number of different application and data sources. Orchestrating web services involves coordination (including asynchronous communications support by the Business Transaction Protocol), management (including administration, change management, and controlling versions), and activity monitoring (including business reporting, or web service auditing). Some tools allow developers to integrate web services into enterprise systems to perform complex transactions and processes. Orchestration is an implementation of choreography within the context of a workflow or business process.

18.9 ELS Interface

J2EE/.NET file authentication/authorization module interfaces are provided in Chapters 10 and 11.

18.10 Access Control List

Data for the ACL originates with the communities of interest (COI). The service must register the ACR described in detail in Chapter 10. The service must have a corresponding ACL. Formats for both of these are provided in Chapter 10.

Chapter 19

Vulnerability Analyses

The sheer volume of regulations that have been created to reduce cyberspace threats is astounding. U.S. Department of Defense [90,91], NIST [2c], Common Criteria [4], and various others [92–94] are just a few. Threat mitigation is undertaken to reduce the attack space and to minimize losses due to cyber activities, either malicious or accidental. From hackers to nation-states, these threats continue to attempt to penetrate networks every day. These threats are growing, evolving, and sophisticated. Loss of information capability, information integrity, and intellectual property is a significant security risk. The material in this chapter is not original and is an adaptation of the Common Criteria methodology first published in 2014 [97].

The goal of this chapter is to describe a process for mitigating many known vulnerabilities and being responsive in mitigating new or newly discovered vulnerabilities. Vulnerability identification is a continuous process whereby threats are reviewed, prioritized, and mitigated through either flaw remediation or modifications to the operating environment. The analyses are reviewed either periodically or on demand as new threats evolve or are identified.

19.1 Vulnerability Causes

The causes of vulnerabilities are numerous. The Common Weakness Enumeration (CWE) [96] was developed to track the causes of vulnerabilities as a guide to their elimination. Vulnerabilities are of concern because they may be turned into exploits that in turn can be used to disrupt IT systems or ex-filtrate their information. Figure 19.1 shows some of the more common causes of these vulnerabilities among nonwebsite software as derived from Reference 96.

Figure 19.2 shows the more common causes of vulnerability among middleware software elements as derived from Reference 96.

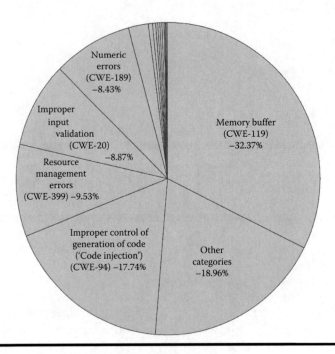

Figure 19.1   Vulnerabilities in nonwebsite software.

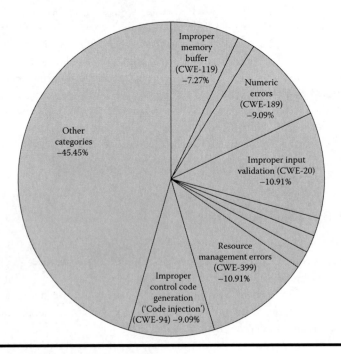

Figure 19.2   Vulnerabilities in middleware.

Identifying discovered and existing vulnerabilities as they relate to software allows software development practices and tools to look for software structures and processes that are exploitable. Many of these tools also check for susceptibility to specific exploits. Proper software development practices will eliminate many of these vulnerabilities. Formal design practices offer additional capabilities to avoid buffer overflows, improper data acceptance, and other software flaw-based vulnerabilities [97]. Nonetheless, tools must be used to verify that the formal methods have been properly used and correctly implemented, or remediation must be applied. These tools are not perfect, and the analysis may miss some vulnerabilities. Their use should be followed by penetration testing. These analyses will reduce the attack space and eliminate some common attack methodologies for the enterprise.

19.2 Related Work

Vulnerability analyses are usually coupled with software quality assurance and fall into three main categories:

1. Static code analysis
2. Dynamic analysis or execution tracing
3. Penetration testing

19.2.1 Static Code Analysis

Static program analysis is the analysis of computer software that is performed without actually executing programs. In most cases, the analysis is performed on some version of the source code, and in other cases some form of the object code. The term is usually applied to analysis performed by an automated tool, with human analysis being called program understanding, program comprehension, or code review.

The sophistication of the analysis performed by static analysis tools is empirical rules. These rules provide the intellectual property associated with the tool set. A growing commercial use of static analysis is verifying the properties of software used in safety-critical computer systems and locating potentially vulnerable code.

These types of analyses are discussed in References 92, 98, and 99.

19.2.2 Dynamic Code Analysis

Dynamic program analysis is the analysis of computer software that is performed by executing programs on a real or virtual processor. For dynamic program analysis to be effective, the target program must be executed with sufficient test inputs to produce interesting behavior. Care must be taken to minimize the effect that instrumentation has on the execution (including temporal properties) of the target program. The sophistication of the analysis performed by tools is both rule-driven and observational-code-insertion-driven (referred to as instrumentation or debug monitors), which provides the intellectual property associated with the tool set. Some dynamic code checker tools are given below:

- HP Security Suite is a suite of tools at various stages of development. QAInspect and WebInspect are generally considered dynamic analysis tools, while DevInspect is considered a static code analysis tool [100].
- IBM Rational AppScan is a suite of application security solutions targeted for different stages of the development lifecycle. The suite includes two main dynamic analysis products [101].
- Intel Thread Checker is a runtime threading error analysis tool that can detect potential data races and deadlocks in multithreaded Windows or Linux applications [102].

19.2.3 Penetration Testing

A penetration test is a method of evaluating computer and network security by simulating an attack on a computer system or network from external and internal threats. The process involves an active analysis of the system for any potential vulnerabilities that could result from poor or improper system configuration. The analyses include known and unknown hardware or software flaws, or operational weaknesses in process or technical countermeasures. This analysis is carried out from the position of a potential attacker using a threat model and can involve active exploitation of security vulnerabilities.

Mosaic [103] has captured a number of tools (including The Penetrator, SAINTexploit™, Metasploit Pro, Core WebVerify™, CORE INSIGHT™ Enterprise, CORE IMPACT® Pro, Core CloudInspect, and others) that will perform such exploitation; each has its pros and cons.

19.2.4 Code Analysis and Penetration Testing Summary

In the analysis of software code, penetration testing, and both static and dynamic analyses to set up the penetration testing are required. Further, this work is not complete because the discovery of vulnerabilities and exploits once the software is fielded must also be submitted to the flaw remediation system and resolved as quickly as possible. To get ahead of this cycle, many software vendors now offer rewards for vulnerability and exploit discovery [104].

19.3 Vulnerability Analysis

All software procured for the enterprise should undergo vulnerability analysis. This is true for commercial, enterprise-developed, and legacy systems to be ported to the enterprise. The developer should perform these analyses as well as provide the flaw remediation (an adaptation of Common Criteria [3]).

While formal methods in the development process and the obtaining of software development credentials such as Capability Maturity Model [105] are valuable, they cannot be used to replace the vulnerability analyses. In an adversarial procurement environment, where the developer either cannot or will not perform these analyses, the developer must agree to allow the procuring agency to perform these analyses or hire a competent laboratory to do the analyses. These costs, if not included in a competitive bid, will be added to the price of the evaluated product when evaluating alternative products for procurement.

The level of effort will depend on the product's complexity. Execution of the vulnerability analyses does not require the execution of a full Common Criteria evaluation, although any such Common Criteria evaluation should include these analyses. The vulnerability analysis described here is based upon the product in its operational environment as opposed to the Target of Evaluation described in Reference 3. The flaw remediation process cannot be performed by anyone other than the software developer. It is assumed that license or purchase of a product will include a support contract that includes flaw remediation provisions if these are not provided with the product.

Within the United States, a number of competent laboratories can do these analyses. These laboratories have tools and testing techniques for penetration testing and will provide a level of assurance on the threat mitigation that will inform decisions. Many are able to conduct these analyses at higher security classification levels and have the capability to sign nondisclosure, noncomplete arrangements with the software developers. Contracting for these analyses would have to include a competitive procurement where the developer is unable or unwilling to perform such tasks. In addition, the purchase of such equipment will be dependent upon successful completion of the vulnerability analysis. Prior vulnerability analysis reports may be used to the extent that the operational environments are similar or modifications to the prior analysis are completed and executed.

Seven laboratories in the United States are licensed under the National Voluntary Laboratory Accreditation Program (NVLAP) [106]. The NVLAP provides third-party accreditation to testing and calibration laboratories. NVLAP accreditation programs are established in response to Congressional mandates, administrative actions by the Federal Government, and requests from government agencies and private-sector organizations.

The NVLAP operates an accreditation system that is compliant with ISO/IEC 17011, *Conformity assessment—General requirements for accreditation bodies accrediting conformity assessment bodies*, which requires the competence of applicant laboratories to be assessed by the accreditation body against all of the requirements of ISO/IEC 17025, *General requirements for the competence of testing and calibration laboratories*.

Figure 19.3 shows the basic vulnerability analysis flow.

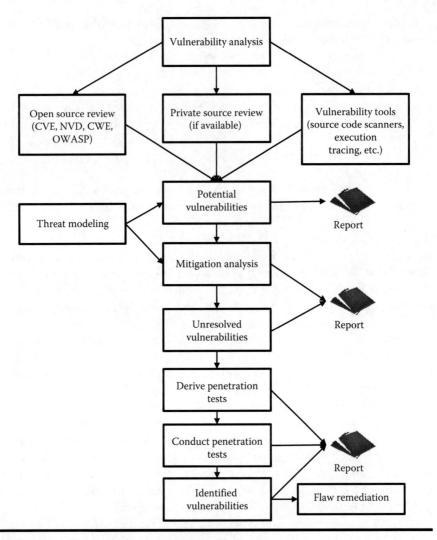

Figure 19.3 Vulnerability analysis process.

19.3.1 Vulnerability Analysis Objective

The objectives of a vulnerability analysis are to do the following:

1. Determine whether the product(s), in its operational environment, has easily identifiable exploitable vulnerabilities
2. Identify those vulnerabilities
3. Begin a remediation process that will close those vulnerabilities

Excessive vulnerabilities may disqualify the product for enterprise use.

19.3.2 Vulnerability Analysis Information

The required information for vulnerability analyses is given below:

- The product(s)
- The guidance documentation
- Identification of all interfaces
- The product(s) suitable for testing
- Harnesses and software instrumentation necessary for testing the product
- Information publicly available to support the identification of potential vulnerabilities

Information that may be used in these analyses is listed below:

- Common Vulnerabilities and Exposures (CVE®) [95] is a dictionary of common names (i.e., CVE identifiers) for publicly known information security vulnerabilities. CVE's common identifiers make it easier to share data across separate network security databases and tools, and provide a baseline for evaluating the coverage of an organization's security tools. If a report from one of the security tools incorporates CVE Identifiers, the tool may quickly and accurately access fix information in one or more separate CVE-compatible databases to remediate the problem.
- National Vulnerability Database (NVD) [107] is the U.S. Government repository of standards-based vulnerability management data represented using the Security Content Automation Protocol (SCAP). This data enables automation of vulnerability management, security measurement, and compliance. NVD includes databases of security checklists, security-related software flaws, misconfigurations, product names, and impact metrics.
- Common Weakness Enumeration (CWE™) [96] is International in scope and free for public use. CWE provides a unified, measurable set of software weaknesses that is enabling more effective discussion, description, selection, and use of software security tools and services that can find these weaknesses in source code and operational systems as well as better understanding and management of software weaknesses related to architecture and design.
- Others include the Open Web Application Security Project [107].

The product developer or evaluator performs additional tests as a result of potential vulnerabilities encountered during the conduct of other parts of the evaluation. The use of the term *guidance* in this process refers to operational guidance and preparative guidance. Potential vulnerabilities may be described in information that is publicly available, or not, and may require skill to exploit, or not. These two aspects are related but distinct. It should not be assumed that, simply because a potential vulnerability is identifiable from information that is publicly available that it can be easily exploited.

19.3.3 Obtaining Vulnerabilities

The product developer or evaluator examines sources of information publicly available to identify potential vulnerabilities in the product. There are many sources of publicly available information, which should be considered, but a minimum set is listed above as input to the analysis. The product developer or evaluator should not constrain his consideration of publicly available information to the above, but should consider any other relevant information available.

The product developer or evaluator records in an evaluation report the identified potential vulnerabilities that are applicable to the product in its operational environment. The product developer or evaluator may use manual methods, source code scanning, execution tracing tools, or all in this analysis, but each of the vulnerabilities described in the evaluation report should be addressed. Each of the vulnerabilities identified as appropriate to the product in its operational environment, is assigned a category and rationale as follows:

1. No further consideration of the potential vulnerability is required if, for example, the product developer or evaluator identifies mitigations in the operational environment, either IT or non-IT, that prevent exploitation of the potential vulnerability in that operational environment. This may include mitigations within the product itself.
2. For any reasons, the potential vulnerabilities may be excluded from further consideration if the potential vulnerability is not applicable in the operational environment.
3. Otherwise, the evaluator records the potential vulnerability for further consideration. This list of potential vulnerabilities applicable to the product in its operational environment, which can be used as an input into penetration testing activities, is reported in the evaluation report.

19.3.4 Deriving Penetration Tests

The product developer or evaluator derives penetration tests that are based on the search above for potential vulnerabilities, threat modeling activities, and other analysis methods. The product developer or evaluator prepares for penetration testing as necessary to determine the susceptibility of the product, in its operational environment, to the potential vulnerabilities identified during the search of the sources of information publicly available.

The product developer or evaluator produces penetration test documentation for the tests based on the list of potential vulnerabilities in sufficient detail to enable the tests to be repeatable. The test documentation includes the following:

1. Identification of the potential vulnerability the product is being tested for
2. Instructions to connect and set up all required test equipment as required for conducting the penetration test

3. Instructions to establish all penetration test prerequisite initial conditions
4. Instructions to stimulate the product
5. Instructions for observing the behavior of the product
6. Descriptions of all expected results and the necessary analysis to be performed on the observed behavior for comparison against expected results
7. Instructions to conclude the test and establish the necessary posttest state for the product

The product developer or evaluator conducts penetration testing based on the list of potential vulnerabilities identified above and prepares an evaluation report on these tests. Where, as a result of evaluation, the product developer or evaluator discovers a potential vulnerability, and this is reported in the evaluation report as a residual vulnerability. The vulnerability is reported as a flaw in the flaw remediation system with a priority commensurate with its potential for exploit and the consequences of a successful exploit.

19.3.5 Continuous Updating

The product developer or evaluator reexamines sources of information publicly available to identify potential vulnerabilities in the product, either periodically or on demand. The analysis may be on demand when critical vulnerabilities or damaging exploits in similar products have been identified, changes in the operational environment are made, or other changes requiring further analysis are made.

19.3.6 Review and Approve

The enterprise representative examines the results of the evaluation report and all penetration testing to determine that the product, in its operational environment, is resistant to an attacker appropriate to the environment. If the results reveal that the product, in its operational environment, has vulnerabilities exploitable by an attacker appropriate to the environment, then remedial action must be taken by the product developer. The enterprise representative ensures that periodic reevaluation as provided above is undertaken.

For critical and trusted software such as the STS or services within the EAS, the enterprise representative may, at his option, conduct or procure independent penetration testing, including repeating some of the described and independently derived tests. The results of these tests may lead to the identification of vulnerabilities that are subject to the flaw remediation processes described below.

19.4 Flaw Remediation

The flaw remediation process is the responsibility of the product developer—an adaptation of Common Criteria [3].

19.4.1 Flaw Remediation Objectives

The objective of this flaw remediation is to demonstrate that the product developer has established procedures that describe the tracking of security flaws, the identification of corrective actions, and the distribution of corrective action information to product users. Additionally, this process demonstrates that the product developer's procedures provide for the corrections of security flaws, the receipt of flaw reports from product users, assurance that the corrections introduce no new security flaws, establishment of a point of contact for each product user, and timely issue of corrective actions to product users. The administrative tracking and reporting of flaws may be outsourced, but the developer must be involved in the corrective actions and must be included in the developer's quality control system.

For the developer to be able to act appropriately upon security flaw reports from product users, product users need to understand how to submit security flaw reports to the product developer and product developers need to know how to receive these reports. Flaw remediation guidance addressed to the product user ensures that product users are aware of how to communicate with the developer; flaw remediation procedures describe the product developer's role in such communication.

The flaw remediation process as applied to security issues is shown in Figure 19.4.

19.4.2 Flaw Remediation Information

The required information for evaluation of flaw remediation processes is given below:

1. The flaw remediation procedures documentation
2. Flaw remediation guidance documentation

The product developer may use automated flaw remediation tracking systems such as trouble ticketing software or may manually track such flaws. However, it is expected that any flaw not remedied with 10 working days will be referred to the quality assurance tracking system for formalized assignment of actions and priorities, and timely reviews to ensure progress in resolution of open items. Security flaws normally have the highest assigned priority for remediation in high assurance systems. Remediation may be code changes, patch updates, configuration changes, or other remedies outside of the product in the operational environment. The enterprise representative may reject the last approach depending on its impact.

19.4.3 A Flaw Remediation Process

The product developer provides a flaw remediation process:

1. That describes the procedures used to track all reported security flaws in each release of the product. The procedures describe the actions that are

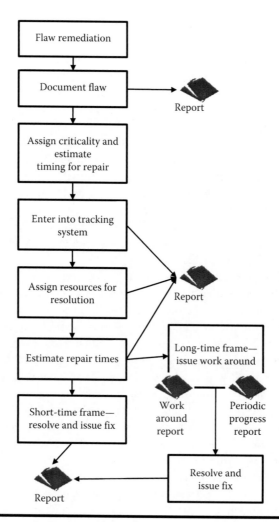

Figure 19.4   Flaw remediation process.

taken by the product developer from the time each suspected security flaw is reported until the time that it is resolved. This includes the flaw's entire time frame, from initial detection, through ascertaining that the flaw is a security flaw, to resolution of the security flaw. If a flaw is discovered not to be security-relevant, there is no need (for the purposes of the flaw remediation requirements) for the flaw remediation procedures to track it further; however, there must be an explanation of why the flaw is not security-relevant.

2. That describes the nature and effect of each security flaw, as well as the status of finding a correction to that flaw. The procedures identify the actions that

are taken by the product developer to describe the nature and effects of each security flaw in sufficient detail to be able to reproduce it. The description of the nature of a security flaw addresses whether it is an error in the documentation, a flaw in the design of the product, a flaw in the implementation of the product, etc. The description of the security flaw's effects identifies the portions of the product that are affected and how those portions are affected.

3. That when applied, these procedures would identify the status of finding a correction to each security flaw. The flaw remediation procedures identify the different stages of security flaws. This differentiation includes, at least, suspected security flaws that have been reported, suspected security flaws that have been confirmed to be security flaws, and security flaws whose solutions have been implemented. It is permissible that additional stages (e.g., flaws that have been reported but not yet investigated, flaws that are under investigation, security flaws for which a solution has been found but not yet implemented) be included.

4. That requires corrective actions to be identified for each of the security flaws. Corrective action may consist of a repair to the hardware, firmware, or software portions of the product, a modification of product guidance, or both. Corrective action that constitutes modifications to product guidance (e.g., details of procedural measures to be taken to obviate the security flaw) includes both those measures serving as only interim solutions (until the repair is issued) as well as those serving as permanent solutions (where it is determined that the procedural measure is the best solution). If the source of the security flaw is a documentation error, the corrective action consists of an update of the affected product guidance. If the corrective action is a procedural measure, this measure includes an update made to the affected product guidance to reflect these corrective procedures.

5. That describes the methods used to provide flaw information, corrections, and guidance on corrective actions to product users. The necessary information about each security flaw consists of its description, the prescribed corrective action, and any associated guidance on implementing the correction. Product users may be provided with such information, correction, and documentation updates in any of several ways, such as their being posted to a website, their being sent to product users, or arrangements being made for the product developer to install the correction. In cases where the means of providing this information requires action to be initiated by the product user, product guidance must be adequate to ensure that it contains instructions for retrieving the information. The only metric for assessing the adequacy of the method used for providing the information, corrections, and guidance is that there is a reasonable expectation that product users can obtain or receive it.

6. That describes a means by which the product developer receives from product users reports and enquiries of suspected security flaws in the product.

The procedures ensure that product users have a means by which they can communicate with the product developer. By having a means of contact with the developer, the user can report security flaws, enquire about the status of security flaws, or request corrections to flaws. This means of contact may be part of a more general contact facility for reporting non security-related problems.

7. That includes a procedure requiring timely response and automatic distribution of security flaw reports and the associated corrections to registered users who might be affected by the security flaw. The issue of timeliness applies to the issuance of both security flaw reports and the associated corrections. However, these need not be issued at the same time. It is recognized that flaw reports should be generated and issued as soon as an interim solution is found, even if that solution is as drastic as turning off the product. Likewise, when a more permanent (and less drastic) solution is found, it should be issued without undue delay. It is unnecessary to restrict the recipients of the reports and associated corrections to only those product users who might be affected by the security flaw; it is permissible that all product users be given such reports and corrections for all security flaws, provided such is done in a timely manner.

8. That results in automatic distribution of the reports and associated corrections to the registered product users who might be affected. Automatic distribution does not mean that human interaction with the distribution method is not permitted. In fact, the distribution method could consist entirely of manual procedures, perhaps through a closely monitored procedure with prescribed escalation upon the lack of issue of reports or corrections. It is unnecessary to restrict the recipients of the reports and associated corrections to only those product users who might be affected by the security flaw; it is permissible that all product users be given such reports and corrections for all security flaws, provided such is done automatically.

19.4.4 Flaw Remediation Quality System

The product developer provides reporting processes:

1. That ensure reported security flaws are remediated and the remediation procedures are issued to product users. The flaw remediation procedures cover not only those security flaws discovered and reported by developer personnel, but also those reported by product users. The procedures are sufficiently detailed so that the developer describes how remediation of each reported security flaw is ensured. The procedures contain reasonable steps that show progress leading to the eventual, inevitable resolution. The procedures describe the process that is made from the point at which the suspected security flaw is determined to be a security flaw to the point at which it is resolved.

2. That ensure that the product users are issued remediation procedures for each security flaw. The procedures describe the process that is taken from the point

at which a security flaw is resolved to the point at which the remediation procedures are provided. The procedures for delivering remediation procedures should be consistent with the security objectives.

3. That provide safeguards that any corrections to these security flaws do not introduce any new flaws. Through analysis, testing, or a combination of the two, the developer may reduce the likelihood that adverse effects are introduced when a security flaw is corrected.

19.4.5 Flaw Remediation Reporting

The product developer provides remediation guidance:

1. That describes a means by which product users report to the developer any suspected security flaws in the product. The guidance ensures that product users have a means by which they can communicate with the product developer so they can report security flaws, enquire about the status of security flaws, or request corrections to flaws.

2. That describes a means by which product users may register with the developer, to be eligible to receive security flaw reports and corrections. Enabling the product users to register with the developer simply means having a way for each product user to provide the developer with a point of contact so the developer can provide product users with information related to security flaws that might affect them, along with any corrections to the security flaw. Registering the product user may be accomplished as part of the standard procedures that product users undergo to identify themselves to the developer, for the purposes of registering a software license, or for obtaining updates and other useful information.

There need not be one registered product user per installation of the product; it would be sufficient if there were one registered product user for an organization. It should be noted that product users need not register; they must only be provided with a means of doing so. However, users who choose to register must be directly sent the information (or a notification of its availability).

19.4.6 Review and Approve

The enterprise representative examines the results of the above actions to determine that the product, in its operational environment, has sufficient flaw remediation. If the results reveal that the product, in its operational environment, has insufficient flaw remediation, then remedial action must be taken by the product developer or the product may be replaced.

19.5 Summary

This chapter has provided a set of processes by which the enterprise can field relatively vulnerability-free software, at least to the extent of known vulnerabilities and exploits. New exploits are subject to temporary solutions and become part of the flaw remediation system where they are reported and monitored until a satisfactory solution is achieved. It is not anticipated that the enterprise will be 100% exploit free as a result of this process alone. Additional measures, including firewalls, ports and protocol restrictions, and some communication scanning may be required. This process should, however, reduce the attack space significantly. The implementation will have to be monitored and evaluated as it proceeds. This includes the tracking of exploits, the response of the software remediation system, and the degree to which the vulnerability was knowable before the exploit, as well as newly discovered vulnerabilities. It is expected that the analyses listed in this chapter will need refinement based upon that feedback.

Chapter 20

An Enterprise
Support Desk

The ESD is the combination of people, hardware, deployed software agents, and software displays that maintain the health of the enterprise web service operations. The ESD is a consumer of the monitoring data. It is both proactive and reactive. It requires integration with hardware and software monitoring systems, including the expected functioning of the applications and services in the enterprise. It was realized early on that an integrated help desk function would be needed for enterprise solutions. It was also clear that many of the details of the enterprise solution needed to be in place. The details began to emerge in 2011 with the initial monitoring requirements [109] and the help desk architecture [110].

20.1 Monitoring

This chapter will initially deal with monitoring processes and required monitoring data. The structure of the support desk follows in Section 20.9. In order to facilitate the ESD as an information user in the enterprise, a series of agents on desktops and service machines, a knowledge base system, display workstations, and alert policies are needed. These requirements are varied and must be integrated with hardware and operating system health monitoring data. For this reason, the enterprise will use service monitoring software, which is flexible, configurable, expandable, and adaptable and includes information from health state monitoring activities. Further, every desktop or laptop within the enterprise will have embedded agents

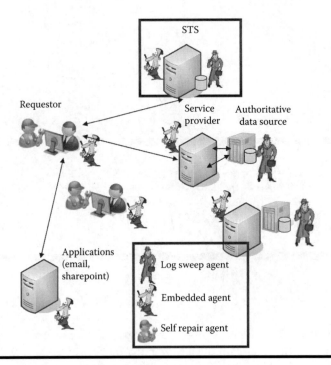

Figure 20.1 Deployed agent architecture.

for self-help and repair of common problems, as well as software that allows ESD principals to take control of the hardware unit for the following purpose:

- Auditing hardware and software configurations
- Providing troubleshooting assistance

Figure 20.1 shows the architecture of the agents for services management. There are separate agents for hardware health monitoring and two types of agents for each service. The first agent is embedded in the service itself for provision of alerts and internal monitoring of service data. The second agent is installed on the server and provides a sweep of monitor files, either periodically or on demand. There is a commercial implementation of this process [111].

All ESD personnel must abide by enterprise security policies, including certification, bilateral authentication, and SAML authorization for access control.

Figure 20.2 illustrates how the ESD accesses the stored data repository.

20.2 Data Repository System

The data repository system is an integrated source of all information on the operation of the enterprise. It will be updated by the ESD and accessible to all the ESD

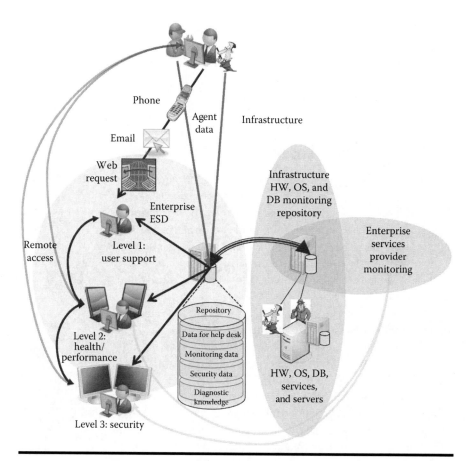

Figure 20.2   Support desk and information repository.

and other entities with appropriate access credentials. Instrumented agents feed the database on a schedule or on demand. This subsection deals with information requirements for the service monitoring.

20.3 Information for Service Monitoring

The knowledge base is where all information related to the enterprise web services is stored. This includes the following

- Hardware/software current status from computing center
- Current reports on test activities, including response times, frequency of test, health state monitors, etc.
- Current reports of usage data from service agent monitors and service monitors, including number of users, session times, response times, etc.

- Hardware/software historical data
- Current and past trouble reports
- A list of current alerts for the entire enterprise
- Historical data on alerts
- Configuration information

20.4 Centralized Repository

Agents have been discussed previously. Two specific agents support the ESD.

Embedded agents: The embedded agent sits on the Java or .NET stacks and monitors the performance of the server and its threads. It should be configured to provide performance, connectivity, and anomaly data to the log file for the service. It is unaware of sequence numbers or events transpiring within the service itself. It will be also be configured to provide alert data as discussed below.

Monitor sweep agents: Figure 20.3 shows the placement of monitor sweep agents in the confines of the enterprise, even though they may reach outside the enterprise on external calls. It is the job of the monitor sweep agents to read, translate, and submit monitor records to the centralized database. There will be no translation for enterprise-developed services, and translation will be minimal when commercial products allow for standard configurations. However, translation may be extensive for proprietary types of monitor data in external sources.

Data provided by the agents is insufficient to maintain high availability and to monitor security. The services themselves, which have the context for many events, must provide inputs to the monitoring data.

20.5 Services by Type

Within the enterprise, there are three basic types of services:

- Web applications
- Aggregation services
- Exposure services

The web application is set up to communicate with a user's browser in HTML. It may call aggregation services or exposure services. Each of these communicates using SOAP/XML. For the purposes of this chapter, the web application will be treated as an aggregation service.

For external services, monitor sweep agent: Uses interface for external log and monitor files, translates, and submits to relational data base for recording periodically or on demand

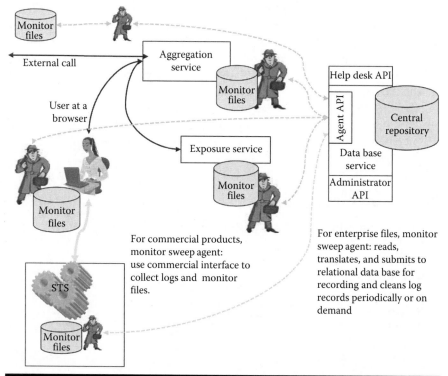

Figure 20.3 **Web service monitoring sweep model.**

An aggregation service is defined as a service whose function is to provide data to the user from a number of authoritative data (AD) sources using a series of exposure services or aggregation services and may include a number of widgets or other display code segments.

An exposure service is defined as a service whose primary function is to provide synthesized data to the user from one or more authoritative content sources. This service may not call other exposure services or aggregation services, but it may directly interface with one or more ACSs.

20.6 Data Keeping Requirements

In order for the agents and administrators to keep the various monitor and configuration files straight, the files must follow a naming scheme and a location scheme as well as a specific file pattern.

20.7 Naming Schema

Each application will have a root name from which other names are derived. The root name should be reflective of the application and include within it a unique identifier of the original applications for which the code was initially developed; for example, meta data environment (root name = MDE), enterprise finance system (root name = EFS). After some time, the number of applications may force the consultation of a registration list to avoid ambiguity.

The extended name will include the root name concatenated to the code name related to the service or usage of the code; for example, EFS web application (EFSWebApp), MDE search application service (MDESearch).

20.8 Monitor Activities

Security monitors involve several classes or monitor issue areas as follows:

- Data generation
- Automatic response
- Records analysis
- Records review
- Event selection
- Record storage

Monitor files: Monitor files will be stored in application storage files similarly to configuration files as follows:

Activity logs as defined below:

```
{Storage root}: /{root name} files/{extendedname}Monitor/
{extendedname}Monitor.log
Ex: Root:/EFSfiles/EFSWebAppMonitor/EFSWebAppMonitor.log
```

An agent present on the server will either periodically or on demand be configured to sweep the log file and send it to the enterprise database for storage and later analysis.

Developer debug files: Debug and other messages added to the required monitoring files are permitted and will be sent to the file:

```
{Storage root}:/{root name} files/{extendedname}Monitor/
{extendedname}MonitorSUP/ {extendedname}MonitorSUP.log
Ex: Root:/EFSfiles/EFSWebAppMonitor/EFSWebAppMonitorSUP/
EFSWebAppMonitorSUP.log
```

Debug files will follow the log4j format provided. An agent present on the server will either periodically or on demand be configured to sweep the monitor file and send it to the enterprise database (or to a database of the developer's choice) for storage and later analysis.

20.8.1 Data Generation

This activity defines requirements for recording the occurrence of relevant events that take place. The security level of recording is the default and must be recorded in the file name described above. It may be supplemented by the basic level of data recording as ordered by the ESD. The basic level is selectable through administrative API with administrator privilege. The activity identifies the level of monitoring, enumerates the types of events that will be monitorable by the service (except as noted—some data may come from agents), and identifies the minimum set of monitor-related information that should be provided within various monitor record types. The enhanced level is selectable through administrative API with administrator privilege and invokes additional details in the monitor records. This Verbose level (the greatest level of data provided in monitor records) is selectable and is automatically triggered with any security alert. For enterprise systems, monitor records are required for all security-relevant events. Basic monitoring will add those events to the security events. Enhanced monitoring will record all events in Table 20.1. A Sequence Number, which is a 16-digit alphanumeric, identifies the overall transaction stream uniquely (Sn). Sn is given by
Concatenate:

> ip address of application server +
> URI of service operation +
> timestamp[yyyyMMddHHmmssSSS] +
> thread ID +
> Common Name of initial service requester

Any error messages returned to a requester inviting them to call the help desk would refer to the Common Name + URI + time approximation yyyyMMddHHmm.

```
If Sequence Number.eq.Null) then Sequence Number = ip
address//'$.'//URI//'$.'//timestamp//'$.'//thread ID//'$.'//
Common Name
```

Table 20.1 provides the events that require monitor records for this area:
Note:
Let Tn =Thread Number
Let Sn =Sequence Number
Let AN = Active Entity Name
Let EV = Event Name
Let ID = ID of Service Requester
Let IDr = ID of Service Requested

Let d = date/time in [yyyy-MM-dd-hh-mm-ss-"."ff(5digits)] (26 characters)
Let OP1 = Other Pertinent Data 1
Let OP2 = Other Pertinent Data 2
Let OP3 = Other Pertinent Data 3
Let OP4 = Other Pertinent Data 4
Let OP5 = Other Pertinent Data 5
Let EM = Exception Message
Let Gp = Group or Role for Access
Let CDN = Cert Domain Name
Let CPK = Cert Public Key
Let CAPII = Complete API Input
Let CAPIR = Complete API Request
Let CAPIr = Complete API Return
Let SAML = Complete SAML Token
Let OPEN = Complete Open Token
Let IDR = ID of Service Requested
Let Rf = Reason for Authorization Failure
Enumeration (Expired SAML, Tampered SAML, Expired Open Token, Timeout, No Matching Groups, Unrecognized SAML, Unrecognized Open Token, Other)
Let Rfi = Reason for Failed Session Initiation
Enumeration (Timeout, Server Error, Corrupted Input, Unknown, Other)
Let Rfe = Reason for Premature Shutdown
Enumeration (Timeout, Hardware Issue, Server Error, Corrupted Input, Unknown, Other)
Let SV = Other Security Violation
Enumeration (Timeout, Luna Hardware Issue, Server Error, Corrupted Input, Unknown, Other)
Let Ta = Monitor Storage Threshold Exceeded
Enumeration (80%, 90%, 100%)
Let XMLDSig = XML Digital Signature Block

Content for all records includes: Thread Number, Sequence Number, Active Entity Name, Event Name, ID of Service Requester, Date/Time, Other pertinent data, XMLDSig.*

In addition, the service developer must meet any requirements of the enterprise.

The developer will determine the content of the enhanced and verbose monitor providing information necessary for debugging and forensics that apply to the service itself.

---

* The XMLDSig is for tamper protection and may be inserted by the service or the logging routine using the private key and certificate of the service.

Table 20.1 Partial List Monitor Records[a]

Event/Category	Content
Start-up of the monitor functions within the service Monitor Levels: • None • Alerts and Inputs • Trace **Category = Basic** **Responsibility = Embedded Agent**	Event Name = "Start Up Monitor" OP1 = ID of Service Requester OP2 = Level of Monitor OP3 = {developer use} OP4 = {developer use} OP5 = {developer use}
Change in monitor functions within the service **Category = Basic** **Responsibility = Web Service**	Event Name = "Shut Down Monitor" OP1 = ID of Service Requester OP2 = Level of Monitor OP3 = {developer use} OP4 = {developer use} OP5 = {developer use}
Session initiation activities **Category = Basic** **Responsibility = Web Service**	Event Name = "Session Initiated" OP1 = ID of Service Requester OP2 = {developer use} OP3 = {developer use} OP4 = {developer use} OP5 = {developer use}
Input malformed **Category = Basic[b]** **Responsibility = Web Service**	Event Name = "Malformed Input" OP1 = ID of Service Requester OP2 = input that triggered the error OP3 = {developer use} OP4 = {developer use} OP5 = {developer use}
Output malformed **Category = Basic[c]** **Responsibility = Web Service**	Event Name = "Malformed Output" OP1= ID of Service Requester OP2 = output that triggered the error OP3 = {developer use} OP4 = {developer use} OP5 = {developer use}
Session complete **Category = Basic** **Responsibility = Web Service**	Event Name = "Session Complete" OP1 = ID of Service Requester OP2 = {developer use} OP3 = {developer use} OP4 = {developer use} OP5 = {developer use}

(Continued)

Table 20.1 (*Continued*)   Partial List Monitor Records[a]

Event/Category	Content
Any exceptions due to Java or supporting programs **Category = Basic[c]** **Responsibility = Web Service and all Handlers as well as web server**	Event Name = "Exception" OP1 = ID of Service Requester OP2 = Exception Message OP3 = data specific to exception or cure OP4 = data specific to exception or cure OP5 = data specific to exception or cure Return to Next level Server Problem—call help desk (Sequence Number = SN) {Unless self-healing} or Server Problem—retry (Common Name + URI + time approximation yyyyMMddHHmm.) {Unless self-healing}
Any known violations of security policy, including all instances of alerts and others as needed. **Category = Security** **Responsibility = Web Service and all Handlers as well as web server**	Event Name = "Security Violation" OP1 = ID of Service Requester OP2 = {developer use} OP3 = {developer use} OP4 = {developer use} OP5 = {developer use} Return to Next level Server Problem—call help desk (Common Name + URI + time approximation yyyyMMddHHmm.)
Authorization **Category = Enhanced** **Responsibility = SAML Validation Handler**	Event Name = "Authorization" OP1 = ID of Service Requester OP2 = SAML OP3 = Open Token OP4 = {developer use} OP5 = {developer use}
Failed authentication **Category = Security** **Responsibility = web server**	OP1 = ID of Service Requester OP2 = Requester Cert identity OP3 = Requester Cert Public Key OP4 = Requester Cert Revocation Date OP5 = Result of Cert Validation Check Return to Next level Server Problem—call help desk (Common Name + URI + time approximation yyyyMMddHHmm.)
Authentication **Category = Enhanced** **Responsibility = web server**	Event Name = Authentication OP1 = ID of Service Requester OP2 = Requester Cert Identity OP3 = Requester Cert Public Key OP4 = Requester Cert Revocation Date OP5 = Result of Cert Validation Check

(*Continued*)

Table 20.1 (*Continued*)   Partial List Monitor Records[a]

Event/Category	Content
Failed authorization **Category** = **Security** **Responsibility** = **SAML Validation Handler**	OP1 = ID of Service Requester OP2 = SAML OP3 = Open Token OP4 = {developer use} OP5 = {developer use} Return to Next level Server Problem — call help desk (Common Name + URI + time approximation yyyyMMddHHmm.)
Thread Establishment[c] **Category** = **Enhanced** **Responsibility** = **Embedded Agent**	Event Name = Thread Established OP1 = ID of Service Requester OP2 = Complete API Input OP3 = {agent developer use} OP4 = {agent developer use} OP5 = {agent developer use}
Service Request — each **Category** = **Enhanced** **Responsibility** = **Web Service**	Event Name = Service Request OP1 = ID of Service Requester OP2 = Complete API Request OP3 = {developer use} OP4 = {developer use} OP5 = {developer use}
Service Response — each If the thread, and sequence as well as the ID of the service are the same the wait time is the time difference between this and the previous record **Category** = **Enhanced** **Responsibility** = **Web Service**	Event Name = "Service Response" OP1 = ID of the Service Requester OP2 = Complete API return OP3 = {developer use} OP4 = {developer use} OP5 = {developer use}
Content download[d] — used when notification or other messages are sent to requester. **Category** = **Basic** **Responsibility** = **Web Service**	Event Name = "Content Download" OP1 = Content Name OP2 = Unique ID, if one assigned OP3 = {developer use} OP4 = {developer use} OP5 = {developer use}

(*Continued*)

Table 20.1 (*Continued*)   Partial List Monitor Records[a]

Event/Category	Content
Message Acknowledgment— used when notification or other messages are sent to requester. May be MAC notices, download restrictions, etc. **Category = Basic** **Responsibility = Web Service**	Event Name = "Message Acknowledgment" OP1 = Acknowledgment Message OP2 = Acknowledgment Response (Yes, No, etc.—may only be one (ok)) OP3 = {developer use} OP4 = {developer use} OP5 = {developer use}
Health State Performance Monitors	
Final Rollout Performance Data A program segment could be computational or waiting for inputs, etc. **Category = Enhanced** **Responsibility = Web Service**	Event Name = "Performance" OP1 = Program Segment Name 1 plus delta t1 OP2 = Program Segment Name 2 plus delta t2 OP3 = Program Segment Name 3 plus delta t3 OP4 = Program Segment Name 4 plus delta t4 OP5 = Program Segment Name 5 plus delta t5
Timeouts and work around Timeouts may or may not occur **Category = Enhanced** **Responsibility = Web Service**	Event Name = "Timeouts" OP1 = Timeout occurrence location OP2 = Timeout delta t OP3 = Workaround (e.g., cache data, default value, etc.) OP4 = {developer use} OP5 = {developer use}
Developer Debug Records	
Developer Debug Records[e] Stored in: {Storage root}:/{root name} files/{extendedname}Monitor/ {extendedname}MonitorSUP/ {extendedname}MonitorSUP. log **Category = Enhanced** **Responsibility = Web Service—optional**	Event Name = [Name Provided by Developer] OP1 = {developer use} OP2 = {developer use} OP3 = {developer use} OP4 = {developer use} OP5 = {developer use}

[a] Each record is digitally signed by the service.
[b] The developer requirements for these errors are covered in a separate section, following alert data.
[c] The Java agent must trap it on the thread, or the server must report it.
[d] Content objects here are meant to include doc, ppt, pdf, jpeg, etc. and not the normal data transfers associated with authoritative databases.
[e] Optional.

20.8.2 Log 4j Specification

Let Tn = Thread Number
Let Sn = Sequence Number
Let AN = Active Entity Name
Let EV = Event Name
Let ID = ID of Service Requester
Let d = date/time in [yyyy-MM-dd-hh-mm-ss-"."ff(5digits)]
Let TZ = Time Zone 3 char
Let OP1 = Other Pertinent Data 1
Let OP2 = Other Pertinent Data 2
Let OP3 = Other Pertinent Data 3
Let OP4 = Other Pertinent Data 4
Let OP5 = Other Pertinent Data 5
Let Dl = Delimiters ['!!']
Let XMLDSig = the XML Digital Signature Block

For both
If M = printf (%AN%Dl %EV%Dl %OP1%Dl %OP2 %Dl%OP3 %Dl %OP4%Dl %OP5%Dl %XMLDSig)
Then M transfers to the logging server handler (see Table 20.2).

Table 20.2 Example from Monitor Table

Start-up of the monitor functions within the service Monitor Levels: • None • Alerts and Inputs • Trace **Category = Basic**	Thread Number, Sequence Number, Active Entity Name, Event Name, ID of Service Requester, Date/Time, Other pertinent data, XMLDSig
	Event Name = "Start Up Monitor" OP1 = ID of Service Requester OP2 = Level of Monitor OP3 = {developer use} OP4 = {developer use} OP5 = {developer use}
Change in monitor functions within the service **Category = Basic**	Thread Number, Sequence Number, Active Entity Name, Event Name, ID of Service Requester, Date/Time, Other pertinent data, XMLDSig
	Event Name = "Shut Down Monitor" OP1 = ID of Service Requester OP2 = Level of Monitor OP3 = {developer use} OP4 = {developer use} OP5 = {developer use}

20.8.3 Alerts and Automatic Response

Certain activities that may happen are considered security violations and will require the computer or network to send alerts and automatically respond. Activities such as failed authentication, attempts to access data beyond access authority, and the potential loss of data due to resource constraints are typical examples. Automated responses may include, among other things, session termination, suspension of privileges, and in extreme cases, shutting down computers and other equipment. Table 20.3 provides the events that require alerting and automatic response. Italicized events are not the responsibility of the service.

20.8.4 SMTP Format for Alerts

The service, at boot-up, should be configured to open a mutually authenticated TLS session with the help desk mail processor (see Table 20.4).

Let Tn = Thread Number
Let Sn = Sequence Number
Let AN = Active Entity Name
Let EV = Event Name
Let ID = ID of Service Requester
Let d = date/time in [yyyy-MM-dd-hh-mm-ss-"."ff(5digits)]
Let OP1 = Other Pertinent Data 1
Let OP2 = Other Pertinent Data 2
Let OP3 = Other Pertinent Data 3
Let OP4 = Other Pertinent Data 4
Let OP5 = Other Pertinent Data 5
Let XMLDSig = the XML Digital Signature Block

20.8.5 Requirements for Java and Service Exception Errors

The developer should be required to provide a number of assurance processes before deploying a service in the operational environment.

Requirement 1: The developer must do a static code analysis and source code scan for vulnerabilities that is based on the CVE.* This report is to be delivered to the enterprise operators with mitigation and/or the rationale for not mitigating for all identified vulnerabilities.

---

* Common Vulnerabilities and Exposures (CVE) and their usage are described in Chapter 18.

Table 20.3 Alert Data[a]

Event	Alert Content	Response	Message Body[b]
Failed authentication **Responsibility = web server**	Thread Number, Sequence Number, Active Entity Name, Event Name, ID of Service Requester, Date/Time, User Entity Identity, Other pertinent data	Server Problem—call help desk (Common Name + URI + time approximation yyyyMMddHHmm.)	Subject: Alert message—EV OP1 = ID of Service Requester OP2 = Requester Cert identity OP3 = Requester Cert Public Key OP4 = Requester Cert Revocation Date OP5 = Result of Cert Validation Check XMLDSig
Failed authorization **Responsibility = SAML Validation Handler**	Thread Number, Sequence Number, Active Entity Name, Event Name, ID of Service Requester, Date/Time, Reason for failure of the event, Other pertinent data	Server Problem—call help desk (Common Name + URI + time approximation yyyyMMddHHmm.)	Subject: Alert message—EV OP1 = ID of Service Requester OP2 = SAML OP3 = Open Token OP4 = {developer use} OP5 = {developer use} XMLDSig
Failed session initiation activities **Responsibility = whoever has visibility**	Thread Number, Sequence Number, Active Entity Name, Event Name, ID of Service Requester, Date/Time, Reason for failure of the event, Other pertinent data	Server Problem—call help desk (Common Name + URI + time approximation yyyyMMddHHmm.)	Subject: Alert message—EV OP1 = ID of Service Requester OP2 = Complete API Input OP3 = Indicated data OP4 = {developer use} OP5 = {developer use} XMLDSig

(Continued)

Table 20.3 (*Continued*) **Alert Data**[a]

Event	Alert Content	Response	Message Body[b]
Abnormal or Premature Session Shutdown[c] **Responsibility = Agent Produced**	Thread Number, Sequence Number[d], Active Entity Name, Event Name, ID of Service Requester, Date/time, Reason for shutdown of the event, Other pertinent data	Server Problem – call help desk (Common Name + URI + time approximation $yyyyMMddHHmm$.)	Subject: Alert message-EV OP1 = ID of Service Requester OP2 = Reason for Shutdown OP3 = Indicated data OP4 = {agent developer use} OP5 = {agent developer use} XMLDSig
Any known violations of security policy not otherwise listed here. **Responsibility = Web Service and all Handlers as well as web server**	Thread Number, Sequence Number, Active Entity Name, Event Name, ID of Service Requester, Date/Time, Violation, Other pertinent data	Server Problem – call help desk (Common Name + URI + time approximation $yyyyMMddHHmm$.)	Subject: Alert message-EV OP1 = ID of Service Requester OP2 = Security Violation OP3 = {developer use} OP4 = {developer use} OP5 = {developer use} XMLDSig
Monitor Data Full[e] (Indicated by file write error) **Responsibility = Agent Produced**	Thread Number, Sequence Number,[d] Active Entity Name, Event Name, ID of Service Requester, Date/Time, Other pertinent data	Activity shutdown	Subject: Alert message-EV OP1 = ID of Service Requester OP2 = Ta OP3 = Indicated data OP4 = {agent developer use} OP5 = {agent developer use} XMLDSig

(Continued)

Table 20.3 (Continued) Alert Data[a]

Event	Alert Content	Response	Message Body[b]
Record has been tampered with[f] **Responsibility = Monitor Agent or database produced**	Thread Number, Sequence Number,[d] Active Entity Name, Event Name, ID of Service Requester, Date/Time, Missing Monitor Record, Other pertinent data	Server Problem—call help desk (Common Name + URI + time approximation yyyyMMddHHmm.)	Subject: Alert message—EV OP1 = ID of Service Requester OP2 = Missing numbers OP3 = Indicated data OP4 = {agent developer use} OP5 = {agent developer use} XMLDSig

a Any service-detected unrecoverable event in this table automatically triggers enhanced monitor mode for the particular service.

b SMTP; see below—all alerts use the same message format.

c If the error routine does not trap the need for shutdown, then the Java agent must trap it on the thread, or the server must report it.

d May not be available.

e This data may not be available, and if it is, it will come from the Log4J routine—probably from a write error if the disk full error does not occur. Log4J is a Java-based logging utility. It was originally written by Ceki Gülcü and is now a project of the Apache Software Foundation.

f This record must come from the signature check when the agent uploads the record to the database—not required of service developer.

Table 20.4 Example from Alert Data

Failed authentication	Thread Number, Sequence Number, Active Entity Name, Event Name, ID of Service Requester, Date/Time, Type of Event, User Entity Identity, Service Entity Identity, Other pertinent data, XMLDSig	Server Problem— call help desk (a Sequence Number may be provided) to user

Requirement 2: The developer must scan all inputs and outputs for "nominal" and report malformed inputs or outputs. The malformed information may be corrected or rejected before any transmitted information is acted upon.

Requirement 3: The developer must provide a list of all Java runtime exception errors that will be relevant and provide the rationale for any Java runtime exception errors not on the list.

Requirement 4: Each relevant error must be documented as to how it is handled, including self-healing errors, and how each non-self-healing error will be handled within the service and how its reports should be handled in after-action analyses.

Requirement 5: Each relevant Java exception error must be trapped and logged. Errors that terminate a session must increase the monitoring category to **Enhanced** until reset.

20.8.6 Record Storage

Additional requirements are placed upon the service to supply a clear monitor trail.

Requirement 6: Protected monitor trail storage requirements are placed on the monitor trail. It will be protected from unauthorized deletion and/or modification. Authorized deletion or modification is monitored, and monitor records are generated.

Requirement 7: Assurances of monitor or log record availability that the system maintains given the occurrence of an undesired condition. This requires resource planning, and the enterprise should generally require 3 months of online data and 2 years of archived data.

Requirement 8: Action in case of possible loss of monitor and log records specifies actions to be taken if a threshold on the monitor trail is exceeded. This includes appropriate notifications under automated response when thresholds are approached.

Requirement 9: Prevention of monitor data loss specifies actions in case the monitor trail is full. This should not happen, but the response should be to preserve the most recent records and to shut down nonessential activity until monitor capability is restored.

20.9 Help Desk Breakdown

There are breakdowns for help desk solutions in the literature [112]; however, the following breakdown is believed to be unique and is based on the other architectural details of the enterprise in this book. The ESD attempts to resolve 90% of customer issues within 20 minutes, and averages less than 15 minutes to resolve all issues. The ESD in this case consists of four basic levels and three separate groups:

1. Level 0—Client self-help. Assistance is provided to the client in the form of knowledge repository (KR) access, frequently asked questions (FAQ), and diagnostic software. Failure to resolve issues at this level leads to a call to the help desk.
2. Level 1—Customer support and help desk. A client may ask for assistance through a help desk phone number, e-mail, or web form entry. This is the unit that will develop a trouble report (TR) and see most through to completion.
3. Level 2—Proactive monitoring of services. This unit will monitor network activities and the performance of services using a testing tool and a series of embedded agents. This level will assist Level 1 when resolution of help desk requests has not been completed at that level. It may also generate technical reports before clients call to report problems.
4. Level 3—Active monitoring and security. This unit will monitor all security alerts sent by agents, and based upon heuristics developed within the enterprise, will perform remote desk audits and dispatch a security monitoring team for physical audit of indicated desktops. This level will assist Level 1 and Level 2 when they have not been able to resolve help desk requests.

20.10 Customer Support and Help Desk

After initial self-help is unsuccessful, the client will turn to the help desk. Three levels of service are provided. Level 1 will be the entry point to the system. At this level, a client will call the help desk about a problem or other issue. The help desk assistant will collect some information, such as name, address, rank, Social Security Number, etc., from the client, verify the client's identity, and attempt to quickly solve the issue using a predefined script and access to the KR. If this does not resolve the issue, it is categorized and escalated to the appropriate level (Level 2). At Level 2, a knowledgeable person will go through a more detailed script to collect information from the client and use the agent-based monitoring process to gain more detailed information about the situation. Level 2 personnel will have more access and privileges, allowing them to make changes and attempt to fix the problem. If Level 2 personnel are able to solve the problem, they will close the TR and update the KR with information about the TR resolution. If the issue cannot be resolved at this level, the TR will be escalated to Level 3, where in-depth analysis and coding are involved. If this resolves the issue, any code fixes will be pushed to the patch/configuration management (CM) team and a temporary quick fix will be generated for future issues and added to the KR. This describes the basic help desk flow in the figures below.

The rest of the section is structured as follows:

- Levels of service
- Identity verification system
- Trouble report management system
- Knowledge repository system
- Error reporting
- Administrator duties
- Trouble report scenarios and data requirements

Details of the agent-based architecture are complex and discussed in Chapter 17.

20.11 Levels of Service

As previously described, there are four basic levels of support, and three basic units or groups to assist in that support.

20.11.1 Level 0: Client Self-Help

Before executing the well-structured help desk levels, there is a loosely defined "Level 0," which refers to the clients' ability to solve their own issues through the KR or other means. Some tools exist and can provide configuration checking and other simple troubleshooting that will solve a percentage of the problems encountered by enterprise users. Resorting to personal responsibility can resolve another significant percentage of the problems encountered by enterprise users. FAQs alone may solve many problems before labor-intensive help desk personnel are involved. The KR is primarily a help desk resource. Developing a culture within the client base of first checking the KR when an issue is encountered can further act as a filter, reducing the load on Level 1. The relationship of levels is shown in the next three figures.

20.11.2 Level 1: Basic Information

Level 1 is where most of the TRs are created. All help desk requests will be recorded in a help desk TR. The Level 1 operator will follow a simple script, which will involve collecting basic information from the client, entering it into a TR, and creating the TR. At this point, the operator will start to address the client's issue. If the issue is resolved, the method of resolution will be entered in the TR. Often this will involve listing a link to the KR article that helped resolve the issue. Other times, it will be an operator text entry based on information personally provided to the client (Figure 20.4).

This process ensures that all interactions are logged appropriately. An issue that is resolved quickly by a link to the KR is important to document. This provides positive feedback to the higher levels that create and maintain these KR articles. A high frequency of access can indicate that this is an important issue that clients need to understand. As a result, a more client-friendly KR article might be created to reduce call volume to the help desk or an enterprise-wide memo might be released addressing the issue. If the article addresses a bug and its workaround, a high access rate might indicate that this is a high priority for a permanent fix. In any case, the proper documentation of client requests, even for seemingly trivial issues, is an important part of the role of Level 1 operators.

In addition to the KR, Level 1 has access to basic live feeds from Units 2 and 3 of the ESD. These feeds indicate the current health, performance, and security situation of the network, and also include hardware and operating system failure information. This feed is one-way, providing current information to the Level 1 operators. This information is intended for use when there are significant network issues. If a client calls and asks about a slow connection, this feed could provide a quick answer for that client if there is significant network traffic at the time. The TR could then be closed without escalation by verifying that Unit 2 knows about the issue and is working to fix it.

Not all issues will be resolved by a KR article link at Level 1. For more difficult problems and problems that require an administrator or other access, the TR is escalated to Level 2. Responsibility of the TR is passed to someone in Level 2, and Level 1's obligations for that TR are complete.

20.11.3 Level 2: Interactive Support

When a TR is escalated to Level 2, it is first scanned to determine the general issue. Although all operators in Level 2 are trained and capable of resolving issues, there will be some areas of expertise that people or levels develop within Level 2, so matching the problem with the person or group addressing it will be helpful for certain types of TRs. When a help desk level has taken ownership of a TR, they contact the client by phone to authenticate them, confirm the information collected by Level 1, and collect more detailed information to address the issue. This interaction follows a script much like Level 1, but it is more detailed in terms of the authentication steps and the information collected. Level 2 operators all have the ability to remotely access a client's desktop. This is provided by agents running on the clients' desktops, which may be part of a standard desktop

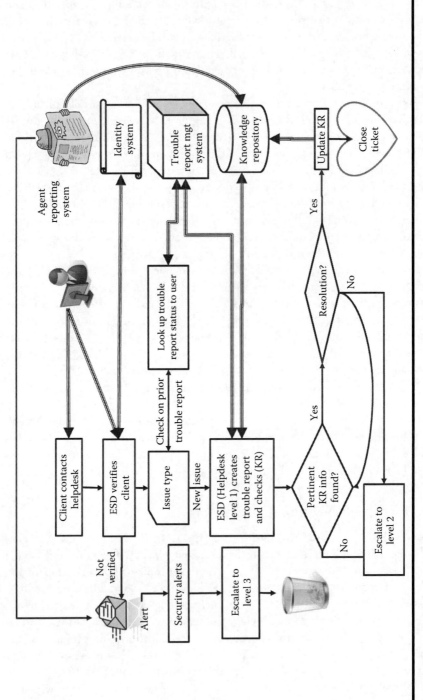

Figure 20.4   Help desk—Level 1.

configuration. If needed, the Level 2 operator will access the client's desktop, collect information directly from their desktop, and make changes to the client's desktop. Examples of changes are software updates, installation of certificates or other security-relevant information, and removal of unauthorized device drivers or other software. All authorized software will be signed and certificated, so detection of unauthorized code should be easily accomplished by an automated scan (Figure 20.5).

The level of expertise at Level 2 is very high. The baseline training for Level 2 operators provides them an ability to resolve almost all issues faced. Specialized training for certain specific issues may be limited to a smaller group within Level 2, but this group will be consulted or given the TR when appropriate. Such specialized training might be for key services. Although the issues addressed might be difficult to diagnose and fix, by having these specialized groups within Level 2 for the most common problem area it is possible to avoid the very costly escalation to Level 3. However, sometimes there is just a fundamental problem with the code, either enterprise code or vendor code, or there is a fundamental architectural problem that must be changed, perhaps at the service provider facility not accessible directly from Level 2. In this case, the issue is escalated to Level 3 and/or sent to the service provider.

20.11.4 Level 3: Security, Serious Bugs, and Vendor Support

Level 3 is not as well defined as Levels 1 and 2. It consists of a collection of developers, security experts, architects, and vendor support channels for all commercial software and hardware. These experts are typically very costly to utilize, but their expertise and skills can resolve any issue properly diagnosed and allocated to them. The goal of the ESD is to address all TRs at the lowest level possible. Essentially, Level 1 acts as a filter to weed out all issues that are a waste of Level 2 resources. Level 2 acts as a further filter to weed out all issues that are a waste of Level 3 resources.

Level 3 does not actually take ownership of any help desk TRs. The one exception is security TRs opened by Level 3. The Level 3 administrator, in consultation with other Level 3 subject matter experts (SME), may decide to call a computer security incident response team (CSIRT) and is responsible for managing this team in its work. Level 3 is contacted by Level 2 when there is a serious issue to resolve, but Level 2 maintains ownership of the TR. Level 3 is treated more like a consultant that the Level 2 operator can call on to solve serious problems. Although the TR does not change hands, the Level 2 operator contacts the client before escalating to Level 3 to inform them that their issue is more serious and may take some time to resolve. Level 3 issues are expected to take days or weeks to resolve instead of the minutes or hours expected at Level 1 or Level 2 (Figure 20.6).

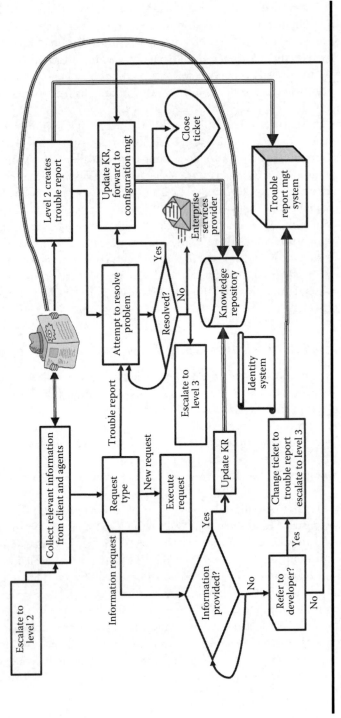

Figure 20.5 Help desk—Level 2.

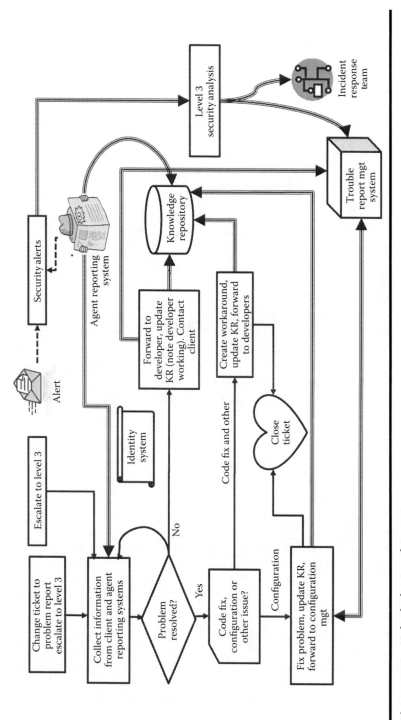

Figure 20.6   Help desk—Level 3.

20.12 Using the Knowledge Repository

The KR is a single integrated source of all information on the operation of the enterprise. It will be updated by all three units within the ESD and accessible to all three units within the ESD. The KR consists of a database, and tools to import and categorize agent-based data, as well as tools for search and discovery. The KR is access-controlled at all levels.

20.12.1 Information for Help Desk Operations

The KR is where all information related to TRs is stored. This will include the following

- Hardware/software current status from the service provider
- Hardware/software historical data
- A list of current alerts for the entire enterprise
- Historical data on alerts
- Reference material for all hardware components
- Reference material for all software components
- Reference material for all protocols and standards
- Configuration information
- All closed TRs
- All reference material that closed TRs link to
- Articles useful for setting up HW/SW, troubleshooting, etc.
- Frequently asked questions

Configuration information will consist of the standard desktop configuration, service configuration, infrastructure component configuration, and any other hardware, software, protocol, or standards settings or choices that have been established across the enterprise.

Closed TRs will be available in the KR. This will allow the help desk to search for similar TRs and use past experience to aid with current issues. Every TR will be added to the KR when it is closed. Access to these closed TRs will be discussed, since this is a potentially sensitive area. However, for now, it is sufficient to note that all closed TRs will be in the KR and available to someone, if not everyone.

In addition to closed TRs, any other documents referenced by the TRs should be included in the KR. Articles written internally by the ESD or other entities within the enterprise will be added to the KR if they would be useful for ESD activity. FAQs will be established, and configuration information will consists of the standard desktop configuration, service configuration, infrastructure component configuration, and any other hardware, software, protocol, or standards settings or choices that have been established across the enterprise. This includes the choice of which ports to open or close, when to use the various WS-* protocols, and which services should run at startup on a Windows Vista machine. For hardware, software, protocol, and standard elements there is an associated set of configurations and settings.

Closed TRs will be available in the KR. This will allow the help desk to search for similar TRs and use past experience to aid with current issues. Every TR will be added to the KR when it is closed. Access to these closed TRs will be discussed, since this is a potentially sensitive area.

In addition to closed TRs, any other documents referenced by the TRs should be included in the KR. This should be done not when the TR is closed but when the links are added to the open TR. The data should be added to the KR, then the link should be established, and then when the TR is closed, the data and link are already there, so no additional work needs to be done. External links (websites, etc.) will be captured in some way (like a Google cache) so that access is assured even when network connectivity is limited.

Articles written internally by the ESD or other entities within the enterprise will be added to the KR if they will be useful for ESD activity. FAQs will be established and probably be used when searching for general information on a topic, which might include KR data as well as other information. The KR search will be more for clients contemplating starting a TR or for ESD/ESU personnel who want specific information for an existing TR.

Different levels of access will be established. These would correspond to different groups and roles that determine KR access. For TRs, the following levels are defined:

5. No closed TRs are viewable by callers.
6. Callers can only view their own TRs.
7. All TRs without any sensitive information are visible.
8. All TRs are visible (exception—security-sensitive TRs), but fields designated sensitive are blanked out.
9. Everything is visible.

The ability to update the KR will be restricted to Level 2 and Level 3 personnel. Level 1 is essentially a firewall for these people, weeding out all the previously solved and documented issues. Because of this, Level 1 will only read the KR, much like the enterprise clients. When a new issue is found that cannot be addressed by the existing KR information, it is resolved at Level 2 or Level 3. After this issue is resolved, the Level 2 administrator writes enough information in either the TR or a KR article so that the issue can be discovered in the KR and resolved by Level 1 support the next time it happens.

For example, if a specific configuration must be used to access a particular new service, Level 2 will field all calls relating to this issue until a KR article is added or the prior TRs provide enough information for Level 1 to solve the problems. As new issues are discovered, the Level 2 people will continue to resolve them and add more information to the KR. Eventually, a client attempting to access the service will find a wealth of information either through reading articles specifically about configuration for the service or through reviewing closed TRs with similar problems.

The main goal is to solve problems as few times as possible, since every level to which an issue is escalated is more costly than the previous one. The most preferable is for clients to solve their own problems through KR articles. When this is not possible, Level 1 tries to resolve it. If it is a new issue, Level 2 must address it. If it is a fundamental change, Level 3 will be involved. However, once an issue makes it to a certain level, it should stop at a lower level the next time it arises because the expert attention provided the previous time should be documented in a way that the levels below can use it without escalating the issue again.

Although only Level 2 and Level 3 can update the KR, anyone can suggest something be added to the KR. A simple way to implement this is through a web page, where any client can enter the information for a KR article, submit it to the appropriate group at Level 2, and let the people at Level 2 review the article and take the appropriate action. This allows people to provide input on issues they may have that are not addressed by the KR, perhaps because they rarely occur or they relate to a specific service that a client not in the ESD happens to know very well. However, Level 2 personnel have the final say because they ultimately are the maintainers of the KR.

20.13 ESD Summary

This chapter discussed monitoring activities and using those activities in a help desk environment. The lists of alerts and monitored events are incomplete and need to be tailored to enterprise activities. This chapter also presented a multitiered approach to enterprise support services.

Chapter 21

Network Defense

With the exception of Chapter 7, we have ignored most of the network aspects. In fact, until we began the standup of our enterprise environment, we did not realize just how intrusive some of the devices can be. Much of this was published as recently as 2014 [121] and 2015 [122].

21.1 Expected Behavior

Entities in the enterprise are deployed with a standard configuration. Over time, patches, updates, new software versions, and mistakes or malicious activity all lead to deviations across the enterprise from this standard baseline. Malicious or unknown software on a system can cause harm or unexpected behavior.

To mitigate these problems where possible, and help fix them in other cases, an enterprise plan for quality of protection is needed. This involves eliminating certain actions on machines that could harm the machine itself or the enterprise. The level of protection is dependent upon the type of enclave (an enclave is defined as a collection of entities with a common set of security and assurance mechanisms in place). Certain mitigations will be exercised based upon the cyber environment and enclave, and they may be exercised in different ways when communication is needed across enclaves of differing security and assurance. Mitigations include virus scanners and disabling of devices or interfaces. These mitigations also involve identifying and fixing issues that were not stopped. This requires a central visualization of the enterprise to quickly identify potential issues and a method of remotely taking action to either fix the affected system or freeze it until further action can be taken.

21.2 Introduction

Enterprise protection is based upon the device, the environment, and the enclave type. An enclave is a collection of entities and assurance mechanisms that uniformly employ the same security. Protection includes on-device software, in-line monitoring of communications, and the particular security model that provides confidentiality, integrity, and availability. Many times this security model is compromised in trying to provide basic levels of protection. These compromises may include policy-based instructions to configure intrusion detection devices that provide the capability for selecting which attacks are being monitored. These policy selections can provide capabilities to select what responses will be taken for each detected intrusion.

21.3 Current Protection Approaches

Elements involved in implementing quality of protection are numerous and complicated. A wide range of appliances are used to provide functionality ranging from the quality of service to the user to the quality of protection of network resources and servers. These appliances are often placed in-line, and some require access to content to provide their service. Figure 21.1 illustrates how these appliances are installed between the user and the application.

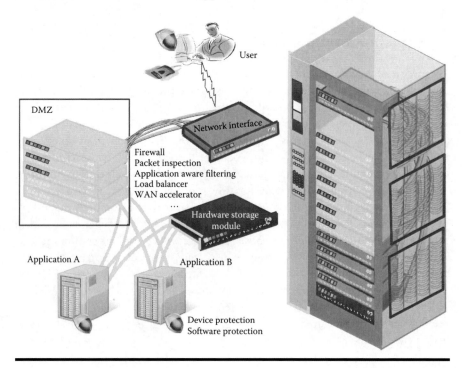

Figure 21.1   End-point access.

The number of appliances can be quite high [32–53]. Below is a partial list of functional types:

- Header-based scanner/logger:
  - Views only unencrypted portion of traffic
  - Synchronous or asynchronous operation
  - Scans for suspicious behavior, logs traffic
- Content-based scanner/logger:
  - Views decrypted content
  - Synchronous or asynchronous operation
  - Scans for suspicious behavior, logs traffic, and/or content
- Header-based firewall:
  - Views only unencrypted portion of traffic
  - Synchronous operation
  - Scans for and blocks suspicious behavior
- Content-based firewall—block only:
  - Views decrypted content
  - Synchronous operation
  - Scans for suspicious behavior and blocks (terminates) connection
- Content-based firewall—modifies malicious content:
  - Views decrypted content
  - Synchronous operation
  - Scans for suspicious content, and blocks connection or removes suspicious content while preserving the connection
- Web accelerator:
  - Views decrypted content
  - Synchronous operation
  - Modifies content for performance
- WAN accelerator:
  - Views decrypted content
  - Multiparty system
  - Synchronous operation
  - Modifies content representation between parties, but no end-to-end modification
- Load balancers:
  - Distributes load among destination end points to improve throughput and reduce latency
  - May decrypt content
  - May combine encrypted flows through an "encryption accelerator"
  - May distribute content by request to different servers based on load
  - Are considered active entities
  - May not decrypt content

- Using "sticky" or end point balances may route all requests from an entity to the same server
- These load balancers are considered passive entities

Each of the appliances above offers some functionality and increases the threat exposure. None of these are bullet-proof from a security standpoint, and they do increase the threat surface and the vulnerability space. Use of any appliance must be balanced by the increased functionality and the increased vulnerability. The situation is further complicated by vendor offerings of load balancers with firewall capability, "smart" accelerators that scan content, and software-only offerings that provide most of these functionalities in a modular fashion.

21.3.1 Current: Unencrypted Traffic

To clarify the current paradigm, a review of what is done through a portal for unencrypted traffic is provided. HTTP traffic is unencrypted from browser to portal, and unencrypted from portal to web applications providing content.

1. Examples:
   www.amazon.com
   www.va.gov
   www.af.mil
2. MITM model for appliances (e.g., firewalls, deep packet inspection, and accelerators) that perform analysis of headers and content (IP, TCP, HTTP, HTML, XML, JavaScript, etc.)
3. The portal is the end point for browser requests

The process is shown in Figure 21.2.

Note that while the traffic is unencrypted, the requester may or may not be authenticated using a smart card with public key infrastructure credentials.

The traffic is pulled in-line through a number of appliances to protect ports and inspect content. We have included a web accelerator in Figure 21.2 because it has a number of characteristics in common with these other appliances. Other appliances, including load balancers and WAN accelerators, may also be included in this stack. Load balancers and some firewalls may be treated as passive entities in this treatment. WAN accelerators are covered later in this chapter.

21.3.2 Current: Encrypted Traffic

When traffic is encrypted, the same basic approach is adapted to handling traffic inspection. HTTPS traffic is successively decrypted and re-encrypted when

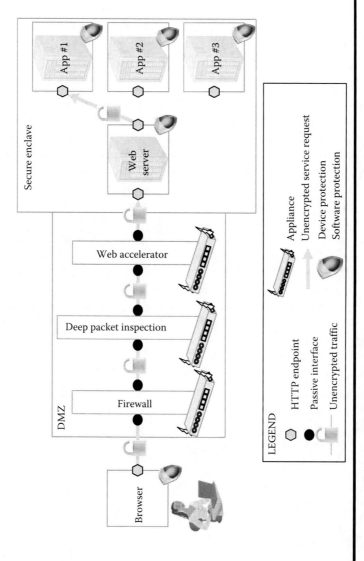

Figure 21.2 Current paradigm for unencrypted traffic.

needed. End-to-end HTTPS traffic is encrypted using TLS from browser to portal and using separate TLS sessions from portal to web applications.

1. Example: https://www.mybank.com
2. MITM model for appliances
3. Some can function without decryption (e.g., firewall)
4. Some require decryption, using portal private key (e.g., deep packet inspection, accelerator)
5. Portal is the end point for browser requests

The process is shown in Figure 21.3.

The appliances of course need to view the unencrypted information. To be able to decrypt the packages, the private key and initialization vectors (IV) from the target services are provided to the in-line appliances. As such, they see the handshake and exchange and have access to the keying material sufficient to compute the session and message authentication code (MAC). A MAC is a cryptographic checksum on data that uses a session key to detect both accidental and intentional modifications of the data (for integrity). While sharing private keys is an easy way to provide the appliance's visibility to the content, it is a singularly bad idea from a security standpoint. Loss of a private key will compromise identity and all sessions and will allow an adversary to impersonate the entity. Further, in high assurance systems, the private keys are locked in a HSM and are not shareable. Loss of a session key will entail loss of session confidentiality only. The situation is a bit more complicated in that some of the devices need to see content and some do not. For example, the following data is available for all encrypted packets in the header without decryption:

1. IP header:
   a. Time to live
   b. Source IP
   c. Destination IP
   d. IP version and flags
2. TCP header:
   a. Source port
   b. Destination port
   c. Sequence number
   d. Acknowledgment number
   e. Windows size
   f. TCP flags
3. TLS handshakes and header:
   a. Version, cipher suite, compression algorithm, extensions
   b. Server certificate and partial chain to root CA

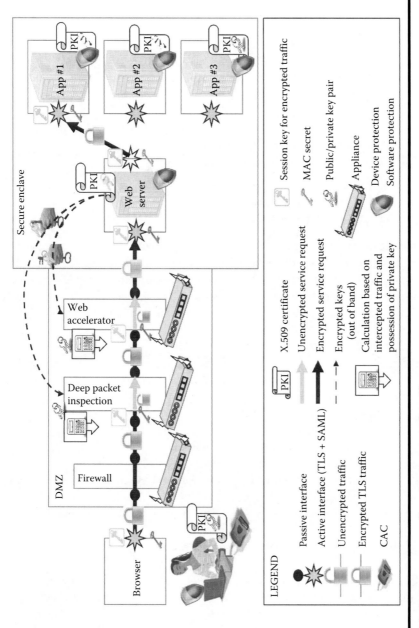

Figure 21.3   Current paradigm for encrypted traffic.

    c. Client certificate and partial chain to root CA
    d. Session IDs, client and server random values
    e. Alerts (full content) sent prior to encryption
    f. Message types and lengths
    g. Renegotiations
    h. Trusted CA list at server
    i. Client-supported cipher suites list and preference
    j. Client-supported compression algorithms
4. Firewall capabilities not requiring decryption:
    a. Blacklist/whitelist based on IP/port numbers
    b. Block unacceptable TLS versions, cipher suites
    c. Block insecure TLS renegotiations
    d. Block compromised or unknown CAs

21.4 An Alternative to Private Key Passing

For most interactions using strong encryption approaches, traffic does not need to be inspected. The firewall functionality will still be available using the headers that are not encrypted. However, it is recognized that certain circumstances, including cyber-attack indications and/or insider suspicions, and others may require content inspection. For these conditions, we recommend an alternative to the sharing of private keys as follows:

1. HTTP traffic is encrypted using TLS from the browser to the web application; the gateway router at enclave boundary provides access to all internal IP addresses.
2. Web application shares only the TLS session keys that are needed for each appliance to function.
    a. Firewall: no keys needed, uses headers.
        Deep packet inspection: encryption key only, no modification needed.
        Accelerator: encryption key and MAC secret, to inspect and modify content.
3. No shared private keys—each active entity has its own unique public/private key pair.
4. Web application is end point for browser requests.

Figure 21.4 shows the alternative recommendation. The figure illustrates the importance of key management. The users have a life equal to the user session. The web server and appliance keys have a fairly long life to accommodate passing of multiple session keys. The public and private keys have a life specified by the certificate.

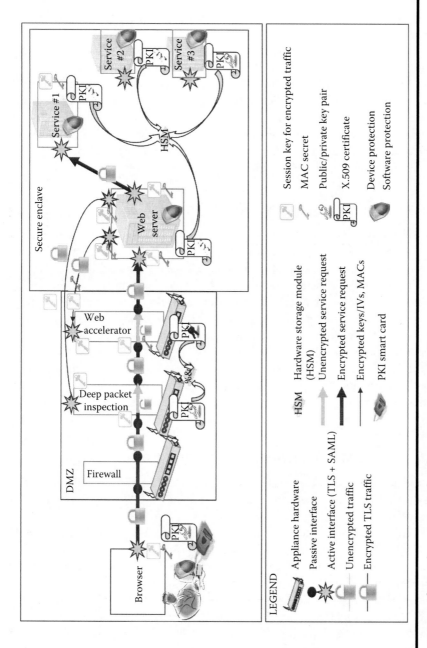

Figure 21.4 Alternative encrypted web server communications.

21.5 A Distributed Protection System

The protection system has the capability to monitor, filter, and shut down traffic to given ports. It scans for malicious code. It examines incoming and outgoing traffic for anomalies or known exploits. The protection system checks ports and protocols and can perform other functionality.

The protection system acts in the security context of the end point for both requester and provider and examines not only the encrypted traffic but also the unencrypted TLS traffic for malicious behavior or code. This requires access to the unencrypted traffic as well as the encrypted traffic. Not all of the checks are provided by the protection system. Figure 21.5 walks through checks in a high assurance enclave provided by the protection system, the server handlers, the service handlers, and the service itself, minimizing the need for in-line appliances.

21.5.1 Appliance Functionality In-Line

For enclaves that are characterized by full bilateral-based authentication, private keys should be required to be under the control of hardware storage modules, and the end-to-end paradigm cannot be broken by a passive entity. In-line appliances may be configured as active entities but this is not recommended. The in-line system can only observe headers, apply white and black lists, and pass through encrypted content without inspection unless it is provided assistance from the service, as shown in Figure 21.5. This assistance is in the form of passing the session keys where appropriate.

The in-line device may decrypt and inspect incoming traffic. It should either deny the communication (with appropriate logging of information and/or security alerts as appropriate) or pass the communication (unmodified) on to the server. The device may also scan outgoing traffic (Figure 21.6).

21.5.2 Appliance Functionality as a Service

The appliance system may be used as a service by the application and as such follows full bilateral authentication and the TLS security paradigm, as shown in Figure 21.7.

In order to prevent attackers from gaining access to networks, each device must monitor DHCP requests and report all such requests to the central monitor. This provides monitoring devices throughout the network to determine whether it is a known and trusted device or a rogue entity, and take action accordingly.

Any system that is found on the network, through DHCP or other traffic, must identify itself to the protection system before any services are provided to it. This identification is through protection system communications, through which each device authenticates to the central authority and also authenticates the central authority. All such traffic uses end-to-end security, and all devices and their

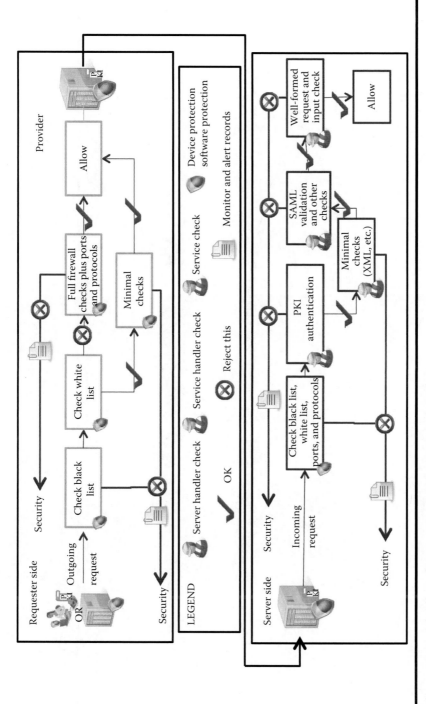

Figure 21.5   Distributed protection without in-line appliances.

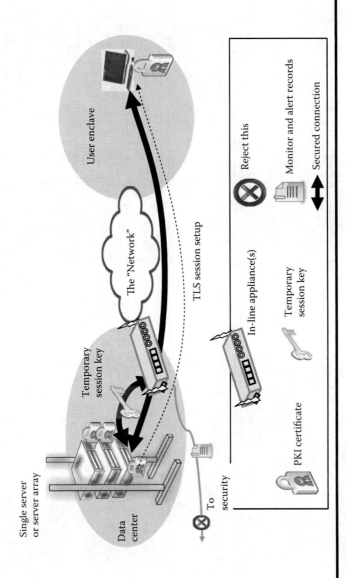

Figure 21.6 In-line appliance functionality.

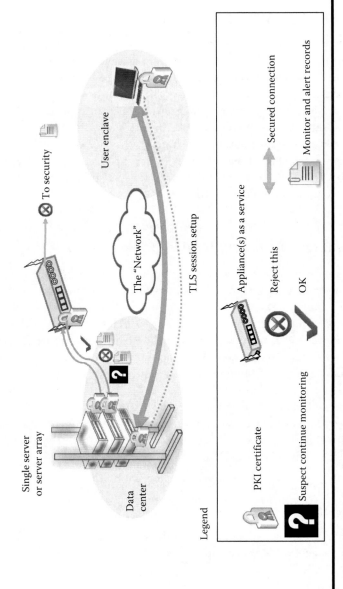

Figure 21.7 Appliance functionality as a service.

protection systems are registered with the enterprise. Unknown entities are not given services and are marked as rogue, which enables local devices to ignore their traffic.

21.6 Next Steps for Appliances

We have reviewed the basic approaches to communication protection in computing environments. We have also described high assurance architectures and the protection elements they provide. In many instances, the high assurance elements provide equivalent protection. In cases in which additional protective measures are needed, we have provided two mechanisms for their incorporation. Neither of these mechanisms requires distribution of a private key, which is often done with today's appliances. The distribution of private keys is a fundamental violation of a high assurance model. Fortunately, many of the appliances are now provided in software. This affords us an opportunity to avoid key distribution and decryption of content before the end point altogether.

21.6.1 Real Demilitarized Zone

However, we must first view the actual complexity of the process to appreciate the dilemma. Figure 21.8 shows how the cabinets full of appliances are wired at the front end of a computing center. The traffic is so great that a myriad of load balancers and routers is employed to provide a routing to each service cluster that has the appropriate inspection capability. In the figure, we have shown a path through the maze to server 9, which is an enterprise application. The content is decrypted right at the top and passed around in unencrypted form all the way to server 9, leaving a large gap in the end-to-end process.

In Figure 21.9, we have taken the individual path that a packet would take to arrive at server 9, including each of the stops along the way. There is one option included in Figure 21.9, and that is shown as a separate path to re-encrypt the packet after the traffic leaves the DMZ.

21.6.2 Security Issue

The current approach violates almost all of the security elements that we strive to maintain in the enterprise security approach:

- Communication is between two active entities that are
  - Unique identity:
    - Private key passing makes identity ambiguous

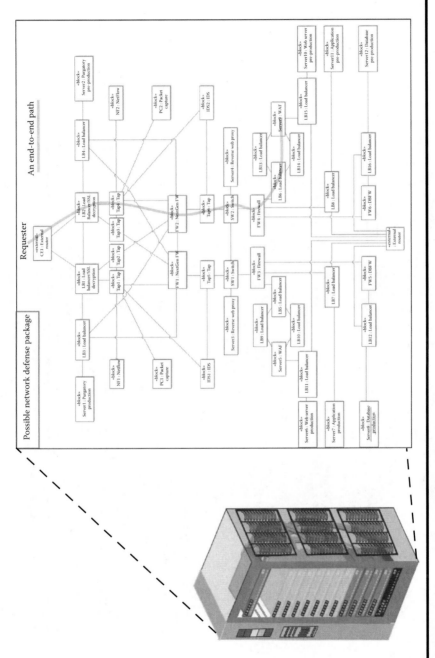

Figure 21.8 Actual complexity of appliance setup.

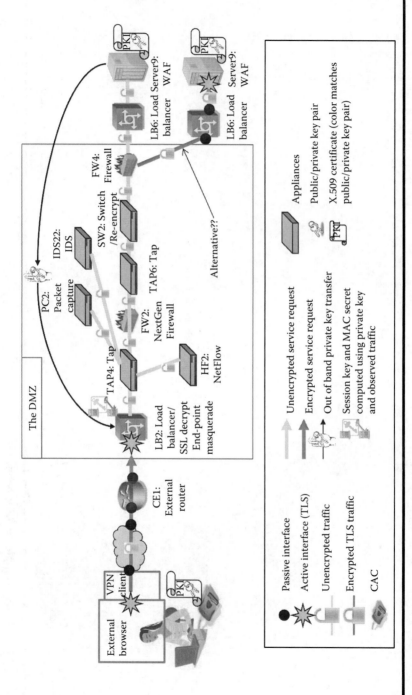

Figure 21.9 Current end-to-end exchange.

- Credentialed:
  - Private key passing shares credentials
- Mutually authenticated:
  - Authentication requires unique identity
- Message integrity:
  - Message sent from active entity A can be verified to be the message received by active entity B
  - Message could have been changed at any time
- Active entities act on their own behalf:
  - Unable to determine who is doing the action
- Confidentiality during transmission:
  - Unencrypted transmission of message throughout

There is a further drawback in that all traffic in the enterprise passes through one bottleneck.

21.6.3 Taking Advantage of Software-Only Functionality

The important point is that most appliance functionality is available as software only. Figure 21.10 shows the conversion of the particular piece of the DMZ that applies to a pseudo-appliance.

The packets are decrypted on entry into the pseudo-appliance and stay that way with the exception of an offload to an external source (such as a network monitoring appliance where packets are counted and graded, etc.). This offloading will be done by full ELS communication (for security, of course). This sounds pretty similar to the current approach. How does this change anything? The difference is in where the pseudo-appliance lives. For the moment, let us assume that the software appliance lives in the application server.

21.6.4 Protecting the Server

Of course we cannot send all of the incoming packets to server 9. That would be inefficient and dangerous. Some packets can wreak havoc before they are even processed, so we would want to be sure that the server 9 was the intended recipient and that server 9 is communicating with a credentialed entity with valid credentials.

Figure 21.11 has identified an intelligent tagging device that will identify the traffic by observing the first few packets. In the case of official enterprise traffic, the first few packets are not encrypted; these involve the exchange of PKI certificates that can be identified, and the owners can be compared to a white list. The target will be the destination for traffic. Before identification, the packets can be passed through the DMZ. If no identification is made, the packets will continue through the DMZ. When identified, they can be passed directly to the server or the load balancer in front of the server.

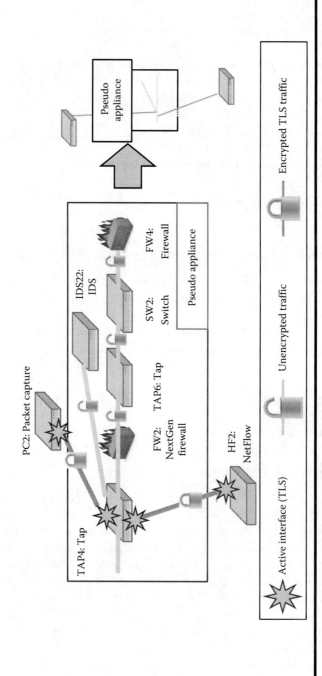

Figure 21.10 Creation of the pseudo-appliance.

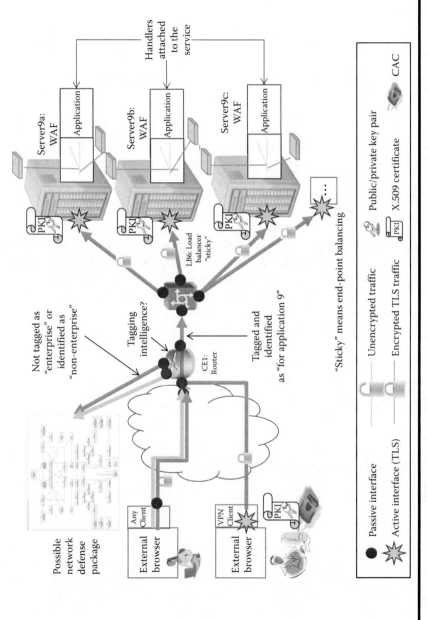

Figure 21.11   Tagged and embedded functionality.

21.6.5 Handlers in the Server

The only remaining problem is to reduce the software functionality to handlers in the handler chain, as shown in Figure 21.12.

Note that the handlers are embedded in the server handler chain at the point that the communication is prepared for their use and that the functionality has been divided along those lines as opposed to the previous functionality such as virus scan, ports and protocols, intrusion detection, or blacklist/whitelist, etc. These are distributed to packet header inspection, packet content inspection, and message content inspection. Each of these may perform inspection related to intrusion detection or blacklist blocking, etc. This is the preferred embodiment for enterprise applications. It moves the inspections to the point of the application itself by inserting handlers within the server and service to do the inspections at the point that it makes most sense. The inspections that can be done without decrypting the packets may be done at the front of the web server because they are passive entities. Moving inspections of decrypted traffic inside the server not only preserves the end-to-end paradigm but also encapsulates the security and allows tailoring for the application itself.

The following paragraphs describe how that process is evolved. The incoming packets are distributed to packet header inspection, packet content inspection, and message content inspection. Each of these may perform inspection related to intrusion detection or blacklist blocking, etc. The handlers may hand off the task to appliances through an enterprise connection if development of the handler is incomplete. It is assumed that the configuration of these handlers is tailored to material relevant to the application and that these configuration files are read in at system startup. Changes to the configurations would require an update to the configuration files and a restart of the application. In cases in which frequent changes are needed, updates may be obtained through a publish–subscribe service.

21.7 Appliances That Change Content

Content-changing appliances were considered late in the development of the enterprise architecture and presented quite a dilemma. The material here was first published in 2015 [123]. Even the server handler chain cannot solve this problem. The class includes web accelerators and wide area network accelerators. Bandwidth continues to be a problem for the active enterprise. Accelerators, prepositioning of data, and integrated solutions that use caches of commonly used data are expanding at an alarming rate. The major problem is maintaining the security principles we have discussed throughout this book. To illustrate, we will discuss the WAN acceleration problem.

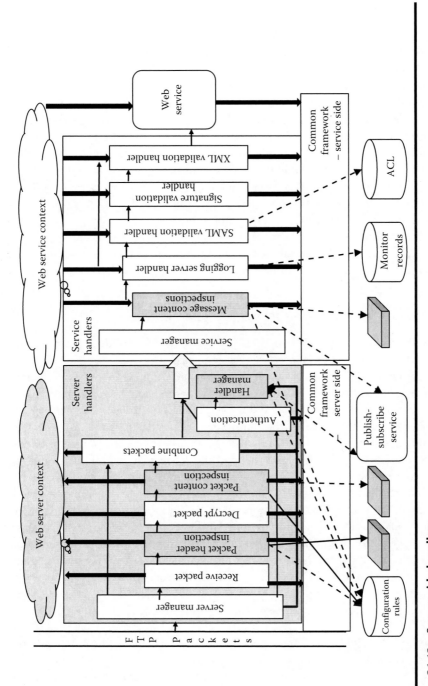

Figure 21.12   Server-side handlers.

21.7.1 Wide Area Network Acceleration

One solution to bandwidth problems over long-haul distances with restricted bandwidth is the WAN accelerator. This accelerator works by tokenizing blocks of information that are sent multiple times in network traffic. Because many such communications include previously transmitted material, the accelerator traffic quickly damps out to transmissions that include tokens instead of the original communication. The tokens are reconstituted before delivery, and the receiver has a seamless connection and is unaware of the process. The acceleration is not without its drawbacks. The process does not work on encrypted traffic due to the random nature of encryption. For high assurance systems using an end-to-end paradigm, there are two main areas of concern. The first is security (how do we handle the decryption/re-encryption process?), and the second is integrity (how do we maintain end-to-end integrity when encryption is broken?).

This section discusses the current approach to WAN acceleration and the changes that are required by a high assurance end-to-end approach. The high assurance end-to-end approach relies on a well-formed security paradigm for the enterprise.

21.7.2 An Introduction to WAN Acceleration

A WAN accelerator [124] is an appliance that optimizes bandwidth to improve the end user's experience on a WAN. The appliance, which can be a physical hardware component, software program, or an appliance running in a virtualized environment, reduces the time it takes for information to flow back and forth across the WAN by using compression and data deduplication techniques to reduce the amount of data that needs to be transmitted. Basically, an accelerator works by caching duplicate files or parts of files so they can be referenced instead of having to be sent across the WAN again. Many of the products have evolved beyond the core acceleration techniques. The WAN optimization controllers (WOC) further optimize the WAN link by accounting for known problems with common network protocols. Protocol optimization cleans up chatty protocols used in common enterprise standards, such as Common Internet File System (CIFS), Microsoft Exchange, and even TCP/IP, to eliminate the typical overhead found in these communication protocols. These optimizations require a deeper understanding of the protocols and can only be accomplished through significant collaboration with application vendors or reverse engineering by the WAN accelerator vendor.

WAN optimization encompasses the following ones [125]:

- Traffic shaping, in which traffic is prioritized and bandwidth is allotted accordingly
- Data deduplication, which reduces the data that must be sent across a WAN for remote backups, replication, and disaster recovery
- Compression, which shrinks the size of data to limit bandwidth use

- Data caching, in which frequently used data is hosted locally or on a local server for faster access
- Monitoring the network to detect nonessential traffic
- Creating and enforcing rules about downloads and Internet use
- Protocol spoofing; this is a method of bundling chatty protocols so they are, in effect, a single protocol

WAN optimization vendors include Blue Coat Systems, Cisco, Expand Networks, F5 Networks, Juniper, and Riverbed Technology.

21.7.3 Current WAN Accelerator Approaches

Acceleration of unencrypted traffic is not of interest in the high assurance end-to-end paradigm, so we will concentrate on the steps involved in handling encrypted traffic. Initially, there is a need to decrypt the traffic since tokenization is ineffective for encrypted traffic. This is due to the randomization of bit streams that are a property of encryption. This is normally done by passing the private key of the server to the server-side WAN accelerator appliance, as shown in Figure 21.13.

As shown in Figure 21.14 (this is an expansion of Figure 8.2, placed here for convenience), the TLS keys are computed and then passed between the accelerator units. The premaster secret keying material that is passed is protected by the private key of the server.

The sharing of the server's private key allows the server-side appliance to extract the premaster secret and compute the session's master secret, just as the end points compute it. This is used to generate the encryption keys and MAC secrets for each TLS connection within this session. As shown in Figure 21.15, the session keys and MAC secrets are then transmitted to the client-side WAN accelerator.

A MAC is a cryptographic checksum on data that uses a shared secret key to detect both accidental and intentional modifications of the data (for integrity). With this MAC secret and the encryption key and initialization vectors (IV), the client-side WAN accelerator can send TLS content to the client that can be decrypted and validated properly.

While sharing of private keys is an easy way to provide the appliances visibility to the content, it is a singularly bad idea from a security standpoint. First, in high assurance systems, the private keys are locked in a HSM and are not shareable. Second, loss of a private key will compromise identity, break integrity, and confidentiality of all TLS traffic to the server (past, present, and future), allow an adversary to impersonate the entity on existing connection, and allow the adversary to impersonate the entity on new connections initiated by the adversary. In contrast, loss of a session key will entail the loss of only confidentiality for a single connection within a TLS session, with no risks for identity impersonation.

Figure 21.15 shows the basic flows. This includes the logical end-to-end client-to-server TLS connection and its three secure component connections to, between,

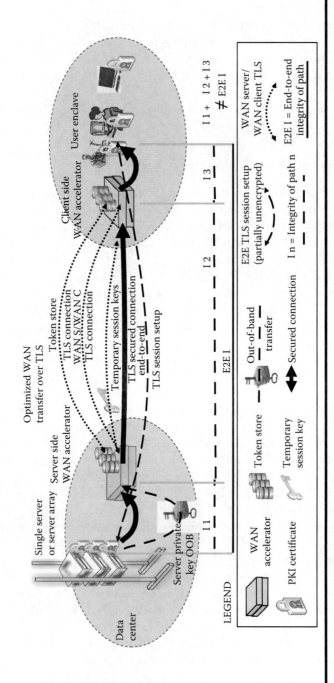

Figure 21.13 WAN accelerator current process server to user.

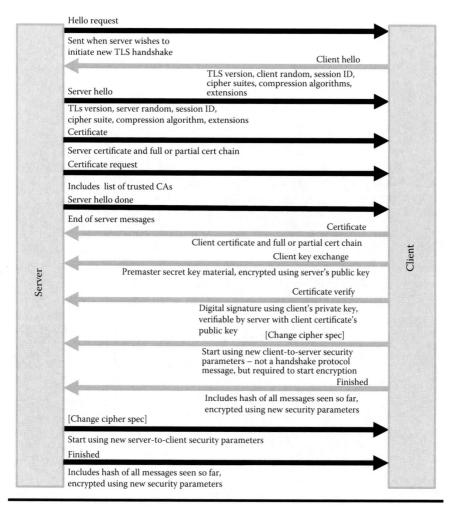

Figure 21.14   TLS handshake.

and from the WAN accelerators. It also includes TLS sessions to provide the session keys to the client-side accelerator, to transmit the tokenized packets to the client-side accelerator, and optionally to keep the tokenization stores in synchronization. Although shown as separate TLS connections between the same end points, these may instead be implemented as separate logical flows within a single TLS connection. Aside from key management issues, the difference is not important.

Figure 21.13 also shows the concern of integrity. The piecewise integrity of the component connections (I1, I2, and I3) does not amount to overall end-to-end integrity (E2E I).

$$I1 + I2 + I3 \neq E2E\ I \tag{21.1}$$

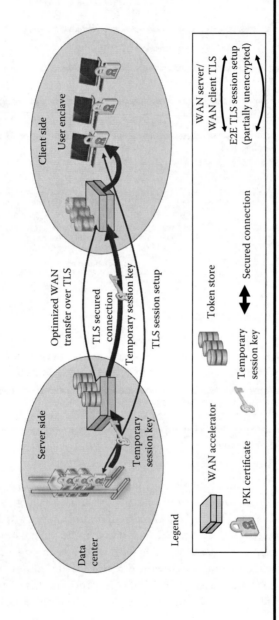

Figure 21.15 Alternative encrypted web server communications.

In an end-to-end security paradigm, the goal is that the receiver can verify that the message sent from the server is identical to the message received at the client. Even when TLS MACs are included in all component connections, the integrity of the end-to-end transmission is not preserved unless we undertake some extraordinary measures. When a component connection retransmits data with a new MAC value, any changes made by that component to the original data will go undetected. In order to avoid an explicit trust of the WAN processes, the TLS reconstruction of the server traffic by the client-side WAN accelerator must be modified. To understand this, we must examine the way in which TLS messages are formed.

21.7.4 An Alternative to Private Key Passing

For most interactions using enterprise-level security approaches, traffic content does not need to be inspected. Firewall functionality will still be available using the headers that are not encrypted. However, certain functions, including WAN acceleration, require content inspection. For these conditions, we recommend an alternative to the sharing of private keys as follows:

1. Web application shares only the TLS session keys that are needed for each appliance to function.
2. No shared private keys—each active entity has its own unique public/private key pair.
3. Web application is the end point for browser requests.

Figure 21.15 shows the alternative recommendation. HTTP traffic is encrypted using TLS from browser to web application. The WAN accelerator uses the provided session keys to decrypt TLS traffic. The balance of the transaction works the same, with the exception of the integrity issue. For this, we must examine the TLS package development process.

21.7.5 Integrity in a TLS Session

The message breakdown and TLS packet construction [143–145] are shown in Figure 21.16. The figure includes fragmentation of messages, addition of headers, compression, addition of the MAC and padding, and encryption. The MAC secret and values that depend on it are indicated in orange. The encryption keys and IVs, and values that depend on them, are indicated in red. The ciphertext has both red and orange, since it relies on both the MAC secret and the encryption keys and IVs.

Figure 21.17 shows the reverse process, where the receiver decrypts, validates the received MAC, decompresses, extracts content, and defragments into the original messages.

One important feature of TLS is that the encryption key/IV and MAC secret are separate values with separate functions. With only the encryption key and IV,

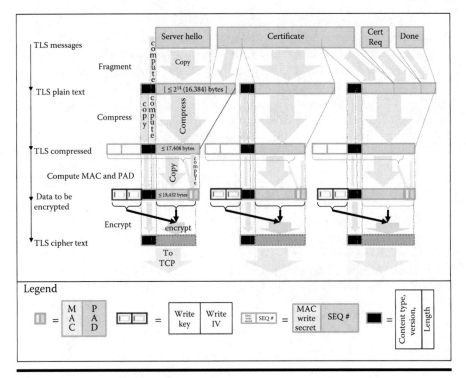

Figure 21.16   TLS transmission steps.

an intermediate node can view the content but not modify it. It cannot compute a valid MAC for the modified content without the MAC secret. Also relevant is that the fragmentation boundaries of the original messages are important for MAC computation. Identical messages that are fragmented differently will have different MACs, since the MACs depend on the fragments to which they are appended.

21.7.6 Flows in a High Integrity System

The overall recommended flows for the high assurance WAN accelerator on the server side are provided in Figure 21.10. The TLS session keys are passed to the server-side WAN accelerator as shown in Figure 21.18 and subsequently passed on to the client-side accelerator through the WAN Server/WAN Client TLS. The primary addition is the transmission of the original message fragmentation, padding, and MACs. These are needed to make an identical reconstruction of the original message. The original MACs can be added to the reconstructed message, for which the targeted end point has the MAC key.

The original TLS MAC digests, paddings, and fragmentation are used to construct TLS packets in lieu of the values that would normally be computed by the

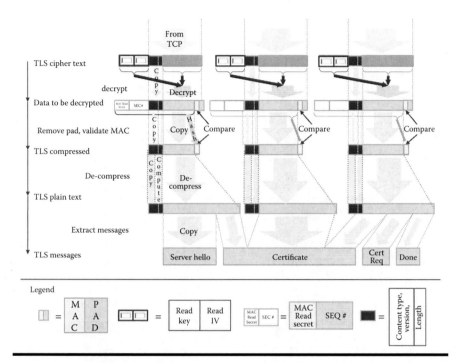

Figure 21.17   TLS reception steps.

TLS protocol. The client-side flows are given in Figure 21.19 and show the same transmission of the fragmentation, paddings, and MACS for the reconstruction of the message on the server side.

To ensure end-to-end integrity, it is necessary that the MAC secret is not available to the WAN accelerator. The receiving WAN accelerator node uses the original content, as received and reconstructed from the WAN connection, the original TLS fragmentation information, and the associated MAC and padding values to construct valid TLS messages to the receiving end point. Because only the sending end point has the MAC secret, the receiving end point has an end-to-end integrity guarantee.

21.7.7 Summary of WAN Acceleration

We have reviewed the basic approaches to WAN acceleration security when dealing with encrypted traffic. These have been found lacking in the specific areas of key protection and message integrity. Key protection is lacking, in that out-of-band passing of the private keys of the servers violate specific security tenants. Message integrity is lacking, in that piecewise integrity is substituted for overall end-to-end integrity. We have also described the high assurance architectures and protection elements they provide. In order to preserve the high assurance key security and

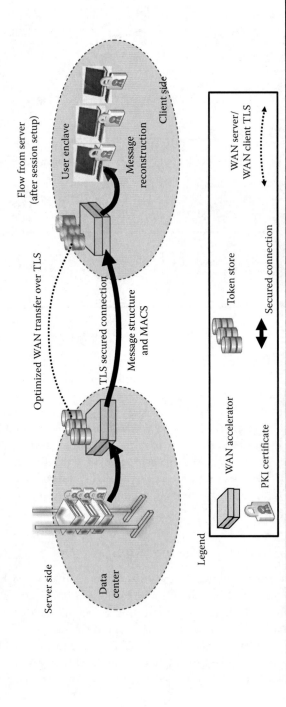

Figure 21.18 Flow from server side.

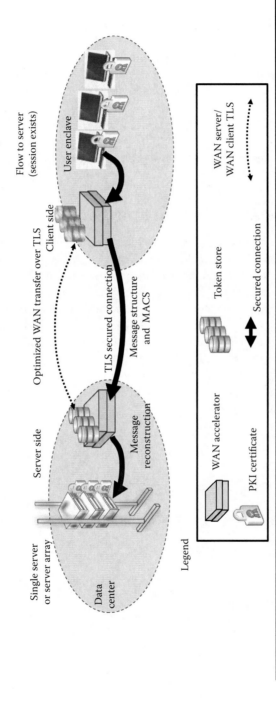

Figure 21.19 Flow from client side.

integrity elements, changes to the basic flows must be made. Key security can be maintained by passing only the session key, which provides a lower risk than passing the private key of the server, and maintains the unique identity of the server. Overall message integrity can be maintained by conspicuously reconstructing the original messages, including the message authentication codes. The development of WAN accelerator mechanisms does not require distribution of a private key, which is often done with today's appliances. The distribution of private keys is a fundamental violation of a high assurance model. What remains is the need for high reliability and secure code for passing of session keys, as well as secure means of transporting TLS plans and MACs for the establishment of service interfaces on the appliances. Pilots are in the process of being undertaken, and we expect some modifications as we learn more about how these devices work.

21.8 Appliances: A Work in Progress

The issue of sharing private keys with appliances has not yet been solved. The network system security is broken, malicious activity is pervasive, and greater resources are being allocated to chase the hope of identifying and mitigating the security threats that are corrupting this system security. The network has such high functionality that it cannot be abandoned. However, the current approach of sharing private keys so that every packet and every transaction can be inspected, even when we do not know what we are looking for, violates primary security properties, and the hunt for solutions is absolutely necessary.

Chapter 22

Concluding Remarks

If you made it here by working through the chapters, congratulations! It actually has taken the author 14 years to arrive at this point, and as you can see, there is considerably more to do. If you came here looking for bottom lines, hang on and we will get there. I hope that you at least read Section I of this book that discusses security topics in more general terms. If you think you have gleaned a few techniques that may help you in setting up your enterprise, all well and good. But you should understand that you may have missed the most important part of this body of work. Many of the techniques do not work alone and need for the complete architecture is high. We discuss that at some length below.

22.1 Where We Have Been and Where We Are Going

What is most impressive is that we spent nearly 350 pages and the topics we didn't discuss at length are more numerous than the ones we did. This book did not cover virtualization, operating systems, hypervisors, ports and protocols, asynchronous communication, name servers, routers, web servers, thread management, quality of service, data synchronization, governance, orchestration, insider behavior, forensics, incident response, continuous operations, and disaster recovery to name a few. All are important topics and all need to be adjusted to the new security model. But understanding the approach and what is different in this model of security is a good start on solving the other problems.

22.2 Understanding the Approach

The system is broken. The bad guys are among us. We have daily bad news on the cyber front. The current approaches are not working, and many of our IT professionals are doubling down by investing more and more in what has not worked in the past. The first step in the process is to recognize the situation. IT systems are invaded, and using the tactics that the invaders have used, in the name of securing or IT systems, is not working. This book has been about recognizing the situation and proposing alternative approaches including, where practical, an abandonment of conventional wisdom. The complexity of the problem precludes a design by formal methods with formal proofs, but it does not preclude a methodical analysis and a set of experiments to validate conclusions.

The processes in this book were developed and continue to be developed on a set of first principles we titled as tenets in the first chapter. Because it is assumed that covertly controlled code is present in the system, we put our emphasis on positive identification of all entities in every transaction. The transactions must be executed with confidentiality and integrity. Furthermore, we expect that identify alone is insufficient evidence to provide access and privilege and require an additional credential for that purpose. We view those items in the current system that would interrupt that model as obstacles to be worked around or through. This includes proxies and portals and "friendly" man-in-the-middle instantiations as well as nefarious masquerades and impersonations. Automated systems are preferred to manual administrator functions although we recognize that some things need an administrator to provide capabilities despite our best efforts at trying to anticipate all contingencies. One goal is to use every case of intervention as a learning experience to reduce the need for intervention.

It is recognized that the techniques herein are not familiar to those already involved in IT architectures and security issues. The enterprise described has no passwords and no accounts. Everything uses encryption as a tool in security, not an end or as a replacement for other techniques. Integrity and accountability are given a high priority. It relies on credentials that can be verified and validated. The first rule is to trust no entities or processes if it is at all possible to treat them as untrusted. The last point is especially true of legacy systems that have not had the benefit of this security model.

The model is exceptionally strong in integration and consistency. The techniques in Section II of this book were designed to work the same way through many different scenarios. They are designed to be extensible and accommodating while maintaining a strong security posture. This is especially true of federation and personal delegation, which we view as indispensable facts of life.

22.3 About Those Takeaways

Complexity is a fact of life. It is too late to put that genie back in the bottle. Complexity does not need to be feared but it does need to be accommodated.

Reality changes over time. If what you are doing is not working you should consider other alternatives. Often standing back and looking at the problem fresh will aid, in at least recognizing, what reality currently is.

The author hates checklists. They are a necessary evil, and several are provided in this book. However, no checklist is complete. IT systems are not stationary and all contingencies have not been considered. Checklists do not substitute for a good understanding of principles.

Rely on experts and their experience, but do not delegate all of your critical thinking to their solutions. Consider where the benefit is and who reaps the rewards.

The concepts are simple but the devil is in the details. Work things through on white boards and paper before configuring end points. Talking it through with another knowledgeable individual will often help crystalize concepts and critical thinking. Meticulously, checking and reviewing will actually save your time in the long run.

Accountability is absolutely necessary in IT systems. Any procedure or process that causes ambiguity or lack of accountability will be exploited by both friends and foes. Informal delegation, proxies, reverse proxies, and sharing of private keys all dilute accountability.

Security is painful and is not needed for achieving the functionality in the tools you need to do your job. Security does not matter unless there is an incident. If you have no security, you will have an incident. If you have strong security, you may have an incident, but at least you will be accountable for your actions.

Trust is a terrible thing to waste. Start with no trust and give in only when it is proven you have to. This applies to everything including certificate authorities who are sometimes victims of exploits too. Verify and validate—always—as a matter of course. Check for expired and revoked certificates whenever a certificate is used (like on signatures and such). This will encourage everyone in your enterprise to keep their credentials current.

Obscurity is not a security method. Publish what you do so that everyone in your organization knows what is going on. Be sure the security will work even if the bad guys know what you are doing. Hiding things only insures that the bad guys know it, because they are insiders, got it from an insider, or stole the information. When your guys don't know what's going on, they may misconfigure or make other mistakes making you more vulnerable.

Time—being in a hurry can cost your time, especially when dealing with complex issues.

When it comes to security don't settle for suggestions that do not seem right. You will sleep better and be blamed less.

Check for all the obvious errors. Misconfigurations, wrong settings, using defaults, you know what they are. Most intrusions start by finding one of those.

Security professionals are righteously paranoid. Assume the worst—you will be right more often that way. Security cannot be compromised in a successful system. The situation is not hopeless, only difficult.

Confidentiality is most useful when it is enforced end-to-end. Breaking encryption before you get to the delivery point is a compromise. When it comes to compromise see the point above.

Integrity is not negotiable. Each party in a transaction should be able to verify that they received the message that was sent by the known party on the other end of the transaction.

Anonymous is not an identity.

Appendix

Acronyms

ABAC	attribute-based access control
ACID	atomicity, consistency, isolation, durability
ACL	access control list
ACR	access control requirement(s)
ACS	authoritative content source
ADP	automated data processing
AE	attribute ecosystem
AES	Advanced Encryption Standard
AMIDS	audit monitoring and intrusion detection system
ANSI	American National Standards Institute [1]
API	application programming interface
APP	application
ASM	application security module
ASP	application service provider
AV	antivirus
AVA	assurance vulnerability assessment
BIOS	basic input–output system
CC	common criteria
CDS	cross-domain solution
CEM	common evaluation methodology
CERT	computer emergency response team
CIO	chief information officer
CISO	chief information security officer
CMA	certificate management authority
CMAC	cipher-based message authentication code
CNA	computer network attack
CND	computer network defense
COI	community of interest
COOP	continuity of operations
COTS	commercial "off-the-shelf"

CPU	central processing unit
CRL	certificate revocation list
CS	cloud system
CT	cipher text
CTO	chief technology office
CWE	common weakness enumeration
CVE	common vulnerabilities and exposures
DAC	discretionary access control
DB	database
DC	domain controller
DDoS	distributed denial of service
DES	Digital Encryption Standard
DH	Diffie–Hellman
DHCP	dynamic host configuration protocol
DIT	directory information tree
DMZ	demilitarized zone
DN	distinguished name
DNS	(1) domain name server
	(2) domain name system
DOB	date of birth
DoS	denial of service
DQ	data quality
DR	disaster recovery
DSA	digital signature algorithm
DSS	digital signature services, a technique to support the processing of digital signatures [1]
DTD	document type definition, the building blocks of an XML document [1]
ER	entity relationship
EA	enterprise architecture
EAS	enterprise attribute store
ECA	external certification authority
ECC	error correcting code
EKU	extended key usage
ELS	enterprise level security
ESD	enterprise support desk
FIPS	Federal Information Processing Standard
FQDN	fully qualified domain name
FTP	file transfer protocol
GB	giga byte
GBAC	group-based access control
GPU	graphics processing unit
GUI	graphical user interface
HAIPE	high-assurance Internet protocol encryptor

HMAC	HashMAC
HSM	hardware security modules
HTML	Hypertext Markup Language
HTTP	hypertext transfer protocol
HTTPS	hypertext transfer protocol secure
I&W	indications and warning
I/O	input/output
IA	(1) information assurance
	(2) information asset
IaaS	infrastructure as a service
IAM	information assurance manager
IANA	Internet assigned numbers authority
IAP	Internet access point
IATFF	Information Assurance Technical Framework Forum
IAW	(1) indications and warnings
	(2) in accordance with
IBAC	identity-based access control
ICMP	(1) Internet control message protocol
	(2) implementation of RFC 1256[4]
ID	identity (also a credential asserting identity)
IDEA	international data encryption algorithm
IdP	identity provider
IEC	International Electrotechnical Commission
IEEE	Institute of Electrical and Electronics Engineers
IETF	Internet Engineering Task Force
IIS	(Microsoft) Internet Information Services
IM	instant messaging
IMAP	Internet message access protocol
INFOSYS	information systems
IO	information operations
IP	Internet protocol
IPC	inter-process communication
IPR	(1) Internet protocol router
	(2) intellectual property rights [1]
IPS	intrusion prevention system
IPSec	Internet protocol security
IPv4	Internet protocol version 4
IPv6	Internet protocol version 6
IRI	internationalized resource identifier
IRM	information resource management
IRS	incident reporting structure
IRT	incident response team
ISE	information sharing environment
ISO	International Organization for Standards
ISS	information systems security

IT	information technology
JAAS	Java Authentication and Authorization Service
JAR	Java Archive
JAX-WS	Java API for XML web services
JCE	Java cryptographic extensions
JDBC	Java database connectivity
JDK	Java development kit
JMS	Java messaging service
JSR	Java specification requests
KDC	key distribution center
KEA	key exchange algorithm
KMI	key management infrastructure
LAN	local area network
LDAP	lightweight directory access protocol
LDAPS	LDAP over SSL
MAC	(1) mandatory access control
	(2) message authentication code
MDC	metadata catalogue
MDD	metadata discovery
MDE	metadata environment
MDR	metadata registry
MIME	multipurpose Internet mail extensions
MITM	man in the middle
MLDB	multilevel database
MLS	multilevel security
MOE	measures of effectiveness
MOP	measures of performance
MSL	multi-security levels
.NET	a software framework that can be installed on computers running Microsoft Windows operating systems
NAC	network access control
NetBIOS	file sharing and name resolution protocol—the basis of file sharing with Windows
NFS	network file system
NID	network intrusion detector
NIDS	network intrusion detection systems
NIST	National Institute of Standards and Technology
NOC	network operating centers
NOSC	network operation security center
NVD	National Vulnerability Database
NVLAP	National Voluntary Laboratory Accreditation Program
OASIS	Organization for the Advancement of Structured Information Standards
OCSP	online certificate status protocol
OMI	open model interface [1]

OO	object oriented
OOB	out of band
OS	operating system
OSD	Office of the Secretary of Defense
OSI	(1) open source initiative
	(2) open system interconnection
OWASP	The Open Web Application Security Project, an Open Source community group dedicated to helping government and industry understand and improve the security of web applications and services [1]
OWL	Web Ontological Language
P2P	peer-to-peer
PaaS	platform as a service
PBAC	policy-based access control
PGP	pretty good privacy
PKCS	Public-Key Cryptography Standards
PKI	public key infrastructure
PKINIT	public key cryptography for initial authentication
POLA	principle of least authority
POP3	Post Office Protocol Version 3
PT	plain text
QoS	quality of service
RA	registration authority
RBAC	role-based access control
RC2	a block cipher designed by Ron Rivest in 1987
RC4	a stream cipher designed by Ron Rivest for RSA data security
RCERTs	regional computer emergency response teams
RDF	resource description framework
RFC	request for comment [4,5]
RIP	routing information protocol
RM	(1) reliable messaging
	(2) reference model
ROI	return on investment
RS-232	a serial line interface originally developed to connect modems and computer terminals
RSA	Rivest, Shamir, Adelman (encryption algorithm)
RST	request for SAML token
RSTR	request for SAML token response
S/MIME	secure/multipurpose Internet mail extensions
SaaS	software as a service
SAML	Security Assertion Markup Language [1]
SDK	software development kit
SEI	Software Engineering Institute
SF	security function
SFP	security function policy

SFR	security functional requirement
SHA	secure hash algorithm
SIGINT	signals intelligence
SLA	service level agreement
SME	subject matter expert
SMTP	simple mail transfer protocol
SNMP	simple network management protocol
SOA	service-oriented architecture
SOAP	simple object access protocol [1]
SOF	strength of function
SPARQL	query language for pattern matching against RDF graphs
SQL	Structured Query Language—an ANSI standard computer language for accessing and manipulating database systems.
SRM	system reference model
SSH	secure shell
SSL	secure socket layer
SSO	single sign on
STIGs	security technical implementation guides
STP	spanning tree protocol
STR	security token reference
STS	security token service
TCB	trusted computer base
TLS	transport layer security
TRM	technical reference model
UBAC	use-case-based access control
UDDI	universal description and discover integration, technical foundation for publication and discovery of web services implementations both within and between enterprises [1]
UDP	user datagram protocol
UI	user interface
UID	unique identifier
UML	Unified Modeling Language
URI	uniform resource identifier
URL	uniform resource locator
URN	uniform resource name
VM	virtual machine
VPN	virtual private network
W2k	Windows 2000
W3C	World Wide Web Consortium [1]
WAN	wide area network
WAS	web application security, a classification scheme for web security vulnerabilities that can be used by both assessment and protection tools [1]
WASP	web application service provider
WCF	Windows Communication Foundation

WiFi	IEEE 802.11
WiMAX	IEEE 802.16
WOC	WAN optimization controller
WS	web services
WS2k3	Windows Server 2003
WS2k8	Windows Server 2008
WSDL	Web Services Description Language
WS-Federation	web services federation protocols
WS-Policy	web services policy protocols
WS-RM	web services reliable messaging, message delivery to software applications with a chosen level of quality of service (QoS). [1]
WSS	web services security offers a trusted means for applying security to web services by providing the necessary technical foundation for higher-level services [1]
wsse	token to indicate a WS-Security package in a SOAP envelope [1]
WS-SEC	web services security
WS-Trust	web services trust protocols [1]
XACML	Extensible Access Control Markup Language, an XML specification for expressing policies for information access over the Internet [1]
XML	Extensible Markup Language
XSD	XML schema document [1]

Terminology

Access	To interact with a system entity in order to manipulate, use, gain knowledge of, and/or obtain a representation of some or all of a system entity's resources.
Access control	(1) Access control is the protection of resources against unauthorized access; a process by which the use of resources is regulated by a security policy and is permitted by only authorized system entities according to that policy. [4]
	(2) Protection of resources against unauthorized access; a process by which use of resources is regulated according to a security policy and is permitted by only authorized system entities according to that policy. [4]
Access control list	A specific file that provides access controls for a given service that are in accordance with the access control requirements for that service.

Access control information	(1) Any information used for access control purposes, including contextual information. [4, X.812] (2) Contextual information might include source IP address, encryption strength, the type of operation being requested, time of day, etc. Portions of access control information may be specific to the request itself, some may be associated with the connection via which the request is transmitted, and others (for example, time of day) may be "environmental." [4]
Access control requirement (ACR)	A specific file in the service registry that provides access controls for a given service that are in accordance with the access control list for that service.
Access rights	A description of the type of authorized interactions a subject can have with a resource. Examples: read, write, execute, add, modify, and delete. [1]
Accreditation	(1) Formal recognition that a laboratory is competent to carry out specific tests or calibration or types of tests or calibrations. (2) Confirmation by an accreditation body as meeting a predetermined standard of impartiality and general technical, methodological, and procedural competence.
Accreditation body	An independent organization responsible for assessing the performance of other organizations against a recognized standard, and for formally confirming the status of those that meet the standard.
Accountability	Accountability means being able to definitively identify and track what entity in the enterprise performed any particular operation (e.g., accessed a file or IP address, invoked a service).
Active role	A role that a system entity has donned when performing some operation, for example accessing a resource. [1]
Actor	(1) A person or organization that may be the owner of agents that either seek to use web services or provide web services. [5] (2) A physical or conceptual entity that can perform actions. Examples: people; companies; machines; running software. An actor can take on (or implement) one or more roles. An actor at one level of abstraction may be viewed as a role at a lower level of abstraction. [5]

Administrator	(1) An individual trusted with full access to a service, enclave or other functional group, for the maintenance of records and policies.
	(2) A person who installs or maintains a system (for example, a SAML-based security system) or who uses it to manage system entities, users, and/or content (as opposed to application purposes; see also End User). An administrator is typically affiliated with a particular administrative domain and may be affiliated with more than one administrative domain. [1]
Agent	(1) An entity that acts on behalf of another entity.
	(2) A background service running for the gathering of data or enforcement of policy.
	(3) An agent is a program acting on behalf of a person or organization.
Anonymity	The quality or state of being anonymous, which is the condition of having a name or identity that is unknown or concealed. [4]
Architecture	(1) Architecture is the structure of components, their interrelationships, and the principles and guidelines governing their design and evolution over time.
	(2) The software architecture of a program or computing system is the structure or structures of the system. This structure includes software components, the externally visible properties of those components, the relationships among them and the constraints on their use.
	(3) A software architecture is an abstraction of the run-time elements of a software system during some phase of its operation. A system may be composed of many levels of abstraction and many phases of operation, each with its own software architecture. [4c]
Assertion	A piece of data produced by a SAML authority regarding either an act of authentication performed on a subject, attribute information about the subject, or authorization data applying to the subject with respect to a specified resource. [1]
Assurance	Grounds for confidence that an entity meets its security objectives.

Asymmetric	Property in encryption where different keys are used for encryption and decryption.
Asynchronous	An interaction is said to be asynchronous when the associated messages are chronologically and procedurally decoupled. For example, in a request–response interaction, the client agent can process the response at some indeterminate point in the future when its existence is discovered. Mechanisms to do this include polling, notification by receipt of another message, etc. [5]
Attribute	(1) An attribute is a distinct characteristic inherent in or ascribed to an entity; an entity's attributes are said to describe it.
	(2) A distinct characteristic of an object. An object's attributes are said to describe the object. Objects' attributes are often specified in terms of their physical traits, such as size, shape, weight, and color, etc., for real-world objects. Objects in cyberspace might have attributes describing size, type of encoding, network address, etc. [1]
Attribute assertion	An assertion that conveys information about attributes of a subject. [1]
Attribute ecosystem	The collection of services and stores needed to create and maintain a claims-based authorization system.
Authentication	(1) Authentication refers to the verification of the claims of an entity as to their identity, using an agreed upon credential.
	(2) Authentication is the process of verifying that a potential partner in a conversation is capable of representing a person or organization. [5]
Authentication assertion	An assertion that conveys information about a successful act of authentication that took place for a subject. [1]
Authoritative	Recognized by appropriate governing authorities to be valid or trusted (e.g., the United States [U.S.] Postal Service is the authoritative source for U.S. mailing ZIP codes).
Authorization	(1) Authorization is establishing that the requesting entity has privileges to access a requested resource or perform a particular operation.

(2) The process of determining, by evaluating applicable access control information, whether a subject is allowed to have the specified types of access to a particular resource. Usually, authorization is in the context of authentication. Once a subject is authenticated, it may be authorized to perform different types of access.

Availability

(1) Property of being accessible and usable upon demand by an authorized entity.

(2) Prevention of unauthorized withholding of information resources.

Binding

(1) An association between an interface, a concrete protocol and a data format. A binding specifies the protocol and data format to be used in transmitting messages defined by the associated interface. [5]

(2) The mapping of an interface and its associated operations to a particular concrete message format and transmission protocol. [5]

(3) See also SOAP binding. [5]

(4) Generically, a specification of the mapping of some given protocol's messages, and perhaps message exchange patterns, onto another protocol, in a concrete fashion. For example, the mapping of the SAML <AuthnRequest> message onto HTTP is one example of a binding. The mapping of that same SAML message onto SOAP is another binding. In the SAML context, each binding is given a name in the pattern "SAML xxx binding." [1]

Certification

(1) the procedure by which a third party gives written assurance that a product, process, or service conforms to specified requirements or standards.

(2) A comprehensive assessment of the management, operational and technical security controls in an information system, made in support of security accreditation, to determine the extent to which the controls are implemented correctly, operating as intended, and producing the desired outcome with respect to meeting the security requirements for the system.

Certifying authority (CA)

The senior official having the authority and responsibility for the certification of ISs governed by a DoD Component IA program.

Cipher	The algorithm that is used to apply a key and a cryptographic operation.
Ciphertext	The material that results from encryption of a plaintext.
Claim	A statement that one subject makes about itself or another subject. For example, the statement can be about a name, identity, key, group, privilege, or capability. Claims are issued by a provider, and they are given one or more values and then packaged in security tokens that are issued by a security token service (STS). They are also defined by a claim value type and, possibly, associated metadata. [1i]
Claim name	A user-friendly name for the claim type. [1i]
Claims-based identity	A unique identifier that represents a specific user, application, computer, or other entity. It enables that entity to gain access to multiple resources, such as applications and network resources, without entering credentials multiple times. It also enables resources to validate requests from an entity. [1i]
Claims provider	A software component or service that can be used to issue one or more claims during sign-in operations and to display, resolve, and provide search capabilities for claims in a card selector (for example, the People Picker control in SharePoint). For more information, see Claims Provider. [1i]
Claims record	The stored form of an ELS claim for a given distinguished name and web service or web application.
Common Criteria	Common Criteria for Information Technology Security Evaluation, the title of a set of documents describing a particular set of IT security evaluation criteria.
Composability	Mathematical problem where several evaluated products are used to make up a system. Their security features and metrics and the way they are combined are then used to compute a system security set of metrics. The problem is not yet solved.
Computer network exploitation	Enabling operations and intelligence collection capabilities conducted through the use of computer networks to gather data from target or adversary automated information systems or networks. Also called CNE.

Computer security	(1) Preventing, detecting, and minimizing the consequences of unauthorized actions by users (authorized and unauthorized) of a computer system.
	(2) Measures and controls that ensure confidentiality, integrity, and availability of information system assets including hardware, software, firmware, and information being processed, stored, and communicated.
Confidentiality	(1) The prevention of unauthorized disclosure of information.
	(2) Assuring information will be kept secret, with access limited to appropriate persons.
Connection	A transport layer virtual circuit established between two programs for the purpose of communication. [4]
Connectivity	Property that allows interaction with IT entities external to itself. This includes exchange of data by wire or by wireless means, over any distance in any environment or configuration.
Credential	Data that is transferred to establish a claimed principal identity.
Cryptography	Mathematical transformations of information that provide for a number of functions, including confidentiality, integrity, and accountability and others.
Cybersecurity	The prevention of damage to, the protection of, and the restoration of computers, electronic communications systems, electronic communication services, wire communications, and electronic communications, including information contained therein, to ensure its availability, integrity, authentication, confidentiality, and nonrepudiation.
Cryptographic module	Set of hardware, software, firmware, or a combination thereof that implements cryptographic logic or processes, including cryptographic algorithms and key generation, and is contained within the cryptographic boundary of the module.
Cryptographic module validation	The act of determining if a cryptographic module conforms to the requirements of FIPS PUB 140-2.
Database	A collection of data.
Data integrity	Property that data has not been altered or destroyed in an unauthorized manner.

Delegate	A rich client that is authorized to impersonate another client. For example, consider a situation in which a user-facing website, Web1, calls an infrastructure data service, Data2. It might be advantageous for Web1 to impersonate its users when it accesses Data2. Web1 contacts a federation server to obtain claims that represent one of its users. When it is contacted, the federation server can determine whether Web1 is an authorized delegate and, if so, it can allow the impersonation. If it is authorized, Web1 accesses Data2 while acting as the user. [1i]
Delegatee	The subject being handed a task, usually a subordinate.
Delegation	Delegation is the handing of a task over to another person, usually a subordinate. It is the assignment of authority and responsibility to another person to carry out specific activities.
Delegator	The subject handing the task over to another person, usually a subordinate.
Delegable	The ability to be delegated.
Decryption	The act of applying the cipher to the key and the ciphertext, resulting in plaintext.
Digital signature	(1) A mathematical scheme for demonstrating the authenticity of a digital message or document. Typically a signature is generated by hashing the message, then encrypting the hash with the private key of an asymmetric key pair, or with a previously shared secret symmetric key.
	(2) A value computed with a cryptographic algorithm and appended to a data object in such a way that any recipient of the data can use the signature to verify the data's origin and integrity. (See: data origin authentication service, data integrity service, digitized signature, electronic signature, and signer.) [4]
Discovery	The act of locating a machine-processable description of a web service-related resource that may have been previously unknown and that meets certain functional criteria. It involves matching a set of functional and other criteria with a set of resource descriptions. The goal is to find an appropriate web service-related resource.

Domain	(1) A Microsoft term used in place of realm.
	(2) A domain is an identified set of agents and/or resources that is subject to the constraints of one of more policies. [5]
Domain controller	A server in a Microsoft Windows domain that runs Active Directory Domain Services, that is, plays the role of an "Active Directory server" or "has the Active Directory role."
Elasticity	The ability to scale resources both up and down as needed. Elasticity is another name for scalability.
End point	An association between a binding and a network address, specified by a URI that may be used to communicate with an instance of a service. An end point indicates a specific location for accessing a service using a specific protocol and data format. [5]
Enterprise	(1) The totality of assets under one management system.
	(2) Enterprise is an organization (or cross-organizational entity) supporting a defined business scope and mission. An enterprise includes interdependent resources (people, organizations, and technology) that must coordinate their functions and share information in support of a common mission (or set of related missions).
Enterprise service registry (ESR)	A collection of files for a specific service that include Credentials, WSDLs, XSDs, ACRs, and other information pertinent to the particular service.
Encryption	(1) The act of applying the cipher to the key and plaintext, resulting in ciphertext.
	(2) In cryptography, encryption is the process of transforming information (referred to as plaintext) using an algorithm (called cipher) to make it unreadable to anyone except those possessing special knowledge, usually referred to as a key. To anyone not in possession of the key, the message should appear to be a completely random sequence of bits.
	(3) Cryptographic transformation of data (called "plaintext") into a form (called "ciphertext") that conceals the data's original meaning to prevent it from being known or used. If the transformation is reversible, the corresponding reversal process is called "decryption," which is a transformation that restores encrypted data to its original state. [4]

Extended claim	A statement that a subject has been delegated to provide, the statement has been authorized by a subject that has the claim (delegator) and permission to delegate For example, the statement can be about a name, identity, key, group, privilege, or capability. Claims are issued by a provider, and they are given one or more values and then packaged in security tokens that are issued by a security token service (STS). They are also defined by a claim value type and, possibly, associated metadata.
Extended claims record	The stored form of an ELS extended or delegated claim for a given distinguished name and web service or web application.
Extensibility	The ability to be extended (as in higher levels of the architecture).
Federated identity	A principal's identity is said to be federated between a set of Providers when there is an agreement between the providers on a set of identifiers and/or attributes to use to refer to the Principal Federate To link or bind two or more entities together [15].
Federation	This term is used in two senses in SAML:
	(a) The act of establishing a relationship between two entities [15].
	(b) An association comprising any number of service providers and identity providers. [1]
Geodatabases	A common data storage and management framework. It combines "geo" (spatial data) with "database" (data repository) to create a central data repository for spatial data storage and management. It can be leveraged in desktop, server, or mobile environments and allows storage of geospatial data in a central location for easy access and management.
Governance	The systems, processes, and procedures put in place to steer the direction, management, and accountability of an organization. In the context of the SOA in the DoD, governance means establishing and enforcing how DoD Components agree to provide, use, and operate services.

Hash function	Any algorithm or subroutine that maps plaintext to a value, called keys. For example, a value can serve as an index to list of plaintext items. The values returned by a hash function are called hash values, hash codes, hash sums, checksums or simply hashes. Hash functions are mostly used to accelerate table lookup or data comparison tasks such as finding items in a database, detecting duplicated or similar records in a large file, finding similar stretches in DNA sequences, and so on. In cryptographic services, a hash is used to nearly uniquely identify the content of a plaintext.
Help desk	A facility to assist users in the resolution of problems.
Identity	The collective set of attributes that defines an entity (i.e., subject, resource, etc.) within a given context.

Identifier	(1) An identifier is an unambiguous name for a resource. initial SOAP sender. The SOAP sender that originates a SOAP message at the starting point of a SOAP message path. [5]
	
	(2) This term is used in two senses in SAML:
	   (a) One that identifies [15].
	   (b) A data object (for example, a string) mapped to a system entity that uniquely refers to the system entity. A system entity may have multiple distinct identifiers referring to it. An identifier is essentially a "distinguished attribute" of an entity. [1] See also Attribute.

Identity	The essence of an entity [15]. One's identity is often described by one's characteristics, among which may be any number of identifiers. See also Identifier, Attribute. [1]
Information assurance	Conducting those operations that protect and defend information and information systems by ensuring availability, integrity, authentication, confidentiality, and non-repudiation. This includes providing for restoration of information systems by incorporating protection, detection, and reaction capabilities.
Information hiding	Information hiding involves only exposing the minimum set of information in efforts to make authorized use of a capability.

Information system	A discrete set of information resources organized for the collection, processing, maintenance, use, sharing, dissemination, or disposition of information. Since information systems can comprise multiple products, different C&A schemes for products and systems can sometimes conflict with one another.
Integrity	(1) Prevention of unauthorized modification of information.
	(2) Assuring information will not be accidentally or maliciously altered or destroyed.
Least privilege	Access is restricted to only those elements and resources necessary to perform the assigned task.
Load balancing	A computer networking method to distribute workload across multiple computers or a computer cluster, network links, central processing units, disk drives, or other resources, to achieve optimal resource utilization, maximize throughput, minimize response time, and avoid overload. Using multiple components with load balancing, instead of a single component, may increase reliability through redundancy. The load balancing service is usually provided by dedicated software or hardware, such as a multilayer switch or a domain name system server.
Malware	Software such as viruses or Trojans designed to cause damage or disruption to a computer system.
Markup Language	A set of XML elements and XML attributes to be applied to the structure of an XML document for a specific purpose. A markup language is typically defined by means of a set of XML schemas and accompanying documentation. For example, the Security Assertion Markup Language (SAML) is defined by two schemas and a set of normative SAML specification text. [1]
Message	A message is the basic unit of data sent from one web services agent to another in the context of web services. The basic unit of communication between a web service and a requester: data to be communicated to or from a web service as a single logical transmission. [1,5] See also SOAP message.

Message reliability	Message reliability is the degree of certainty that a message will be delivered and that sender and receiver will both have the same understanding of the delivery status. [5]
Measured service	Cloud computing resource usage can be measured, controlled, and reported providing transparency for both the provider and consumer of the utilized service.
Middleware	(1) In a distributed computing system—the software layer that lies between the operating system and the applications on each site of the system. (2) In the context of this document—the software toolkits and API's that must be leveraged in order to implement the desired secure service-oriented architecture.
Nonrepudiation	(1) Nonrepudiation is that property that ensures actions are attributable to the entity that invokes them. (2) Method by which the sender of data is provided with proof of delivery and the recipient is assured of the sender's identity, so that neither can later deny having processed the data. [5]
Network security	Protection of information systems against unauthorized access to or modification of information, whether in storage, processing or transit, and against the denial of service to authorized users, including those measures necessary to detect, document, and counter such threats.
Orchestration	An orchestration defines the sequence and conditions in which one web service invokes other web services in order to realize some useful function. I.e., an orchestration is the pattern of interactions that a web service agent must follow in order to achieve its goal. [5]
Organizational security policy	One or more security rules, procedures, practices, or guidelines imposed by an organization upon its operations.
Persona	Alternate representation of a user for delegation, least privilege, or concurrent tasking.
Personae	More than one persona.

Plaintext	The unmodified information before any cryptographic operations. It need not be plain American Standard Code for Information Interchange (ASCII), as it could be Extensible Markup Language (XML), Hyper-Text Markup Language (HTML), plain ASCII, symmetric keys, etc. It is the material that may provide information to an eavesdropper.
Platform as a service (PaaS)	Is a category of cloud computing services that provides a computing platform and a solution stack as a service.
Policy	A policy is a constraint on the behavior of agents or person or organization. [5]
Policy decision point (PDP)	A system entity that makes authorization decisions for itself or for other system entities that request such decisions. For example, a SAML PDP consumes authorization decision requests, and produces authorization decision assertions in response. A PDP is an "authorization decision authority." [1]
Policy enforcement point (PEP)	A system entity that requests and subsequently enforces authorization decisions. For example, a SAML PEP sends authorization decision requests to a PDP, and consumes the authorization decision assertions sent in response. [1]
Protocol	(1) A set of semantic and syntactic rules that determine the behavior of entities that interact.
	(2) A set of formal rules describing how to transmit data, especially across a network. Low-level protocols define the electrical and physical standards to be observed, bit- and byte-ordering and the transmission and error detection and correction of the bit stream. High-level protocols deal with the data formatting, including the syntax of messages, the terminal to computer dialogue, character sets, sequencing of messages etc.
Provider	A generic way to refer to both identity providers and service providers. [1]
Proxy	(1) An agent that relays a message between a requester agent and a provider agent, appearing to the web service to be the requester. [5]
	(2) An entity authorized to act for another.
	(a) Authority or power to act for another.
	(b) A document giving such authority. [15]

Pull	To actively request information from a system entity. [1]
Push	To provide information to a system entity that did not actively request it. [1]
Quality of service	Quality of service is an obligation accepted and advertised by a provider entity to service consumers. [1]
Registry	Authoritative, centrally controlled store of information. [5]
Relational database	A data store based on the relational model, which means related sets (as in a mathematical set) of information are stored in tables (relations).
Reliability	Property of consistent intended behavior and results.
Requester, SAML requester	A system entity that utilizes the SAML protocol to request services from another system entity (a SAML authority, a responder). The term "client" for this notion is not used because many system entities simultaneously or serially act as both clients and servers. In cases where the SOAP binding for SAML is being used, the SAML requester is architecturally distinct from the initial SOAP sender. [1]
Role	Predefined set of rules establishing the allowed interactions between a user and the services provided in an enterprise.
Security architecture	A plan and set of principles for an administrative domain and its security domains that describe the security services that a system is required to provide to meet the needs of its users, the system elements required to implement the services, and the performance levels required in the elements to deal with the threat environment. A complete security architecture for a system addresses administrative security, communication security, computer security, emanations security, personnel security, and physical security, and prescribes security policies for each. A complete security architecture needs to deal with both intentional, intelligent threats and accidental threats. A security architecture should explicitly evolve over time as an integral part of its administrative domain's evolution. [4]
Security Assertion	An assertion that is scrutinized in the context of a security architecture. [1]

Security Assertion Markup Language (SAML)	The set of specifications describing security assertions that are encoded in XML, profiles for attaching the assertions to various protocols and frameworks, the request/response protocol used to obtain the assertions, and bindings of this protocol to various transfer protocols (for example, SOAP and HTTP). [1]
Security assurance	Grounds for confidence that an entity meets its security objectives.
Security attribute	Information associated with users, subjects, and objects used for the enforcement of the Security Policy.
Security context	With respect to an individual SAML protocol message, the message's security context is the semantic union of the message's security header blocks (if any) along with other security mechanisms that may be employed in the message's delivery to a recipient. With respect to the latter, and examples are security mechanisms employed at lower network stack layers such as HTTP, TLS/SSL, IPSEC, etc. With respect to a system entity, "Alice," interacting with another system entity, "Bob," a security context is nominally the semantic union of all employed security mechanisms across all network connections between Alice and Bob. Alice and Bob may each individually be, for example, a provider or a user agent. This notion of security context is similar to the notion of "security contexts" as employed in Reference 4, and in the Distributed Computing Environment [DCE], for example.
Security flaw	Condition that alone or in concert with others provides an exploitable vulnerability.
Security token service	(1) A service that: • Provides security tokens for accessing other services when presented requests with proper credentials (Identity Provider component), and/or • Translates security tokens from one form to another, providing a token with the needed attributes for determining authorization to the relying service (Security Provider component). (2) A web service that issues claims and packages them in encrypted security tokens. For more information, see WS-Security and WS-Trust. [1i]

Serializabilty	The property of a database such that there is a valid sequence of events that could have resulted in the database state for all externally visible states of the database.
Service	A service is an abstract resource that represents a capability of performing tasks that form a coherent functionality from the point of view of providers entities and requesters entities. To be used, a service must be realized by a concrete provider agent. [5]
Services	A mechanism to enable access to one or more capabilities, where the access is provided using a prescribed interface and is exercised consistent with constraints and policies as specified by the service description.
Service description	A service description is a set of documents that describe the interface to and semantics of a service. [5]
Service interface	A service interface is the abstract boundary that a service exposes. It defines the types of messages and the message exchange patterns that are involved in interacting with the service, together with any conditions implied by those messages. Service Interface is a logical grouping of operations. An interface represents an abstract service type, independent of transmission protocol and data format. [5]
Service provider	(1) A service provider is an entity (i.e., person or organization) that offers the use of capabilities by means of a service. (2) A role donned by a system entity where the system entity provides services to principals or other system entities. [1]
Service registry or Registry service	Is a platform neutral, network based directory that stores information about services and is searchable based on the descriptive metadata defined in the service specification.
Service requester	See requester agent and requester entity. See also the discussion about service requester in Reference 5.
Service WSDL	A collection of end points. See web service.
Session	A lasting interaction between system entities, often involving a user, typified by the maintenance of some state of the interaction for the duration of the interaction. Such an interaction may not be limited to a single connection between the system entities. [5]

SOAP	The formal set of conventions governing the format and processing rules of a SOAP message. These conventions include the interactions among SOAP nodes generating and accepting SOAP messages for the purpose of exchanging information along a SOAP message path. [1]
Software as a service (SaaS)	sometimes referred to as "on-demand software" supplied by ISVs or "Application-Service-Providers" (ASPs), is a software delivery model in which software and associated data are centrally hosted on the cloud.
Software assurance	The planned and systematic set of activities that ensure that software life cycle processes and products conform to requirements, standards, and procedures.
Standards	Documented agreements containing technical specifications or other precise criteria to be used consistently as rules, guidelines, or definitions of characteristics to ensure that materials, products, processes, and services are fit for their purpose.
Strength of function	A qualification of a security function expressing the minimum efforts assumed necessary to defeat its expected security behavior by directly attacking its underlying security mechanisms.
Symmetric	Property in encryption where the same key is used for encryption and decryption.
Synchronous	An interaction is said to be synchronous when the participating agents must be available to receive and process the associated messages from the time the interaction is initiated until all messages are actually received or some failure condition is determined. The exact meaning of "available to receive the message" depends on the characteristics of the participating agents (including the transfer protocol it uses); it may, but does not necessarily, imply tight time synchronization, blocking a thread, etc. [5]
System entity	An active element of a computer/network system. For example, an automated process or set of processes, a subsystem, a person or group of persons that incorporates a distinct set of functionality. [4]
System integrity	Property that a system performs its intended function in an unimpaired manner, free from deliberate or accidental unauthorized manipulation of the system.

Threat	(1) Any circumstance or event with the potential to harm an IT system through unauthorized access, destruction, disclosure, modification of data, and/or denial of service.
	(2) Potential danger that a vulnerability may be exploited intentionally, triggered accidentally, or otherwise exercised.
	(3) A potential cause of an unwanted incident which may result in harm to a system or organization.
Threat model	A representation of threats and possible attack methods in an operational environment against a specific product or products.
Transaction	Transaction is a feature of the architecture that supports the coordination of results or operations on state in a multistep interaction. The fundamental characteristic of a transaction is the ability to join multiple actions into the same unit of work, such that the actions either succeed or fail as a unit. [5]
Trusted path	Means by which a user and a security function can communicate with necessary confidence to support the security policy.
User	A natural person who makes use of a system and its resources for any purpose [1].
Validation	Activity applied throughout the system's life cycle to confirm or establish by testing, evaluation, examination, investigation, or competent evidence that a DoD IS's assigned IA controls are implemented correctly and are effective in their application.
Verification	(1) Confirmation by examination and provision of objective evidence that specified requirements have been fulfilled.
	(2) Process of comparing two levels of an IT system specification for proper correspondence, such as security policy model with top-level specification, top-level specification with source code, and source code with object code.
Vulnerability	Weakness in the design, operation, or operational environment of an IT system or product that can be exploited to violate the intended behavior of the system relative to safety, security, and/or integrity.

WS-Federation	The Organization for the Advancement of Structured Information Standards (OASIS) standard specification that defines the WS-Federation Passive protocol and other protocol extensions that are used for federation. The WS-Federation standard defines mechanisms that are used to enable identity, attribute, authentication, and authorization federation across different trust realms. For more information about WS-Federation, see Understanding WS-Federation at the MSDN web site. [1i]
WS-Security	The WS-Security standard is a set of protocols designed to help secure web service communication by using SOAP. For more information about WS-Security, see OASIS Web Services Security (WSS) TC on the OASIS site. [1,1i]
WS-Trust	A standard that uses WS-Security to provide web services with methods to build and verify trust relationships. For more information about WS-Trust, see OASIS Web Services Secure Exchange (WS-SX) TC on the OASIS site. [1,1i]
XML schema	The format developed by the World Wide Web Consortium (5) for describing rules for a markup language to be used in a set of XML documents. In the lowercase, a "schema" or "XML schema" is an individual instance of this format. For example, SAML defines two schemas, one containing the rules for XML documents that encode security assertions and one containing the rules for XML documents that encode request/response protocol messages. Schemas define not only XML elements and XML attributes, but also data types that apply to these constructs. [1]
Zeroize	A method of erasing electronically stored data by altering the contents of the data storage so as to prevent the recovery of the data. [2]

Bibliography

1. OASIS open set of Standards:
   a. N. Ragouzis et al., *Security Assertion Markup Language (SAML) V2.0 Technical Overview*. OASIS Committee Draft. Available online at: http://www.oasis-open. org/committees/download.php/27819/sstc-saml-tech-overview-2.0-cd-02.pdf, March 2008.
   b. P. Madsen et al., *SAML V2.0 Executive Overview*. OASIS Committee Draft. Available online at: http://www.oasis-open.org/committees/download. php/13525/ sstc-saml-exec-overview-2.0-cd-01-2col.pdf, April 2005.
   c. P. Mishra et al., *Conformance Requirements for the OASIS Security Assertion Markup Language (SAML) V2.0*. OASIS Standard. Available online at: http://docs.oasis-open.org/security/saml/v2.0/saml-conformance-2.0-os.pdf, March 2005.
   d. S. Cantor et al., *Bindings for the OASIS Security Assertion Markup Language (SAML) V2.0*. OASIS Standard. Available online at: http://docs.oasis-open.org/ security/saml/v2.0/saml-bindings-2.0-os.pdf, March 2005.
   e. S. Cantor et al., *Profiles for the OASIS Security Assertion Markup Language (SAML) V2.0*. OASIS Standard. Available online at: http://docs.oasis-open.org/security/ saml/v2.0/saml-profiles-2.0-os.pdf, March 2005.
   f. S. Cantor et al., *Assertions and Protocols for the OASIS Security Assertion Markup Language (SAML) V2.0*. OASIS Standard. Available online at: http://docs.oasis-open.org/security/saml/v2.0/saml-core-2.0-os.pdf, March 2005.
   g. S. Cantor et al., *Metadata for the OASIS Security Assertion Markup Language (SAML) V2.0*. OASIS Standard. Available online at: http://docs.oasis-open.org/ security/saml/v2.0/saml-metadata-2.0-os.pdf, March 2005.
   h. F. Hirsch et al., *Security and Privacy Considerations for the OASIS Security Assertion Markup Language (SAML) V2.0*. OASIS Standard. Available online at: http://docs. oasis-open.org/security/saml/v2.0/saml-sec-consider-2.0-os.pdf, March 2005.
   i. J. Hodges et al., *Glossary for the OASIS Security Assertion Markup Language (SAML) V2.0*. OASIS Standard. Available online at: http://docs.oasis-open.org/ security/saml/v2.0/saml-glossary-2.0-os.pdf, March 2005.
   j. *WS-Trust Specification 1.4*, http://docs.oasis-open.org/ws-sx/ws-trust/200802 OASIS, February 2009.
   k. *WS-ReliableMessaging Specification 1.2*, http://docs.oasis-open.org/ws-rx/wsrm/ 200702 OASIS, February 2, 2009.

l. *WS-SecureConversation Specification 1.4*, http://docs.oasis-open.org/ws-sx/ws-secureconversation/200512 OASIS, February 2009.

m. *WS-Security Specification 1.1*, OASIS, November 2006. UDDI Version 3.0.2.

n. *UDDI Spec Technical Committee Draft*, Dated 20041019. Document identifier: uddi_v3, Latest version: http://uddi.org/pubs/uddi_v3.htm

2. National Institute of Standards, Gaithersburg, Maryland:

   a. NIST Special Publication 800-38, *Recommendation for Block Cipher Modes of Operation: 38A, Methods and Techniques*, December 2001; 38B, The RMAC Authentication Mode, November 5, 2002 draft; 38C, The CCM Mode for Authentication and Confidentiality, May 2004.

   b. *Recommendation for Block Cipher Modes of Operation: 38A, Methods and Techniques*, December 2001; 38B, The RMAC Authentication Mode, November 5, 2002 draft; 38C, The CCM Mode for Authentication and Confidentiality.

   c. NIST Special Publication 800-53, *Recommended Security Controls for Federal Information Systems and Organizations, Revision 3*, August 2009.

   d. NIST Special Publication 800-67, *Version 1.2, Recommendation for the Triple Data Encryption Algorithm (TDEA) Block Cipher*, Revised January 2012.

   e. NIST Special Publication 800-95, *Guide to Secure Web Services*. Available at: http://csrc.nist.gov/publications/nistpubs/800-95/SP800-95.pdf. (Accessed on February 19, 2011) Federal Information Processing Standards Publication 140, Security Requirements for Cryptographic Modules, May 25, 2001.

   f. NIST Special Publication 800-144, *Guidelines on Security and Privacy in Public Cloud Computing*, Wayne Jansen, Timothy Grance, December 2011.

   g. NIST Special Publication 800-145, *Draft: Cloud Computing*, Computer Security Division, Information Technology Laboratory, National Institute of Standards and Technology, Gaithersburg, MD 20899-8930, Peter Mell, Timothy Grance, January 2011. http://csrc.nist.gov/publications/drafts/800-145/Draft-SP-800-145_cloud-definition.pdf.

   h. Federal Information Processing Standards Publication 140, *Security Requirements for Cryptographic Modules*, May 25, 2001.

   i. Federal Information Processing Standards Publication 180-3, *Secure Hash Standard*, August 2002.

   j. Federal Information Processing Standards Publication 186-3, *Digital Signature Standard*, June 2009.

   k. Federal Information Processing Standards Publication 196, *Entity Authentication Using Public Key Cryptography*, February 18, 1997.

   l. Federal Information Processing Standards Publication 197, *Advanced Encryption Standard (AES)*, November 2001.

   m. Federal Information Processing Standards Publication 188, *Standard Security Label for Information Transfer*, September 6, 1994. http://www.itl.nist.gov/fipspubs/fip188.htm

3. Common Criteria for Information Technology Security Evaluation:

   a. Version 3.1, revision 3, July 2009. *Part 1: Introduction and General Model*.

   b. Version 3.1, revision 3, July 2009. *Part 2: Functional Security Components*.

   c. Version 3.1, revision 3, July 2009. *Part 3: Assurance Security Components*.

   d. *Common Methodology for Information Technology Security Evaluation*, Version 3.1, revision 3, July 2009.

4. Internet Engineering Task Force (IETF) Standards:
   a. STD 5 (RFC0791), *Internet Protocol*, J. Postel, September 1981, and subsequent RFCs 791/950/919/922/792/1112
   b. STD 9 (RFC0959), *File Transfer Protocol*, J. Postel, J. Reynolds, October 1985.
   c. STD 66 (RFC3986), *Uniform Resource Identifier (URI): Generic Syntax*, T. Berners-Lee, R. Fielding, L. Masinter, January 2005.
   d. RFC 1321, *The MD5 Message-Digest Algorithm*, April 1992.
   e. RFC 2104, *HMAC: Keyed-Hashing for Message Authentication*, February 1997. STD 9 (RFC0959) *File Transfer Protocol*, J. Postel, J. Reynolds, October 1985.
   f. RFC 2406, *IP Encapsulating Security Payload*, November 1998.
   g. RFC 2459, *Internet X.509 Public Key Infrastructure Certificate and CRL Profile*, January 1999.
   h. RFC 2560, *X.509 Internet Public Key Infrastructure Online Certificate Status Protocol—OCSP*, June 1999.
   i. RFC 2829, *Authentication Methods for LDAP*. M. Wahl, H. Alvestrand, J. Hodges, R.L. Morgan. May 2000.
   j. RFC 3305, *Report from the Joint W3C/IETF URI Planning Interest Group: Uniform Resource Identifiers (URIs), URLs, and Uniform Resource Names (URNs): Clarifications and Recommendations*, August 2002.
   k. RFC 4120, *The Kerberos Network Authentication Service V5*, updated by RFC 4537 and 5021.
   l. RFC 4510, *Lightweight Directory Access Protocol (LDAP): Technical Specification Road Map*, June 2006.
   m. RFC 5246: *The Transport Layer Security (TLS) Protocol Version 1.2*, August 2008.
   n. RFC 5751, *Secure/Multipurpose Internet Mail Extensions (S/MIME) Version 3.2*, Message Specification, July 2010.
   o. RFC 6151, *Updated Security Considerations for the MD5 Message-Digest and the HMAC-MD5 Algorithms*, March 2011.
   p. Web Services Architecture, *Requirements, W3C Working Group Note*, 11 February 2004. Latest version: http://www.w3.org/TR/ws-arch/
5. World Wide Web Consortium (W3C):
   a. *XML Encryption Syntax and processing*, December 10, 2002.
   b. *XML Signature Syntax and Processing*, June 10, 2008.
   c. *XML Canonical XML Ver. 1*, March 2001.
   d. *XML-Exclusive Canonicalization Ver. 1*, July 2002.
   e. *W3C XML Schema Definition Language (XSD) 1.1 Part 2: Datatypes*, W3C Recommendation, April 5, 2012. Latest version: http://www.w3.org/TR/xmlschema11-2/
   f. *W3C XML Schema Definition Language (XSD) 1.1 Part 1: Structures*, W3C Recommendation, April 5, 2012. Latest version: http://www.w3.org/TR/xmlschema11-1/
   g. *SOAP Version 1.2 Part 1: Messaging Framework* (second edition). World Wide Web Consortium (W3C), April 27, 2007. http://www.w3.org/TR/soap12-part1/
   h. *Web Services Description Language (WSDL) Version 2.0 Part 0: Primer*, W3C Recommendation, June 26, 2007.
   i. *Web Services Description Language (WSDL) Version 2.0 Part 1: Core Language*, W3C Recommendation, June 26, 2007. Latest version: http://www.w3.org/TR/wsdl20

    j. *Web Services Description Language (WSDL) Version 2.0 Part 2: Adjuncts, W3C Recommendation*, June 26, 2007.

    k. Semantic Annotations for WSDL and XML Schema, W3C Recommendation, August 28, 2007.

    l. HTML 4.01 Specifications, W3C Recommendation, December 24, 1999.

    m. XHTML™ 1.1—*Module-Based XHTML—(second edition), W3C Recommendation*, November 23, 2010.

6. ISO/IEC Standards:

    a. *Information Technology—Database Languages—SQL—Part 1: Framework (SQL/ Framework)*, ISO/IEC 9075-1:2011(E), December 15, 2011.

    b. *Information Technology—Database Languages—SQL—Part 2: Foundation (SQL/ Foundation)*, ISO/IEC 9075-2:2011(E), December 15, 2011.

    c. *Information Technology—Database Languages—SQL Multimedia and Application Packages—Part 1: Framework*, ISO/IEC 13249-1:2007(E), February 15, 2007.

    d. *Information Technology—Database Languages—SQL Multimedia and Application Packages—Part 2: Full-Text*, ISO/IEC 13249-2:2003(E), November 1, 2003.

    e. *Information Technology—Database Languages—SQL Multimedia and Application Packages—Part 3: Spatial*, ISO/IEC 13249-3:2011(E), April 15, 2011.

    f. *Information Technology—Database Languages—SQL Multimedia and Application Packages—Part 5: Still Image*, ISO/IEC 13249-5:2003(E), November 1, 2011.

    g. *Information Technology—Database Languages—SQL Multimedia and Application Packages—Part 6: Data Mining*, ISO/IEC 13249-6:2006(E), December 1, 2006.

7. L. Margherio, S. Cooke, S. Montes, *The Emerging Digital Economy*, Secretariat on Electronic Commerce, U.S. Department of Commerce, Washington, DC 20230, September 8, 2010, http://govinfo.library.unt.edu/ecommerce/EDEreprt.pdf, http://www.esa.doc.gov/Reports/emerging-digital-economy.

8. D. W. Davies, CBE, FRS, June 7, 1924, Treorchy, UK, May 28, 2000, Australia, http://www.thocp.net/biographies/davies_donald.htm.

9. D. W. Davies, *Internet Hall of Fame Pioneer*, http://www.internethalloffame.org/inductees/donald-davies

10. *Lawrence Roberts Manages the ARPANET Program*. Living Internet.com. Retrieved November 6, 2008.

11. *ARPANET*, http://en.wikipedia.org/wiki/ARPANET

12. *A Brief History of Network Computing*, http://inventors.about.com/library/weekly/aa091598.htm

13. *Internet Growth Data 1995–2010*, www.internetworldstats.com

14. *MIT Internet Growth 1993–1994*, http://www.mit.edu/~mkgray/net/internet-growth-raw-data.html, *Internet Growth Data* 1971–1992, Extrapolated by Author.

15. *Merriam Webster* online dictionary for identity, http://www.learnersdictionary.com/definition/identity

16. M. Burrows, M. Abadi, and R. M. Needham, A logic of authentication, *ACM Transaction on Computer Systems*, 8(1), 18–36, 1990.

17. W. R. Simpson and C. Chandersekaran, Information Sharing and Federation, in *2nd International Multi-Conference on Engineering and Technological Innovation: IMETI2009*, Vol. I, pp. 300–305, Orlando, FL, July 2009.

18. W. R. Simpson and C. Chandersekaran, Group based access control extensibility, *Electronic Digest of the 2009 Annual Security Application Conference (ACSAC)*, 12 pp., Honolulu, Hawaii, December 2009.

19. W. R. Simpson and C. Chandersekaran, Cryptography for a high assurance Web-based enterprise, in *Proceedings World Congress on Engineering and Computer Science 2013*, Vol. 1, Lecture Notes in Engineering and Computer Science, pp. 23–28, Berkeley, CA, October 2013.

20. *Public Key Cryptography Standard, PKCS #1 v2.1: RSA Cryptography Standard*, RSA Laboratories, June 14, 2002.

21. S. K. Miller, Fiber optic networks vulnerable to attack, *Information Security Magazine*, November 15, 2006.

22. *Additional material may be found at InfoBlox*, http://www.encryptionanddecryption. com/encryption/asymmetric_encryption.html

23. *Additional material may be found at Cryptography World*, http://www.cryptography-world.com/des.htm

24. J. R. C. Cruz, Dr. Dobb's, Keccak: The new SHA-3 encryption standard, *The World of Software Development*, May 2013. http://www.drdobbs.com/security/keccak-the-new-sha-3-encryption-standard/240154037, see http://keccak.noekeon.org/

25. W. Simpson, C. Chandersekaran, and R. Wagner, High assurance challenges for cloud computing, in *Proceedings World Congress on Engineering and Computer Science 2011*, Vol. I, Lecture Notes in Engineering and Computer Science, pp. 61–66, Berkeley, CA, October 2011.

26. W. Simpson, C. Chandersekaran, H. K. Kim, S-L. Ao, and B. B. Rieger, Editors, IAENG Transactions on Engineering Technologies—Special Edition of the World Congress on Engineering and Computer Science 2011, Lecture Notes in Electrical Engineering 170, DOI: 10.1007/978-94-007-4786-9_16, ISBN: 978-94-007-4785-2, Chapter 16, Co-Existence of High Assurance and Cloud-Based Computing, pp. 201–214, May 2012.

27. W. Simpson and C. Chandersekaran, Enterprise high assurance scale-up, in *Proceedings World Congress on Engineering and Computer Science 2012*, Vol. 1, Lecture Notes in Engineering and Computer Science, pp. 54–59, Berkeley, CA, October 2012.

28. *Web Service Security: Scenarios, Patterns, and Implementation Guidance for Web Services Enhancements (WSE) 3.0*, Microsoft Corporation, 2005.

29. SearchSecurity, *Security Resources, computer forensics (cyber forensics)*, http://searchsecurity.techtarget.com/definition/computer-forensics

30. *OASIS Profiles for the OASIS Security Assertion Markup Language (SAML) V2.0*. Available at http://www.oasis-open.org/committees/tc_home.php?wg_abbrev=security

31. Air Force Information Assurance Strategy Team, *Air Force Information Assurance Enterprise Architecture, Version 1.70, SAF/XC*, March 15, 2009. [Not available to all]

32. J. Spealman, K. Hudson, and M. Craft, 2003. *Windows Server 2003: Active Directory Infrastructure*, Microsoft Press. 2003. pp. 1-8–1-9. ISBN: 0-7356-1438-5.

33. Wikipedia, the online encyclopedia.

34. R. Oppliger, May 1997. Internet security: FIREWALLS and BEYOND. *Communications of the ACM*, 40(5), 94.

35. K. Ingham, and S. Forrest, 2002. *A History and Survey of Network Firewalls*. (pdf). p. 4. https://www.cs.unm.edu/~treport/tr/02-12/firewall.pdf. Retrieved November 25, 2011.

36. Firewalls by Dr. Talal Alkharobi. http://www.ccse.kfupm.edu.sa/~talal/Sec/Firewall.pdf.

37. W. R. Cheswick, S. M. Bellovin, and A. D. Rubin, 2003. Google Books Link. *Firewalls and Internet Security: Repelling the wily hacker*. IBSN 0-201-634666-x.

38. C. Duhigg, August 29, 2003. *Virus May Elude Computer Defenses*. Washington Post.

39. R. Conway, 2004. *Code Hacking: A Developer's Guide to Network Security.* Massachusetts: Charles River Media, Hingham, p. 281. ISBN 1-58450-314-9.

40. Chang, Rocky October 2002. Defending against flooding-based distributed denial-of-service attacks: A tutorial, *IEEE Communications Magazine*, 40(10), 42–43.

41. V. Almeida, A. Bestavros, M. Crovella, A. de Oliveira, Characterizing reference locality in the WWW, *Proceedings of the Fourth International Conference on Parallel and Distributed Information Systems*, pp. 92–107, Miami Beach, FL, December 18–20, 1996.

42. A. Mehmet, C. Bornhövd, S. Krishnamurthy, C. Mohan, H. Pirahesh, B. Reinwald, Cache tables: Paving the way for an adaptive database cache, in *Proceedings of the 29th International Conference on Very Large Databases*, pp. 718–729, Berlin, Germany, September 9–12, 2003.

43. K. Amiri, R. Tewari, S. Park, and S. Padmanabhan, 2002. On space management in a dynamic edge cache, in *Proceedings of the Fifth International Workshop on the Web and Databases* (WebDB 2002), Madison, Wisconsin. ACM, New York, 37–42.

44. J. Anton, L. Jacobs, X. Liu, J. Parker, Z. Zeng, T. Zhong, Web caching for database applications with Oracle Web Cache, in *Proceedings of the 2002 ACM SIGMOD International Conference on Management of Data*, Madison, Wisconsin, June 03–06, 2002 [doi: 10.1145/564691.564762].

45. Apache HTTP Server Project, 2003. *Apache HTTP server.* http://httpd.apache.org/

46. BEA Systems, 2003. Weblogic application server. http//www.bea.com.

47. CacheFlow, 1999. *Accelerating E-Commerce with CacheFlow Internet Caching Appliances* (a CacheFlow white paper). http://www.thefreelibrary.com/CacheFlow+Introduces+the+First+Caching+Solution+Optimized+for...-a061550752.

48. B. Cain, O. Spatscheck, M. May, and A. Barbir, 2001. *Request-Routing Requirements for Content Internetworking.* http://www.ietf.org/internet-drafts/draft-cain-request-routing-req-03.txt

49. K. S. Candan, W.-S. Li, Q. Luo, W.-P. Hsiung, and D. Agrawal, Enabling dynamic content caching for database-driven web sites, in *Proceedings of the 2001 ACM SIGMOD International Conference on Management of Data*, pp. 532–543, Santa Barbara, California, May 21–24, 2001 [doi:10.1145/375663.375736].

50. J. Challenger, P. Dantzig, and A. Iyengar, 1999. A scalable system for consistently caching dynamic web data, in *Proceedings of the 18th Annual Joint Conference of the IEEE Computer and Communications Societies (INFOCOM) (New York, NY).* IEEE Computer Society Press, Los Alamitos, California, 294–303.

51. C. Cunha, A. Bestavros, and M. Crovella, *Characteristics of WWW Client-based Traces*, Boston University, Boston, Massachusetts, 1995.

52. ESI Consortium, 2001. *Edge Side Includes.* http://www.esi.org

53. S. Gadde, M. Rabinovich, J. Chase, Reduce, reuse, recycle: An approach to building large Internet caches, in *Proceedings of the 6th Workshop on Hot Topics in Operating Systems (HotOS-VI)*, p. 93, May 5–6, 1997. Harvard University, Boston, MA.

54. E. Gamma, R. Helm, R. Johnson, and J. Vlissides, *Design Patterns: Elements of Reusable Object-Oriented Software*, Addison-Wesley Longman Publishing Co., Inc., Boston, MA, 1995.

55. W. R. Simpson, and C. Chandersekaran, Claims-based authentication for a Web-based enterprise, in *Proceedings World Congress on Engineering 2013, the 2013 International Conference of Information Security and Internet Engineering*, Vol. I, Lecture Notes in Engineering and Computer Science, pp. 524–529, Imperial College, London, July 2013.

56. *Standard for Naming Active Entities on DoD IT Networks, Version 3.5 (or current)*, September 23, 2010.
57. DoDI 8500.2 DoD Instruction 8500.2, *Information Assurance (IA) Implementation*, February 6, 2003.
58. *KRP Key Recovery Policy for the United States Department of Defense, Version 3.0*, August 31, 2003.
59. W. R. Simpson and C. Chandersekaran, World Wide Web Consortium (W3C) workshop on security models for device APIs, *Federated Trust Policy Enforcement by Delegated SAML Assertion Pruning*. 4 pp., London, England, December 2008.
60. W. R. Simpson and C. Chandersekaran, A SAML framework for delegation, attribution and least privilege, *The 3rd International Multi-Conference on Engineering and Technological Innovation: IMETI2010, Volume 2*, Orlando, FL, pp. 303–308, July 2010.
61. W. R. Simpson and C. Chandersekaran, Claims-based enterprise-wide access control, in *Proceedings World Congress on Engineering 2012, The 2012 International Conference of Information Security and Internet Engineering*, Vol. I, Lecture Notes in Engineering and Computer Science, pp. 524–529, Imperial College, London, July 2012.
62. W. R. Simpson and C. Chandersekaran, The case for bi-lateral end-to-end strong authentication, World Wide Web Consortium (W3C) Workshop on Security Models for Device APIs, 4pp., London, England, December 2008.
63. W. R. Simpson, C. Chandersekaran and C. Ebrima, An authentication model for delegation, attribution and least privilege, in *3rd International Conference on PErvasive Technologies Related to Assistive Environments: PETRAE10*, 7pp., Samos, Greece, June 2010.
64. W. R. Simpson and C. Chandersekaran, A persona framework for delegation, attribution and least privilege, in *International Conference on Complexity, Informatics and Cybernetics: CCCT2010*, Vol. II, pp. 84–89, Orlando, FL, April 2010.
65. W. R. Simpson and C. Chandersekaran, Personal delegation by persona creation, *International Journal of Computer Technology and Application (IJCTA)*, 2(6), June 2011, 413–423.
66. W. R. Simpson and C. Chandersekaran, Assured content delivery in the enterprise, in *Proceedings World Congress on Engineering 2012, The 2012 International Conference of Information Security and Internet Engineering*, Vol. I, Lecture Notes in Engineering and Computer Science, pp. 555–560, Imperial College, London, July 2012, coauthored by Coimbatore Chandersekaran.
67. Musings on Digital Rights Management a.k.a. Digital Restrictions Management:
    a. R. Lewis, January 8, 2008. *What Is DRM and Why Should I Care?* Firefox News. http://firefox.org/news/articles/1045/1/What-is-DRM-and-why-should-I-care/Page1.html. Retrieved July 10, 2008.
    b. R. McMillan, May 23, 2006. Article Settlement Ends Sony Rootkit Case. PC World. http://www.pcworld.com/article/id,125838-page,1-c, unresolvedtechstandards/article.html Article. Retrieved April 8, 2007.
    c. S. Marechal, January 9, 2007. *DRM on Audio CDs Abolished.* http://lxer.com/module/newswire/view/78008/index.html.
    d. C. Holahan, January 4, 2008. Sony BMG Plans to Drop DRM. http://www.businessweek.com/technology/content/jan2008/tc2008013_398775.htm.
    e. http://www.locklizard.com/Introduction_to_Digital_Rights_Management.pdf
    f. http://en.wikipedia.org/wiki/Digital_rights_management#Introduction/

    g. http://www.mp3newswire.net/stories/6002/drm.html/

    h. http://creativecommons.org/

    i. http://eff.org/

    j. http://www.spiderrobinson.com/melancholyelephants.html/

68. Authorized Classification and Control Markings Register, Director of National Intelligence (DNI) Special Security Center (SSC), Controlled Access Program Coordination Office (CAPCO) Washington, DC 20511, Vol. 1, edition 2 (Version 1.2): May 12, 2008.

69. DoD 5200.1-PH, DoD Guide to Marking Classified Documents, April 1997, Assistant Secretary of Defense for, Command, Control, Communications and Intelligence, http://www.dtic.mil/dtic/pdf/customer/STINFOdata/DoD5200_1ph. pdf

70. W. R. Simpson, Proceedings of the 19th World Multi-Conference on Systemics, Cybernetics and Informatics: WMSCI, *Database Access – Application-Driven versus Data-Driven*, Volume I, WMSCI 2015, Orlando, Florida, July 12–15, 2015, pp. 187–193.

71. Java:

    a. Oracle Java SE Documentation The Java Database Connectivity (JDBC) API Specification4.1. http://docs.oracle.com/javase/7/docs/technotes/guides/jdbc/

    b. JDBC™ 4.1 Specification, JSR 221, Lance Andersen, Specification Lead, July 2011. Download.oracle.com/otn-pub/jcp/jdbc-4_1-mrel.../jdbc4.1-fr-spec.pdf

72. *ODBC Programmer's Reference*. Available at http://msdn.microsoft.com/en-us/library/windows/desktop/ms714177%28v=vs.85%29.aspx

73. *XML Path Language (XPath) Version 1.0*. Available at http://www.w3.org/TR/xpath/

74. *XQuery 1.0: An XML Query Language* (second edition). Available at http://www.w3.org/TR/xquery/

75. *XSL Transformations (XSLT) Version 1.0*. Available at http://www.w3.org/TR/xslt.

76. *Information Technology—Database Languages—SQL*, ISO/IEC 9075-*:2008. Available at ANSI website: http://webstore.ansi.org/FindStandards.aspx?SearchString=9075&SearchOption=1&PageNum=0&SearchTermsArray=9075|null|null.

77. R. Housley, W. Ford, W. Polk and D. Solo, *Internet X.509 Public Key Infrastructure: Certificate and CRL Profile*. RFC 2459, January 1999.

78. *Serializability Theory*. Available at http://courses.cs.vt.edu/~cs5204/fall99/distributedDBMS/serial.html.

79. S. C. Gupta, *DBMS Fundamentals*. Available at http://www.scribd.com/doc/24578499/29/Checkpoints.

80. J. Ellis and L. Ho, with Maydene Fisher, *JDBC 3.0 Specification*. Available at http://java.cnam.fr/iagl/biblio/spec/jdbc-3_0-fr-spec.pdf.

81. E. F. Codd, 1970. A relational model of data for large shared data banks, *Communications of the ACM Archive*, 13(6), June 1970, 377–387.

82. Introducing databases by Stephen Chu, in Conrick, M. 2006. *Health Informatics: Transforming Healthcare with Technology*, Thomson, ISBN 0-17-012731-1, p. 69.

83. Datanamic, Introduction to Database Design, Online tutorial, http://www.datanamic.com/support/lt-dez005-introduction-db-modeling.html

84. H. Zhuge, 2008. *The Web Resource Space Model. Web Information Systems Engineering and Internet Technologies Book Series* 4. Springer. ISBN 978-0-387-72771-4.

85. *My SQL Stored Programs and Views*, http://docs.oracle.com/cd/E19078-01/mysql/mysql-refman-5.0/stored-programs-views.html#stored-routines-syntax

86. *Purdue on Using Stored Procedures to Set Views*, https://www.cs.purdue.edu/homes/ninghui/projects/Topics/DB_FineGrained.html

87. D. L. Parnas, On the criteria to be used in decomposing systems into modules, *Communications of the ACM*, 15(12), December 1972, pp. 1053–1058.

88. *Enabling Web Services*, http://go.microsoft.com/fwlink/?LinkId=153335

89. *Testing Published Web Services*, (http://go.microsoft.com/fwlink/?LinkId=153336), How to Create a .NET Application to Test a WCF Service Published with the BizTalk WCF Service Publishing Wizard (http://go.microsoft.com/fwlink/?LinkId=202830)

90. Microsoft Knowledge Base Article 815145, HOW TO: Lock down an ASP.NET Web Application or Web Service. http://go.microsoft.com/fwlink/?LinkId=153337

91. *ASP.NET Edit Rule Dialog Box*, (http://go.microsoft.com/fwlink/?LinkID=64566) in the .NET Framework 2.0 documentation.

92. For Windows Server, 2008. See *Network Load Balancing Deployment Guide*. http://go.microsoft.com/fwlink/?LinkId=153139

93. Department of Defense, 2012a. Committee on National Security Systems Instruction (CNSSI) No. 1253, *Security Categorization and Control Selection for National Security Systems' Categories for Moderate or High Risk Impact as Delineated in NIST 800-53*.

94. Department of Defense, 2012b. DOD Directive (DoDD) O-8530.1, Computer Network Defense (CND).

95. B. A. Wichmann et al., 1995. Industrial perspective on static analysis, *Software Engineering Journal*, March, 69–75. http://citeseerx.ist.psu.edu/viewdoc/download?doi=10.1.1.138.4760&rep=rep1&type=pdf

96. B. Livshits et al., 2008. Securing web applications with static and dynamic information flow tracking, in *PEPM '08: Proceedings of the 2008 ACM SIGPLAN Symposium on Partial Evaluation and Semantics Based Program Manipulation*. pp. 3–12, ACM, New York.

97. A. Kiezun et al., 2009. Automatic creation of SQL injection and cross-site scripting attacks, in *ICSE'09, Proceedings of the 30th International Conference on Software Engineering*, Vancouver, BC, Canada, May 20–22.

98. MITRE, 2013. *Common Vulnerability and Exposures*. http://cve.mitre.org/

99. MITRE, 2013. *Common Weakness Enumeration*. http://cwe.mitre.org/

100. W. R. Simpson and C. Chandersekaran, Vulnerability and remediation for a high assurance Web-based, in *Proceedings of the 16th International Conference on Enterprise Information Systems*, Vol. 2, pp. 119–128, Lisbon, Portugal, April 27–30, 2014, SCITEPRESS—Science and Technology Publications, ISBN: 978-989-758-028-4.

101. P. Jones, 2010. A formal methods-based verification approach to medical device software analysis. *Embedded Systems Design.*, http://www.embedded.com/design/prototyping-and-development/4008888/A-Formal-Methods-based-verification-approach-to-medical-device-software-analysis

102. B. Livshits, 2006. Improving Software Security with Precise Static and Runtime Analysis, section 7.3. *Static Techniques for Security*, Stanford doc. thesis.

103. *HP Security Tools*, 2013. http://h20331.www2.hp.com/ hpsub/cache/281822-0-0-225-121.html?jumpid=ex_ 2845_vanitysecur/productssecurity/ka011106

104. *IBM Rational*, 2013. http://www.03.ibm.com /software/products /us/en/appscan

105. *Intel Compilers*, 2013. http://software.intel.com/en-us/intel-compilers/

106. *Mosaic*, 2013. http://mosaicsecurity.com/categories/27-network-penetration-testing

107. M. Finifter, et al., *An Empirical Study of Vulnerability Rewards Programs*, USENIX Security 2013, August 15, 2013.
108. CMMI Institute, 2013, *Standard CMMI Appraisal Method for Process Improvement (SCAMPI) Version 1.3a: Method Definition Document for SCAMPI A, B, and C.* http://cmmiinstitute.com/resource/standard-cmmi-appraisal-method-process-improvement-scampi-b-c-version-1-3a-method-definition-document/
109. NIST, 2006, *National Voluntary Laboratory Accreditation Program.* http://www.nist.gov/nvlap/upload/nist-handbook-150.pdf
110. NIST, 2013, *National Vulnerability Database.* http://nvd.nist.gov/
111. *The Open Web Application Security Project (OWASP)*, 2013. https://www.owasp.org/index.php/Main_Page
112. W. R. Simpson and C. Chandersekaran, CCCT2010, Vol. II, *An Agent Based Monitoring System for Web Services*, Orlando, FL, pp. 84–89, April 2011.
113. W. R. Simpson and C. Chandersekaran, A multi-tiered approach to enterprise support services, in *1st International Conference on Design, User Experience, and Usability, Part of the 14th International Conference on Human-Computer Interaction (HCII 2011)*, Orlando, FL, 10 pp., July 2011. Also published in: A. Marcus (ed.): *Design, User Experience, and Usability*, Pt I, HCII 2011, LNCS 6769, pp. 388–397, 2011. Copyright Springer-Verlag, Berlin, Heidelberg, 2011.
114. *Introduction to Amber Point SOA Management System, Software Manual*, December 2007.
115. D. Boneh, C. Gentry, S. Halevi, F. Wang, D. J. Wu, Private database queries using somewhat homomorphic encryption. In: M. Jacobson, M. Locasto, P. Mohassel, R. Safavi-Naini, (eds.) ACNS 2013. LNCS, vol. 7954, pp. 102–118. Springer, Heidelberg, 2013, *Practical Packing Method in Somewhat Homomorphic Encryption* 49.
116. M. Yasuda, T. Shimoyama, J. Kogure, K. Yokoyama, T. Koshiba, Packed homomorphic encryption based on ideal lattices and its application to biometrics. In: A. Cuzzocrea, C. Kittl, D. E. Simos, E. Weippl, L. Xu, (eds.) *CD-ARES Workshops*, Fribourg, Switzerland, September 8–12, 2014.
117. P. Paillier, Public-key cryptosystems based on composite degree residuosity classes. In: J. Stern, (ed.) *EUROCRYPT 1999*. Lecture Notes in Computer Science, Vol. 1592, pp. 223–238. Springer, Heidelberg, 1999.
118. R. A. Popa, C. M. S. Redfield, N. Zeldovich, and H. Balakrishnan, CryptDB: processing queries on an encrypted database, *Communications of the ACM*, 55(9), Sept. 2012 (also *Proc. of 23rd ACM SoSP*, Sept. 2011).
119. R. A. Popa, F. H. Li, N. Zeldovich, An ideal-security protocol for order-preserving encoding, in *Proc. of the 2013 IEEE Symposium on Security and Privacy*, San Francisco, California, May 2013.
120. Middleton, I. Key Factors in HelpDesk Success (An analysis of areas critical to helpdesk development and functionality), British Library R&D Report 6247, The British Library 1996.
121. *Service Management Solutions White Paper Deliver Service Excellence through the Unique Advantages of IBM Service Management Solutions*, September 2007.
122. J. A. Farrell and H. Kreger, Web services management approaches, *IBM Systems Journal*, 41(2), 2002, 212–227.
123. Managing Information Access to an Enterprise, Information System Using J2EE and Services, Oriented Architecture, *IBM Redbook*, January 2005.
124. *ASP.NET Application Services in Windows Communication Foundation (WCF).* http://msdn.microsoft.com/en-us/library/ms731082(v=vs.110).aspx

125. W. R. Simpson, K. Foltz, and C. Chandersekaran, Distributed versus centralized protection schema for the enterprise, in *Proceedings World Congress on Engineering and Computer Science 2014*, Vol. 1, Lecture Notes in Engineering and Computer Science, pp. TBD, Berkeley, CA, October 2014.

126. W. R. Simpson and Kevin Foltz, Wide area network acceleration in a high assurance enterprise, in *Proceedings of the World Congress on Engineering 2015*, Vol. I, WCE 2015, pp. 502–507, Imperial College, London, U.K., July 1–3, 2015.

127. M. Rouse, WAN optimization (WAN acceleration). http://searchenterprisewan. techtarget.com/definition/WAN-optimization, August 2010.

128. M. Rouse, *WAN Accelerator*, Network management and monitoring: The evolution of network control. http://searchenterprisewan.techtarget.com/definition/WAN-accelerator, December 2009.

129. M. Machowinski, WAN optimization market passes $1 billion in 2008, up 29%; enterprise router market down. *Enterprise Routers and WAN Optimization Appliances.* Infonetics Research. Retrieved July 19, 2011.

130. J. Skorupa, and S. Real 2010. *Forecast: Application Acceleration Equipment, Worldwide, 2006–2014, 2Q10 Update.* Gartner, Inc. Retrieved July 19, 2011.

131. N. Cardwell, S. Savage, T. Anderson, Modeling TCP latency. *INFOCOM 2000. Nineteenth Annual Joint Conference of the IEEE Computer and Communications Societies. Proceedings. IEEE. Dept. of Computer Science & Engineering*, Washington University, Seattle, WA, IEEE.org. Retrieved July 20, 2011.

132. Jacobson, Van. *TCP Extensions for Long-Delay Paths.* Request for Comments: 1072. Internet Engineering Task Force (IETF). Retrieved July 19, 2011.

133. S. Floyd, *High Speed TCP for Large Congestion Windows.* Request for Comments: 3649. Internet Engineering Task Force (IETF). Retrieved July 19, 2011.

134. C. Paris, *Latency & Colocation.* Retrieved July 20, 2011.

135. M. Rabinovich, and I. Gokhman. CIFS acceleration techniques. *Storage Developer Conference*, SNIA, Santa Clara, 2009.

136. A. Datta, D. Vandermeer, K. Dutta, and H. Thomas, *Proxy-Based Acceleration of Dynamically Generated Content on the World Wide Web: An Approach and Implementation (2002).* http://citeseer.uark.edu:8080/citeseerx/viewdoc/summary;jsessionid=D62 7E36FC1E6EF538BAB7500C53C9E7F?doi=10.1.1.15.3182

137. Request for Comments: *The Transport Layer Security (TLS) Protocol Version 1.2*, http://tools.ietf.org/html/rfc5246, August 2008.

138. Request for Comments: *3749, Transport Layer Security Protocol Compression Methods*, http://tools.ietf.org/html/rfc3749, May 2004

139. Request for Comments: *Transport Layer Security (TLS) Extensions*, http://tools.ietf. org/html/rfc4366, April 2006.

140. Authentication Methods for LDAP. M. Wahl, H. Alvestrand, J. Hodges, R.L. Morgan. IETF RFC 2829 May 2000.

141. *United States Department of Defense, X.509 Certificate Policy, Version 10*, March 2, 2009.

142. *FPKI-Prof Federal PKI X.509 Certificate and CRL Extensions Profile, Version 6*, October 12, 2005.

143. *SDN 702, Abstract Syntax for Utilization with Common Security Protocol (CSP), Version 3 X.509 Certificates, and Version 2 CRLs, Revision C*, May 12, 1999.

144. *SDN 706 X.509 Certificate and Certification Revocation List Profiles and Certification Path Processing Rules for MISSI Revision D*, May 12, 1999.

145. DoD Directive 8581.1, *Information Assurance (IA) Policy for Space Systems Used by the Department of Defense*, June 21, 2005.

146. DoD 5200.1-R *Information Security Program*, January 1997.

147. National Security Telecommunications and Information Systems Security Policy No. 11, *National Policy Governing the Acquisition of Information Assurance (IA) and IA-Enabled Information Technology (IT) Products*, June 2003.

148. Vocabulary.com, http://www.vocabulary.com/dictionary/attribute

149. R. M. Needham and R. M. Schroeder, Using encryption for authentication in large networks of computers, *Communications of the ACM*, 21(12), 993–999, 1978.

150. Internet. Shibboleth Project. Available at http://shibboleth.internet2.edu/ (Accessed on February 19, 2011).

151. I. Foster, C. Kesselman, G. Tsudik, and S. Tuecke, A security architecture for computational grids, in *Proceedings of the 5th ACM Conference on Computer and Communications Security Conference*, pp. 83–92, San Francisco, CA, November 2–5, 1998.

152. V. Welch, I. Foster, C. Kesselman, O. Mulmo, L. Pearlman, S. Tuecke, J. Gawor S. Meder, and F. Siebenlist, X.509 Proxy certificates for dynamic delegation, *3rd Annual PKI R&D Workshop*, Gaithersburg, MD, April 12–14, 2004.

153. E. Belani, A. Vahdat, T. Anderson, and M. Dahlin, The CRISIS wide area security architecture, in *Usenix Security Symposium*, San Antonio, TX, January 26–29, 1998.

154. M. Lewis, and A. Grimshaw, The core legion object model, in *Proceedings of the 5th IEEE Symposium. On High Performance Distributed Computing*, pp. 562–571. IEEE Computer Society Press, 1996.

155. Remarks by Debra Charpaty, Corporate Vice President, Global Foundation Services, Microsoft Management Summit, Las Vegas, May 1, 2008, http://www.microsoft.com/Presspass/exec/debrac/mms2008.mspx (Accessed 19 February 2011).

156. B. Johnson, technology correspondent, guardian.co.uk, Cloud computing is a trap, warns GNU founder Richard Stallman, September 29, 2008.

157. A. Plesser, *Executive Producer, Beet.tv, Cloud Computing is Hyped and Overblown, Forrester's Frank Gillett.....Big Tech Companies Have Cloud Envy*, http://www.beet.tv/2008/09/cloud-computing.html, September 26, 2008 (Accessed on February 19, 2011).

158. D. B. Johnson, and D. A. Maltz. Protocols for adaptive wireless and mobile networking. *IEEE Personal Communications*, 3(1), 34–42, February 1996.

159. A. Hills, and D. B. Johnson. A wireless data network infrastructure at Carnegie Mellon University. *IEEE Personal Communications*, 3(1), 56–63, February 1996.

160. Naming and Addressing: URIs, URLs, ..., Dan Connolly, Revision: 1.58 of 2006/02/27 15:15:52, http://www.w3.org/Addressing/

161. Formally Assigned Uniform Resource Names (URN) Namespaces, Last Updated 2011-08-17, This is the Official IANA Registry of URN Namespaces, http://www.iana.org/assignments/urn-namespaces/urn-namespaces.xml

162. Z. Liu, A. Ranganathan, A. Riabov, Specifying and enforcing high-level semantic obligation policies, in 8th *IEEE International Workshop on Policies for Distributed Systems and Networks (POLICY'07)*, pp. 119–128, Bologna, Italy, June 13–15, 2007.

163. W. Yao, Fidelis: A policy-driven trust management framework, *Lecture Notes in Computer Science*, 2692, 301–317, 2003.

164. H. Wang, and S. L. Osborn, Delegation in the role graph model, in *Proceedings of the 11th ACM Symposium on Access Control Models and Technologies*, Lake Tahoe, California, 2006.

165. L. H. Zhang, G. J. Ahn, and B. T. Chu, A rule-based framework for role-based delegation and revocation, *ACM Transactions on Information and System Security (TISSEC)*, 6, 404–441, 2003.

166. J. B. D Joshi, and E. Bertino, Fine-grained role-based delegation in presence of the hybrid role hierarchy, in *Proceedings of the Eleventh ACM Symposium on Access Control Models and Technologies*, Lake Tahoe, California, 2006.

167. J. Wainer, and A. Kumar, A fine-grained, controllable, user-to-user delegation method in RBAC, in *Proceedings of the 10th ACM Symposium on Access Control Models and Technologies*, Stockholm, Sweden, 2005.

168. R. Tamassia, D. Yao, and W. H. Winsborough, Role-based cascaded delegation, in *Proceedings of the 9th ACM Symposium on Access Control Models and Technologies*, Yorktown Heights, New York, 2004.

169. X. Zhang, S. Oh, and R. Sandhu, PBDM: A flexible delegation model in RBAC, in *Proceedings of the 8th ACM Symposium on Access Control Models and Technologies*, Como, Italy, 2003.

170. J. S. Park, Y. L. Lee, H. H. Lee, and B. N. Noh, A role-based delegation model using role hierarchy supporting restricted permission inheritance, in *Proceedings of the International Conference on Security and Management, SAM '03*, pp. 294–302, Las Vegas, NV, June 23–26, 2003.

171. J. Bacon, K. Moody, and W. Yao, A model of OASIS role-based access control and its support for active security, *ACM Transactions on Information and System Security (TISSEC)*, 5, 492–540, 2002.

172. E. Barka, R. Sandhu, A role-based delegation model and some extensions, in *23rd National Information Systems Security Conference*, Baltimore Convention Center, Baltimore, October 16–19, 2000.

173. R. Sandhu, and Q. Munawer, The ARBAC99 model for administration of roles, in *Proceedings of the 15th Annual Computer Security Applications Conference*, Phoenix, AZ, December 6–10, 1999, p. 229.

174. C. Goh, and A. Baldwin, Towards a more complete model of role, in *Proceedings of the 3rd ACM Workshop on Role-Based Access Control*, Fairfax, Virginia, United States, 1998, pp. 55–62.

175. R. S. Sandhu, E. J. Coyne, H. L. Feinstein, and C. E. Youman, Role-based access control models, *Computer*, 29, 38–47, 1996.

176. J. Wainer, P. Barthelmess, and A. Kumar, WRBAC: A workflow security model incorporating controlled overriding of constraints, *International Journal of Cooperative Information Systems,* 12, 455–486, 2003.

177. J. Wainer, A. Kumar, and P. Barthelmess, DW-RBAC: A formal security model of delegation and revocation in workflow systems, *Information Systems,* 32, 365–384, 2007.

178. C. Ruan, and V. Varadharajan, Resolving conflicts in authorization delegations, in *Proceedings of the 7th Australian Conference on Information Security and Privacy*, Melbourne, Australia, July 3–5, 2002, pp. 271–285.

179. V. Atluri, and A. Gal, An authorization model for temporal and derived data: Securing information portals, *ACM Transactions on Information and System Security (TISSEC)*, 5, 62–94, 2002.

180. Å. Hagström, S. Jajodia, P. Francesco, and D. Wijesekera, Revocations—A classification, in *Proceedings of the 14th IEEE Workshop on Computer Security Foundations*, Cape Breton, Nova Scotia, June 11–13, 2001, p. 44.

181. E. Dantsin, T. Eiter, G. Gottlob, and A. Voronkov, Complexity and expressive power of logic programming, *ACM Computing Surveys (CSUR)* 33, 374–425, 2001.

182. R. Fagin, On an authorization mechanism, *ACM Transactions on Database Systems (TODS)*, 3, 310–319, 1978.

183. P. P. Griffiths, and B. W. Wade, An authorization mechanism for a relational database system, *ACM Transactions on Database Systems (TODS)*, 1, 242–255, 1976.

184. Multiple contributors, Delegation, from Wikipedia, the Free Encyclopedia. Available online at: http://en.wikipedia.org/wiki/Delegation, 2011.

185. J. Kemp et al., *Authentication Context for the OASIS Security Assertion Markup Language (SAML) V2.0, OASIS Standard*. Available online at: http://docs.oasis-open.org/security/saml/v2.0/saml-authn-context-2.0-os.pdf, 2005.

186. *Community of Interest (AF COI) Primer, Version 1.0*, Date: 12 July 2011, SAF/US(M), https://cs.eis.af.mil/afdbt/COI/default.aspx

187. W. R. Simpson, C. Chandersekaran, and R. Wagner, IDA Research Notes, Best Publications in the Open Literature, *Secure Cloud Based Computing*, Winter 2012–2013, pp. 21–27.

188. *MSN Glossary for Claims*, http://msdn.microsoft.com/en-us/library/ee534975.aspx

Index

Note: Page numbers followed by "*fn*" indicates footnotes.